Contempor
New Zealand
Ngā Kupu Tītohu o Aotearoa

MIRIAMA EVANS is of Ngati Mutunga and Ngai Tahu descent. She was born in Christchurch in 1944. As a mature student at Victoria University of Wellington she gained a B.A. Honours in Maori Studies. Miriama Evans is one of three women from Spiral who published *the bone people* by Keri Hulme and *The House of the Talking Cat* by J. C. Sturm. She joined Te Ohu Whakatupu, the Maori women's secretariat in the Ministry of Women's Affairs, in 1986.

HARVEY McQUEEN was born in Little River, Banks Peninsula, in 1934. After gaining an M.A. in history from Canterbury University he taught in secondary schools in the Waikato. In 1972 he became an inspector of secondary schools in Hamilton, shifting to Wellington in 1977 to work in the head office of the Department of Education. He took early retirement in 1986 to work as a freelance consultant and to pursue his own writing, but in 1988 accepted an offer to work in the Prime Minister's Department at Parliament as Executive Assistant (Education Media).

Harvey McQueen has edited two anthologies of New Zealand poetry for schools: *Ten Modern New Zealand Poets* (with Lois Cox, 1974) and *A Cage of Words* (1980). With Ian Wedde he edited *The Penguin Book of New Zealand Verse* (1985). He has published four volumes of his own poetry: *Against the Maelstrom* (1981), *Stoat Spring* (1983), *Oasis Motel* (1986) and *Room* (1988).

IAN WEDDE was born in Blenheim in 1946. As a child he lived in East Pakistan, Europe and England, and he has travelled extensively as an adult. Ian Wedde was educated at the University of Auckland, where he gained an M.A. in English. He now lives in Wellington and works as a freelance writer, for the last six years as art critic for the *Evening Post*.

Ian Wedde has published several collections of poetry, including *Spells for Coming Out* (1977), joint winner of the New Zealand Book Award for poetry; and most recently, *Driving into the Storm: Selected Poems* (1987) and *Tendering* (1988). He has also published three novels: *Dick Seddon's Great Dive* (1976), winner of the New Zealand Book Award for fiction, *Symmes Hole* (1986), and *Survival Arts* (1988); and a collection of stories, *The Shirt Factory and Other Stories* (1981). With Harvey McQueen, he co-edited *The Penguin Book of New Zealand Verse* (1985).

He has received several literary awards: the Burns Fellowship (1972), Writers Bursary (1974), New Zealand Literary Fund Scholarships in 1980 and 1989, Arts Council of New Zealand Travel Award (1983), and the Victoria University Literary Fellowship (1984).

THE PENGUIN BOOK OF
Contemporary New Zealand Poetry
Ngā Kupu Tītohu o Aotearoa

Edited by
MIRIAMA EVANS, HARVEY McQUEEN
and
IAN WEDDE

PENGUIN BOOKS

PENGUIN BOOKS

Penguin Books (NZ) Ltd, 182–190 Wairau Road, Auckland 10, New Zealand
Penguin Books Ltd, 27 Wrights Lane, London W8 5TZ, England
Viking Penguin Inc., 40 West 23rd Street, New York, New York 10010, USA
Penguin Books Australia Ltd, 487 Maroondah Highway, Ringwood, Australia 3134
Penguin Books Canada Ltd, 2801 John Street, Markham, Ontario, Canada L3R 1B4

Penguin Books Ltd, Registered Offices: Harmondsworth, Middlesex, England

First published in 1989
1 3 5 7 9 10 8 6 4 2

Copyright © this selection Miriama Evans,
Harvey McQueen and Ian Wedde, 1989
Copyright © introductions Miriama Evans
and Harvey McQueen, 1989

Designed by Richard King
Typeset by Typocrafters Ltd, Auckland
Printed in Hong Kong

CONTENTS

Contents

Contents

Contents

Contents

Contents

Contents

Contents

Contents

INTRODUCTION (1)

If everything is anywhere in flux
perhaps we may not read the same map twice.

— Kendrick Smithyman

Ian Wedde and I always saw this anthology as part of a project which began with the 1985 *Penguin Book of New Zealand Verse*. That anthology took a general overview, it had an historiographic profile. There were new questions with different answers in this compilation.

Both books include material in Maori; this one, however, has a Maori editor, Miriama Evans. (Her introduction to the Maori material follows.) To our ideas Miriama added further issues raised by another way of formalising language. The decision to include Maori material was an *a priori* one, vindicated by discussions with those responsible for collecting and editing the material. Aware of the difficulties and pitfalls of a bi-cultural approach, we remain convinced that it is the right one.

As with the earlier volume we tried to start without a theory, which is in itself a theory, there being no such thing as an unmediated reading. Any selection must be an expression of theoretical, cultural and personal determinants. We could not be unaware of the judgements of other anthologists, nor of our own previous decisions. To have the effrontery to make a selection, one can choose between two approaches: making decisions in the context of received wisdom, or attempting to look anew, through one's own binoculars. So we tried to let what was there in the poetry chart the maps we would use. A sense of direction, if not location, soon emerged from our survey of present and likely future territory.

An example is the boundaries formed by the word 'contemporary'. We began gathering material assuming Baxter as the starting point. Quickly we moved to post-Baxter as several things became clear. Such an anthology would duplicate territory already traversed. Then there was the immense range and quantity of poetry over the last decade and the problem of distinguishing between new and young. By settling for post-Baxter we gained a sense of explored but uncharted freehold.

So the poems themselves shifted us to an approximate date — 1980 — which was about the time we closed the previous volume.

Introduction

This anthology records the poetry of the Muldoon era, the tensions and dynamics which gathered momentum to emerge into a nuclear-free, radical, re-structuring New Zealand. But while we might believe we have cut the apron strings, the islands we occupy are not isolate. As we finished our selection the world's financial markets went into meltdown. Subsequent anthologies will have a different foreground.

Our selection method was the same as last time: independent reading and shortlisting, then discussion, winnowing, arguing, rereading, and eventual agreement. As before, Ian and I were amazed (and pleased) at how often our choices coincided. Where they didn't we had to re-examine and negotiate our judgements. Though Miriama worked independently we continually cross-checked to make sure we were following roughly the same tracks.

It is too soon to pin a theory, or theories, to what is happening in New Zealand verse, except to note that there is a lot happening, and that it reflects a changing, pluralistic society. The resulting diversity includes the increasing appearance of the long poem. Anthologies, by their nature, tend to go for the lyric and the short poem. That so many contemporary New Zealanders attempt sustained poems suggests the form should not be denied. Kendrick Smithyman's 'Reading the Maps' became our touchstone. We debated. If it went in, by the scale of things there would be no space for any other Smithyman. Was this fair? Was it fair to make a selection of what we considered the finest contemporary verse and not include several long poems in their entirety? Long poems by Alistair Campbell, Graham Lindsay, Allen Curnow and Michele Leggott helped us make up our minds.

Questions of hierarchy bedevilled us throughout our collaboration. Obviously major established writers who had been productive throughout the decade would be represented generously, as would certain mid-career writers and significant new writers. But we did make a conscious decision very early on to be as non-hierarchical as possible. Another decision was to include expatriates. Fleur Adcock, Eric Beach, Alan Brunton and Nigel Roberts are still part of the contemporary scene. Their inclusion is appropriate in a book which has less reason than earlier anthologies to be interested in questions of 'national identity' and historical development.

As we narrowed our selections we realised we were dealing with the nature of language more than we had anticipated.

To bring it to scale I was driven
or drove headlong, taking whatever a telltale dial
on an outmoded

dashboard said was nearly true of Then
and There, the literal. Metaphor too, and parable
long since outmoded.

— Kendrick Smithyman

In retrospect it is obvious that a book aiming to look hard at the decade in which we are living will examine the language of that time. The early decision to include 'Reading the Maps' and Campbell's 'Soul Traps' became our signpost. Very different poems, they propose different kinds of reading and desires for language, but in a sense they polarise the poetry in this book. Both are concerned with a kind of archaeology or a recovering of what language can do; both treat language as a tool for research and something active in itself rather than as, primarily, a means of expression. The work of new writers such as Michele Leggott, Leigh Davis and Gregory O'Brien amply demonstrates this development.

Other gifted, new writers — such as Dinah Hawken and John Newton — work from a more testamentary base than Leggott, Davis and O'Brien, but also demonstrate the same approach. Supple and objective, their language expects more from its reading than responses to personal authenticity.

You'd be a brave human who would say where all the influences
come from, but I think the word sets the whole thing up...

— Keri Hulme

An anthology spanning the last two decades would have been more confessional, more personal. By the 1980s, the public voice is more present. As Dinah Hawken says, 'There's no way of holding politics out of this'. Rogernomics, state intervention, land rights, feminism: the issues underpin the discourse and language used to assail the power of privilege. Many poets, Maori and women especially, use these to empower themselves. The 1985 Penguin anthology was criticised for recognising that empowering. In the intervening few years the need for recognition has become even more obvious. However, just as an artificial democratisation of space was not forced upon writers neither did we seek forced parity between the sexes; but we certainly kept an editorial eye on the extent to which parity was being achieved.

Introduction

Alphabetical ordering of the volume's contents seemed to make sense and avoided the hierarchical. When the arrangement was made it took on a further definition: the cross-references added their own vibrations and we had our book.

We acknowledge the support of Penguin Books for continuing to publish the extended anthologies and the New Zealand Literary Fund for research funding. We owe thanks to many people, in particular Penguin's managing editor, Geoff Walker. Jock Phillips, director of the Stout Research Centre, Victoria University of Wellington, gave us hospitality and support. The librarians of the Wellington Public and Victoria University libraries were constructively helpful. Then there are the many poets and critics with whom we've consulted, argued and tested our ideas. In considering the application of the term 'contemporary', we would like to express our gratitude and admiration for the achievement of such senior figures as Allen Curnow and of younger writers like Michele Leggott.

I would like to thank my colleague and friend, Ian Wedde, for his patience, humour and sensitivity. Few people have thought so long and so hard about the nature of poetry. I treasure many late night sessions.

> *All language is a place, all*
> *landscapes*
> *mean something.*

> — Ian Wedde

And Miriama Evans. Shortly after she agreed to work with us she obtained a position which entailed long hours on the job. Then she got promotion. But she still found time to complete her section.

There are times when working on a collaborative anthology that the uncharted terrain is at risk of becoming a battlefield. Not once did we head towards this possibility: the exploration was so rewarding and satisfying.

Harvey McQueen

INTRODUCTION (2)

Tērā ko Rereahiahi, ko te Mahu Tonga
Kōrikoriko mai rā te kiko o te rangi
kori ana, ka pū ake te tau o te ate
Rere ana ki ngā hihi whetū i runga
Kia tiaho iho hei kura, te tara pounamu e tū!

— Merimeri Penfold

E ngā mana e ngā reo e ngā karangatanga maha tēnā koutou. Tangihia rā te āhuatanga kei ngā aituā kei te hunga kua whetū-rangitia i te wā iti nei. Kei te huri ngā mahara ki Te Okanga Huata, ki a Taniwha Waru, ki a Louis Johnson, ki a rātou mā, ētehi pou i rō pukapuka nei: nonanahi i kapohia ai rātou e te ringa kaha o aituā. Haere, ngā mate, ki te poutūtanga nui o Pipiri. Ka tūhono-hono rātou te hunga wairua ki a rātou, haere ana rātou i te ara whānui e huna ai te tini te mano ka ngaro ki te pō.

Kāti, tēnā tātou ngā kanohi ora.

The invitation to join Ian Wedde and Harvey McQueen as Maori editor to this anthology at once filled me with excitement and a sense of immense responsibility. I knew that the usual methods of collecting and editing an anthology would produce a limited range of contemporary Maori poetry. Only fragments have been published. Therefore, while Ian and Harvey set about their library search, I began to enquire about poets' work during hui and turned my ear and eye to performances.

Maori literature retains an oral rather than written form, and Maori audiences continue to judge and appreciate contemporary Maori poetry primarily by its performance rather than by its appearance in print. Indeed, an appreciation of the content, language and literary form is inextricably interwoven with a sense of ihi, wehi and wana, that is the power, awe and inspiration of the occasion and the performance itself.

The interrelationships among the poet, the poem, its performance, the performers, the occasion and the audience raised questions about the boundary of the word 'contemporary' in quite a different manner from those which Ian and Harvey addressed in the selection of poetry in English. From a Maori point of view, what is contemporary can be judged from a cultural perception of time and the indivisibility of past, present and future into discrete segments. Thus a holistic recognition of 'contemporary' is not just confined to the 'here and now' but is enmeshed with the traditional and futuristic.

For example, 'Te Tangi a Taku Ihu / The Sound of My Sneezing Nose' by Te Whetū in 1880, which appeared in the previous volume, *The Penguin Book of New Zealand Verse*, is a poem that still enjoys currency amongst Taranaki people, particularly Te Ati Awa. It is performed regularly by Taranaki groups both as a poi and a waiata. The content remains pertinent to the performers, it continues to inspire them, and it makes a statement to the audience. In this sense Te Whetū's hundred-year-old poem belongs to this period and could be considered contemporary.

While the contemporary nature of such waiata is acknowledged, the Maori poetry for this anthology has been selected predominantly from poets of this decade.

Te Kuru-o-te-marama Waaka's patere about the Tarawera eruption is an example of a contemporary composition firmly linked into and expressive of a traditional style of the past. Perhaps the most graphic example of the 'contemporary continuum' is Ngapo Wehi's 'I Te Tīmatanga / In the Beginning', a poem which in content and style belongs as much to a thousand years ago as it does to its time of composition.

In contrast, poets such as Hirini Melbourne, Piki Kereama and Ranui Ngarimu, whose modern compositions belong to te ao hou, the new world, may take up themes from te ao tawhito, the ancient world.

One poem, 'Te Kōtuku — Te Manu Wairua o Te Toka / White Heron — The Spirit Bird of the South' by Aunty Jane Manahi, carries the Kāi Tahu dialect, which is little heard by the majority of Maori people these days.

While recognising the oral nature of the work and the complexity of defining a boundary for contemporary poetry, it was also important, as Maori editor, not to make assumptions about the availability of material for publishing in this anthology. Many Maori poets, performers, and audiences believe that the vitality and essence cannot be truly appreciated through the written word. Indeed, a number of poets declined to allow their poetry to be published.

Some poets gave 'popular' versions of their work, omitting those sections of particular relevance to specific iwi, hapu or other groups. 'Te Hokinga Mai', a waiata-a-ringa by Pā Max Mariu and Te Taite Cooper, for example, has another verse for Ngāti Kahungunu which is not included in this anthology.

Poets included as Maori contributors had some freedom to select which poems to transcribe for this book. Thus Te Aomuhurangi Temamaka Jones, having declined the inclusion of 'Me he rau', a waiata tangi, in the 1985 volume, requested that it be published here. Other poets, after critical appraisal of their work, set aside suitable and expressive compositions — perhaps because the time was not ripe for their publication.

Inevitably then, the contemporary Maori poetry for this anthology has its own tātai and its own whakapapa, that is, it is layered with its own logic and sense of continuum. This builds on the 1985 *Penguin Book of New Zealand Verse*, with its welcome inclusion of Maori poetry and translations together with Margaret Orbell's observation that contemporary poets were renewing and extending the ancient traditions with songs of protest and celebration.

To some extent, selections were made in recognition of the tremendous variation in style and format, and by limitations imposed through the method of collection. Certainly significant events such as the Te Māori exhibition, the centenary of the Tarawera eruption, and the gifting of Tongariro National Park to the nation by Ngāti Tuwharetoa have produced poems for inclusion. The anthology also reflects current interest in the preservation or restoration of Maori values. In addition, consideration was given to the geographic spread of poets, a desire to achieve parity between the sexes, and a preference to ensure a distribution of contributors across iwi.

Ngā Kupu Tītohu reproduces in microcosm a range of poetry heard in Maori circles. Nevertheless, it is not a comprehensive survey of Maori poetry, but rather a personal selection. It does not, for example, include an oriori, a song of instruction to a child, although Hori Tait's 'He Koha Kī / A Gift of Words from My Grandmother' is reminiscent of this type. 'He Koha Kī' is more universal in theme than traditional oriori, which were whānau or hapu specific. Awe-inspiring poi kāwai, a mnemonic for genealogy, and pao, cryptic poetic comments which punctuate discussion on the marae, were reluctantly set aside.

Contributions for this anthology include haka, ngeri, pokeka, patere, waiata poi, waiata tangi, waiata aroha, and waiata-a-ringa.

Introduction

At one end of the range are dynamic haka, ngeri and pōkeka. These are vigorous and powerful. At the other end of the spectrum are the longer, formal, almost formulaic-styled waiata which provide commentaries on topical issues.

'Tērā Ko Rereahiahi' by Merimeri Penfold is one such poem. The waiata blends contemporary and archaic patterns and themes:

> From the conception the increase
> From the increase the thought
> From the thought the remembrances
> From the remembrance the consciousness
> From the consciousness the desire.
> That canoe was set afloat by Te Hau and Hohepa.

Here the ancient Maori philosophy of creation is expressed in traditional whakapapa style as a rationale for the development and celebration of the new marae at Auckland University — the waiata tells us that Matiu Te Hau and Pat Hohepa conceived the idea of building a marae on campus. Rich in language and content, like others in this anthology, it is an historical source for future generations.

Ruka Broughton's 'He Waiata mō Te Herenga Waka', is also about a university marae. It was composed and first used at the beginning of the building programme to encourage dedication to the project amongst the Maori community at Victoria University. It was initially performed as a waiata with a brisk tempo but has latterly become a waiata tangi, a song of lament in remembrance of the poet.

And so the texture and layers of the Maori poetry for this anthology are varied. Archaic, traditional, modern, and seeds for future compositions: each layer is woven with a contemporary thread.

> I tīmata mai Te Ao
> I roto i Te Pōuri
> Ko Te Kore ko Te Pū
> Te Weu, Te More, me Te Aka
>
> — Ngapo Wehi

I would like to record my deepest thanks to taua, Maaka Jones, who sustained me throughout this long endeavour and who provided many of the translations and invaluable advice on the nuances of Maori phrases and words. The poets themselves also provided explanations and perspectives of their poems that have assisted in editorial decisions, and I thank them for sharing their taonga through this anthology. Throughout the country there are many whom I wish to acknowledge with gratitude: the numerous people who were consulted, who offered ideas, and who acted as 'scouts'.

Ian and Harvey quickly proved to be interested in my editorial idiosyncracies and encouraged me to explore the Maori material in my own style. Harvey was unstinting in his support and encouragement during periods of anxiety about my limited leisure time to work on this anthology. I thank you both for your forebearance.

Finally, my most heartfelt thanks to Penguin editor Geoff Walker, who, apart from his support and interest throughout the project, had the awesome task of negotiating the finalisation of my contribution when other demands on my time were at a premium.

Miriama Evans

FLEUR ADCOCK

(Born 1934)

Downstream

Last I became a raft of green bubbles
meshed into the miniature leaves
of that small pondweed (has it a name?)
that lies green-black on the stream's face:
a sprinkle of round seeds, if you mistake it,
or of seed-hulls holding air among them.

I was those globules; there they floated —
all there was to do was to float
on the degenerate stream, suburbanized,
the mill-stream where it is lost among houses
and hardly moving, swilling just a little
to and fro if the wind blows it.

But it did move, and I moved on, drifting
until I entered the river
where I was comported upon a tear's fashion
blending into the long water
until you would not see that there had been
tear or bubble or any round thing ever.

Lantern Slides

1

'You'll have to put the little girl down.'
Is it a little girl who's bundled
in both our coats against my shoulder,
buried among the trailing cloth?

It's a big haul up to the quay,
my other arm heavy with luggage,

the ship lurching. Who's my burden?
She had a man's voice this morning.

2

Floods everywhere. Monsoon rain
syphoning down into the valley.
When it stops you see the fungus
hugely coiling out of the grass.

Really, in such a derelict lane
you wouldn't expect so many cars,
black and square, driving jerkily.
It's not as if we were near a village.

3

Now here's the bridal procession:
the groom pale and slender in black
and his hair black under his hat-brim;
is that a frock-coat he's wearing?

The bride's as tall as his trouser pocket;
she hoists her arm to hold his hand,
and rucks her veil askew. Don't,
for your peace of mind, look under it.

4

The ceremony will be in a cavern,
a deep deserted underground station
built like a theatre; and so it is:
ochre-painted, proscenium-arched.

The men have ribbons on their hatbands;
there they are, behind the grille,
receding with her, minute by minute,
shrivelling down the empty track.

Mary Magdalene and the Birds

1

Tricks and tumbles are my trade; I'm
all birds to all men.
I switch voices, adapt my features,
do whatever turn you fancy.
All that is constant is my hair:

plumage, darlings, beware of it.

2

Blackbird: that's the one to watch —
or he is, with his gloss and weapon.
Not a profession for a female,
his brown shadow. Thrush is better,
cunning rehearser among the leaves,
and speckle-breasted, maculate.

3

A wound of some kind. All that talk
of the pelican, self-wounding,
feeding his brood from an ever-bleeding
bosom turns me slightly sick.

But seriousness can light upon
the flightiest. This tingling ache,
nicer than pain, is a blade-stroke:
not my own, but I let it happen.

4

What is balsam? What is nard?
Sweetnesses from the sweet life,
obsolete, fit only for wasting.

I groom you with this essence. Wash it
down the drain with tears and water.
We are too human. Let it pass.

5

With my body I thee worship:
breast on stone lies the rockdove
cold on that bare nest, cooing
its low call, unlulled,
restless for the calling to cease.

6

Mary Magdalene sang in the garden.
It was a swansong, said the women,
for his downdrift on the river.

It sounded more of the spring curlew
or a dawn sky full of larks,
watery trillings you could drown in.

Uniunea Scriitorilor

Caterpillars are falling on the Writers' Union.
The writers are indifferent to the caterpillars.
They sit over their wine at the metal tables
wearing animated expressions and eating fried eggs
with pickled gherkins, or, (the dish of the day),
extremely small sausages: two each.

Meanwhile here and there an inch of grey bristles,
a miniature bottle-brush, twitches along a sleeve
or clings to a shoulder. The stone-paved courtyard
is dappled with desperate clumps of whiskers,
launched from the sunlit mulberry trees
to take their chance among literary furniture.

A poet ignores a fluffy intruder
in his bread-basket (the bread's all finished)
but flicks another from the velvet hat
(which surely she must have designed herself —
such elegance never appears in the shop-windows)
of his pretty companion, who looks like an actress.

The writers are talking more and more rapidly.
Not all are writers. One is a painter;
many are translators. Even those who are not
are adaptable and resourceful linguists.
'Pardon!' says one to the foreign visitors.
'Permit me! You have a worm on your back.'

Drowning

'Si qua mulier maritum suum, cui legitime est iuncta,
    dimiserit, necetur in luto' — Lex Burgund., 34, 1
(If any woman has killed her lawfully married husband
    let her be drowned in mud.)

Death by drowning drowns the soul:
bubbles cannot carry it;
frail pops of air, farts
loosed in water are no vessels
for the immortal part of us.
And in a pit of mud, what bubbles?
There she lies, her last breath with her,
her soul rotting in her breast.

*

Is the sea better, then?
Will the salty brine preserve
pickled souls for the Day of Judgement?
Are we herrings to be trawled
in long nets by Saint Peter?
Ocean is a heavy load:
My soul flies up to thee, O God —
but not through mud, not through water.

And so, Bishop Synesius,
how can you wonder that we stand
with drawn swords on this bucking deck,
choosing to fall on friendly steel
and squirt our souls into the heavens
rather than choke them fathoms deep?

29

FLEUR ADCOCK

One more lash of the storm and it's done:
self-murder, but not soul-murder.

Then let the fishes feast on us
and slurp our blood after we're finished:
they'll find no souls to suck from us.
Yours, perhaps, has a safe-conduct:
you're a bishop, and subtle, and Greek.
Well, sir, pray and ponder. But our
language has no word for dilemma.
Drowning's the strongest word for death.

An Epitaph

I wish to apologize for being mangled.
It was the romantic temperament
that did for me. I could stand rejection —
so grand, 'the stone the builders rejected . . .' —
but not acceptance. 'Alas', I said
(a word I use), 'alas, I am taken
up, or in, or out of myself:
shall I never be solitary?'
Acceptance fell on me like a sandbag.
My bones crack. It squelches out of them.
Ah, acceptance! Leave me under this stone.

ROB ALLAN

(Born 1945)

from *Karitane Postcards*

1

For example, Andropov is dead. That was the news
caught in its announcement.
Another world dreaming out a personal life
it's a personal world in successive moments
I saw these features in the coast of Karitane
green dips of distance   a return to the old place
approximating the dream where I started
to desire, entreat, wish myself in the world.
  In New York City 30 cm of snow fell today
I pour myself more tea. I am reading *Rivers and Mountains*
by John Ashbery.
Mr. Leech is 93 years old and wishes to be remembered
to me.
Some plants I know by smell and some by their
feel; in my hands.
Sometimes I can taste them
at times like sunlight   all this going on forever.

2

If I catch myself staring at an object
I must decide what I will tell you
Gertrude Stein struggled to get rid of nouns
— the nouns had to go
I want history to go and politics and art
and images and symbols. I am looking at a plate
of shells named after Captain Cook
and I hear my boy sleeping in the bedroom
next door. I want description to go.
I want multinational companies to go
I want the hoons revving up over the road to go
Captain Hook that's what Richard calls him
and his breath is a small surf through the wall.

ROB ALLAN

Karitane it breathes all around my body
and the stars of the visible universe
I want the past and future_to go
and my single mindedness.

3

In the Book of Hours I found on the shelf
pressed flowers   selfheal, groundsel
speedwell, placed there some twenty years ago
by Betty Bell   to Betty it said in the fly leaf
with love from Bella   San Francisco May 1953.
Such quietness there is space to panic
I like to hear my breath
its noise the noise and heart's clamour
of direction and purpose.
Truby organized the local residents to sandbag
the river so it didn't flow again into old channels.
On wet nights he roused them
under God's full glare, sandbagging the insolent
shadows.

4

We are sunk in history   drilled in it.
The seaweeds have names from war
sea bombs oyster thief
the earth is divided by the names we give
powers genesis
I have dug in five nut trees
it's a plan for peace and not being involved
in future wars.
Groundsel is a rapid growing plant of waste ground
and selfheal a low growing plant
explains itself   simply living
as if I could   be pure and simple and good.

I know how life feels
it's art's disguise   it's a handle on existence
and words' ignorance
I come back to.

5

Houseflies find a way out fast
when I swish at them with the I Ching.
I need quiet to write
this postcard to you. I need
a fight if I'm to say something.
Now someone is singing as they come up the road
it's someone who wants to be in this poem.
Trees outside want an original translation
everything wants to understand
and it's not in language yet
but what have I been expecting all this time?

Silence
the delight and foolish antics of sages.
It's here at Karitane that the surf hits the stars
with loud spray
and the USA and the USSR —
I get these messages like everyone else.

10

The thirsty Irish of Liverpool needed water
the rivers of Rivington and Horwich
Riddlesworth Yarrow and Douglas
slake my thirst the waters of the Liverpool Corporation
Waterworks trespass on the land.
I see Hart's chances are fading.
Words like these down under Marian and Richard
are fishing at Pulling Point.
What will endure of us. I have a sense of
inadequate cover my childhood wants out
of the limits words can give for a start
and not taking directions from anyone.
So ideally here in love
and going into all this
What a catch trevalli squid butterfish and cod
the sweeping acres of the human voice.

ROB ALLAN

Talking to My Neighbour

I was talking to my neighbour
the other day, where his paddock touches
my boundary; — not that we said much.

We are both reasonable blokes
in good favour with our wives

And in reasonable counsel with friends
and relatives; we talked about the economy

— The government and its ways were mentioned;
all the general beefing that might help keep democracy

Alive; for as everyone says
You have to fight for your rights.

We all know this down this way,
my neighbour knows it.

It was a warm spring afternoon
— a gentle sky pressed a claim upon hills

And the sun lit upon flowers
while the trees balanced each careful thrust of wind.

ARAPETA MARUKITEPUA AWATERE

(1910–76); Ngāti Porou, Whānau-ā-Hinetāpora, Uepōhatu)

Ka Huri

Ka huri taku aro ki te tai hauāuru kūreitanga rā o aku tini waka
Kei Mohakatino Tokomaru tēnā puta noa ko te tini o
    Te Āti Awa.

Ka huri au ki Onuku-taipari ko te peka tēnā o Kurahaupo,
Tīmata i kōnā Taranaki iwi nui.

Ka huri ki te Waipārara-kite-uru puta noa ngā iwi o Aotea waka
Kei Pātea rawa ko Ngāti Ruanui, kei Waitotara ko Rauru Kaitangata,
Kei Wanganui rawa ko Te Āti Hau.

Ka mihi au ki Taranaki maunga nui taku waka ruruhau noa
Tuawhakarere ōna wai e rere kia ngoto iho au ko
    Te Ua-Hau-Mene me
Tohu Kākahi ko Te Whiti-o-Rongomai me Titokowaru.

Ngā puna wai kua ūhia noa ko te puna wai o tēnei rā, kua iri ki
Te maunga tītōhea ki rehe o te rangi e rere koutou ki te wai e
Kore nei e mimiti, ahakoa tukitukitia e te poaka, mau tonu tana
Mana Māori motuhake.

Rua tawhito ka puta Kāhui Rua,
Rua te hīhiri
Rua te pupuke
Rua te mahara
Rua te kōrero
Rua te wānanga
Rua te manu
Rua te tira.

Ka moe rā i a Tau tū rangi, ka puta rā ko Rua Taranaki,
Tū mai e Koro te maunga kōrero ngā kuru pounamu a
    ngā tūpuna i
Takahi i te pae ki Wharaurangi

Ki a Hine-nui rā e
Ki a Hine-nui rā e
Ki a Hine-nui-i-te-pō rā e.

I Turn

I turn to face the western tides, the landing point of my many
    canoes.
At Mohakatino is Tokomaru from which came the multitudes of
    Te Ati Awa.

I turn to Onuku-taipari, that is the branch of Kurahaupo,
from there began the populous iwi called Taranaki.

I turn to Waiparara-kite-uru — from where the tribes of Aotea
dispersed: at Patea is Ngati Ruanui, at Waitotara is Rauru
Kaitangata, at Wanganui is Te Ati Hau.

I greet Taranaki, the great mountain — my canoe's shelter
from very ancient times. Its water flows directing me to Te Ua
Hau Mene, Tohu Kakahi, Te Whiti o Rongomai, and
    Titokowaru.

The springs have been widespread — today the spring can
    be heard
on the barren mountain at the fold of the sky. Hurry to the water
that will never dry up, for although it has been abused by the
Pakeha, it holds fast to its special Maori mana.

From Primeval Rua came the flock of Rua
Rua, the desire,
Rua, the increase,
Rua, the thought,
Rua, the conversation,
Rua, the instruction,
Rua, the leader,
Rua, the traveller.

He married Tau Tu Rangi; Rua Taranaki was born.
Stand there, Koro, the mountain of stories, the greenstone
ornaments of the ancestors who have crossed the horizon
    to Wharaurangi,
to Hine-nui,
to Hine-nui,
to Hine-nui-i-te-po there.

Translation by Miriama Evans

ERIC BEACH

(Born 1947)

th build-up to th wet

look out sky
here comes a cloud
don't ring me on th radio phone
here comes lightning
don't play in th gutter kid
here comes old man croc
look out martha
(hic) comes arthur
th build-up to th wet
ski-ing in my sweat
top end lake
horizon about to break
never rains
but it pours
look out marriage
here comes divorce
raindrops like beerguts
bulk on balconies
big blobs in bloomers
wobble on wobbly knees
look out arthur
here comes martha
look out sky
here
     comes
        a
         cloud

in th desert you remember

that th world's round, so that th whirl of ants
in th ring road of honey ants dreaming
is perfectly sensible, & th wheel we walk
doesn't bump along a rut of happiness
towards an absurd fence in a fine cemetery
nor are we left with a notion of prayer
dumped out every sunday with th garbage
so good to see someone arriving
knowing they come from a long line of foot-prints
& laughing at mirages of mountain ranges —
'it goes west, a long way, that one'
but th man who believes in th book
lives in a world too crowded for this kind of humour
preaching to th red earth from his green quarter acre
from behind barbed wire with his guard dog & flowers
walking straight ahead, not seeing th sand painting
that boots & hooves destroy, th man unmaking
in uncomfortable clothes in a church made awkward
by stiff corners, collars, & clean thoughts
that won't last out of sight of water
still, a spiritual people must sing
groping in a new dark, & hearing sticks clicking
in th dry places where th old religion
hums to itself, & may be overheard

Beachy's birdproof fences

th soldier settlement farm went in th depression
th bank grabbed it during th slump, owed them £250
did quite a bit of fencing for others, but not birdproof
my own fences still standing after 60 years
5 puriri posts to th chain
5 or 6 heart rimu battens to th panel & 7 wires
puriri & kinau strainer
worked with bill cowley, bill was fast & neat
& although not a bushman, he could land an axe blade

on a pin head, downhill, & that's a necessity
when splitting posts & battens
we were lucky enough to come across a big rimu
(red pine down your way) with th sap rotted off it
on a clearing & after cleaning away all th debris
& all the hou kou, we decided to try ourselves th following day
battens in sap were worth 4 shillings per hundred at th stumps
& heart 5 shillings, heart rimu or totara £3 to £3 10 shillings
per hundred, wages 12 shillings a day, then, about 1923
hot, & we worked like mad dogs, sawing, wedging & halving
4 foot lengths, & then I hacked off 2 inch thick slabs
& bill humped them to his chopping block & split them
into 2 inch by 2 inches / a lovely straight grain log
and when we had our battens we sawed 6'8" lengths for posts
and got to 64, bill & I were both pretty skinny
but when bill buried his axe in a slab it was with speed and
    precision
and it was satisfying to me after I had wedged off a neat slab
to have it converted into square battens and not 2"×3"s
    & 2"×1½"s
th small ones didn't count anyway, we lost some gravy that day
and according to my mental arithmetic we earned £2 each
oh, and I forgot to mention that we sawed and split 800 battens
(so th fence must've been about 50 chains at 16 battens per chain
and 64 posts so we still had 140 posts to split)
th log was on th ground but we had to square th butt
I got th debt down to £250 and then they took th farm

dinosaur

th dinosaur doesn't stoop to conversation
all grass to him, a feeding scythe —

                    a thousand years
                    a toothpick
& life /
        th biggest watermelon

th dinosaur is his own energy crisis

excess too small a word /
                    ah dope — oh booze
& the beat trying to find th heart
   th blood having to dance
        as over & over
   blood must remember
when to go left, when to go right,
   in a city of blood
having to find a way home

a dinosaur always drives under th influence
& on th wrong side of th road /
                        'suddenly, this moon,
                        coming straight at me'
— spin th wheel & roll —
                    — too fast to feel terror —
that's how to hold yrself together /
                        make yr own
                        whirlpool/
                                NO
everyone's shouting
                & you, triumphant /
                        YES

a dinosaur is a small freeway
3 tons of bones /
                a street directory of evolution
including a church, a bowling green, a cemetery,
                an erector set for palaeontologists
a small fortune /
                to endow a chair for dinosaurs

a dinosaur is here because it has nowhere else to go
after th ultimate, there's only th latest model, all extras,
completely automatic, streamlined, with new safety features,
th modern age doing a wheelie in a dinosaur park
having swallowed a dinosaur
— mammoth side effects /
                    & to counteract th mammoth
                    tyrannosaurus rex
(huge pupils with knees that won't fit under th desk)

ERIC BEACH

psychosis a dinosaur : neurosis, human

dinosaurs don't make love : dinosaurs make dinosaurs
not affect of affection but like to like
above every meat market — cold cuts of blue
                              a transcendent, dirigible dinosaur
toppling from highs, dinosaur days
& dinosaur nights, towering above rage
                              dinosaurs not smashed by windows
dinosaurs shattering th news
not extinct, not cubist, not th ice metaphor

a dinosaur refuses to repeat himself

in occupied territory

th dawn is an illegal gathering
th sun will break no windows today
th blacks will march quietly
to night's blank offices

th man will accept submissions
from th top of th required steps
there's no way you can be heard
with your language so closely watched

you can sleep in your beds at night
in th land of opportunity
you can sleep in your jobs by day
superannuation & th after-life

th memo says 'it is written —
we've worked hard to get where we are'
we, the survivors, with th barbed-wire flag
twisting th stars along fences

old shed

th sun rounds out th window frame, wooden & obedient,
heat bucks along th planks, & th rigid, pitiful nails
jerk like bad sex, surrendering to th marriage rust,
if this were society, planed to fit for a time, not
seeing th world — th iron will of th green

ropes fray from fretting beams, a shadow peaceful in its corner
shifts comfortably with th sun, light & shadow back to back
like two old people exchanging gender, sitting under th eaves
of a treadle sewing machine, on the spiralling anatomy of a sofa
or an old car seat, watching a tendril, tentative, at th door

flipping thru a crate of books, each unique, fantastic,
an alchemy of words, a black sun dancing green & red
on th sunlit page, popular romances that've put on weight,
'scarcely daring to breathe', heavy going, a bumble bee
waddles thru a warp, th plummet of self, impossible & absurd

TONY BEYER

(Born 1948)

Island Waters

separating one by one
this knot of serpents
dadakulaci
              or banded coral
snakes the colour of ambivalence

for fifteen years they have nested
under the jetty in my memory
easing themselves at dusk
out into hard blue water

and we fine combers of the reef
thick river silt had fouled
ran dove and swam there
days before we noticed

toads too were numerous
live heaps of muck at night
that blurted and flopped
across the yacht club lawn

or tossed on a sleeping
mate's face wept slime
that like *yaqona*
numbed the lips and nose

between tides the serious play
of our transect went on
where we scraped chipped and measured
tilling the reef's immobile garden

observing the work light does
or depth and salinity

and the pitted vehemence of species
born at one kind of edge we know

to raise the head was to
acknowledge once again the stale
ingredients of fancy's jigsaw
scurrying into view

the tall palms mopping the wind
and always as if on a loop
some svelte schooner
white moustached offshore

asides of the paradise business
like the smiles and flowers
our limp excuse of science
turned briefly solemn at the airport

and going back now without it
would embrace the slick deal whole
sun surf and sand
and the tourists' glittering tits

no better and no worse
an eden simplified
than that of the boys we weren't
who knew without the aid

of quadrat wires and trowels and formalin
the shape of a habitat
where nothing innocent lasts long
and clean fangs weave and glint

Cut Lilac

the dead smell the rain gives
to bunches of cut lilac
in bay windowed living rooms

is another version of the skull
your mouth feels when you kiss
a lover's or a child's clear forehead

but these are impetuous blue
upon the stems that throng
the vase's throat and splay from it

half captive or as free
as wands of light the recent sun
by peering wetly forth outside

has interspersed among them
divining paths like ours in time
that sprawl and gather haltingly

towards the next blind cervix
of the grave the best of us
will shoulder through with joy

The Kill

days there were bulls
the stink was different
and the darker purple
of their flayed weight
glistened above us
with humps that looked
too solid and thick
for a blade to enter

the season before I had
worked the cattle ramp
herding to death
their bent wet cocks
and wagging sacs
indiscriminate mountings
as they jumped and
bawled at the goad

prime bullocks ran
easily and once inside
hung sleek in their
jackets of creamy fat
when I had my bludger's
job on the air hose
blowing stiff hairs
from slits in the hocks

dazed by the jungle
beat the island boys
rapped with their steels
on sinks and partitions
I watched the stickers
cut and step clear
of the shocking hot
red clatter they released

below my duralumin
perch the brisket breaker
cursed and the pearl grey
shivery bundles
of guts unravelled
along the conveyor belt
dribbling a cud
of half digested grass

I used to day dream
there of men hoist
upside down on hooks
between bone and tendon
my landlord for a start
and maybe the foreman
whose bullet eyes
assessed my every pause

but there was no need
in that tall flickering
shed of bellows and
iron sounds to conjure
worse damnations

than the place itself
where hands were flawed
expendable parts that

served in paltry ways
the cold machinery had
not stooped yet to learn
and those enduring
longest gloved in blood
knew less each day
the powers they once
held to mend and make

obsessed with the sorry
tubes of flesh that hung
in front of them
the lines of bare men
after knock off in the
showers called
other images to mind
and like an abandonment

of soul too casual
to regret what never
seemed to wash away
outside or inside
was the necessary vile
dead breath that went
home with us all on
hair and clothes and skin

Early Weather

1

I was born in a far city
and the speech of trams
and the speech of workmen
grappling out the clay foundations

of a motor parts warehouse
rasped against the windows
of the small brick hospital
where my mother groaned

2

I grew in the house of a man
who had been shot at often
during a long
and singular part of his youth
and couldn't forget

he taught me a wariness
beyond my daily need

it was not easy to be with him
or to watch his love
of the death he had tensed himself
to accept and then mislaid

3

I am one of three brothers
all men now in middle life

our faces are marked by the fingerprints
of our loyalties
our travels and children and lost loves

sometimes we sit together in the sun
and drink beer
and pass around among ourselves
the familiar
wry and insulting language
we invented for another time

TONY BEYER

New Moves

1

this far from the road
a tension in the forest air
as if two men
had conspired to kill a third
and bring him lolling to town
lamenting the accident

it is safest to wear bright clothes
and walk upright
talking aloud to your companions
or the trees if you have none

the starved hiker
peels the soles from his feet
and gags at biting into them

the widow steps from one
short cot to the next
to hear the listless breathing
and twists the flame from the tilley
with a gesture the darkness loves

2

stress that the forest
is not a symbolic forest
and the blood in the splayed cups
of the ferns is actual

then the ground is all of a piece
rat skull and robin skull
and the sidewinding freckled trough
of last night's rain
that burrows out of sight

only the acrid spent
bullet cases may perplex you
and the pall like a dart of midges
hovering above them

you follow the tufts
of tartan wool snagged on branches
occasional smears
of heel prints in the mud
until you are certain
no one has been this way before

and the thin sun at your
back has its own
miraculous way with wounds

PETER BLAND

(Born 1934)

Two Family Snaps

1 *In a Council-House Backyard* (circa 1925)

Here's mum modelling her Susan Lenglen gear
with the penny-a-week insurance man
looking amazed at this ripe
housewife in white silk stockings leaning
over the clothesline. Over

the fence the neighbours' kids
mime her poses. They wink and strut
waving their Great Exhibition mugs. Mum
was much admired by a neighbourhood
that knew a bit of class when they saw it.

Talent will out, they all said.
It never did, but the neighbours
still applauded — being more
than faithful to those of their own
who always made the most of their lot.

2 *Big Game* (circa 1928)

Here's dad in Africa living it up
with a dead pig under his foot.
He's got a big cigar and an ever bigger gun.
All around him there's space
and hordes of naked black lasses.

Just the place for a Bradford lad
brought up on Wesley and smog.
No wonder he's enjoying himself,
killing and screwing and making a profit.
When this was taken he was nearly forty.

Another few months and they shipped him home
to work on the ledgers. He packed life up
but took another twenty years to drop off.
I'm looking at an Empire in its hey-day.
Even the dead pig is laughing.

Letters Home — New Zealand 1885

for Allen Curnow

1

Flocks sway, packed tight against the rails.
We boil them down for soap. Each
ewe's worth fourpence for her fat alone:
twice what we'd get by shipping them back home.
(How patiently they wait, heads bowed
like girls at Sunday School.) I try
to catch up on my notes
describing specimens of plant and stone
picked up on my walks. We hacked
cross-sections from live kauri trunks
before we burned the slopes. I hope
to show them at Kew that decent work's being done
out here in the colonies. The smell
of blood and melting bones
fouls the verandah where I smoke.
(My notes on fault-lines are especially good.)
The lake's almost dried up. It's been
like Africa this year. The black
swans die in hundreds, eating
their own yolk. Eels
glut the crimson mud for scraps
tipped from the vats. I've seen
them crawl across the lawn
to grab a live sheep's foot. At night
I read the psalms . . . *The Lord's
my Shepherd*. It's most apt. Two
years here now. It almost feels like home.

PETER BLAND

2

Dear *friend* (there's no one here
called that) I intend
to write a natural history
of these hills. (Most plants
are primitive, some unique. My wife
says we are Adam and Eve.)
My mind's escaped old ways of seeing,
strict categories of breeding, station, class:
it roams, almost unprincipled, between
these tremendous horizons
and the new small print
used in the bibles that you've sent.
Much thanks. I wish
you could see my lake. I've made
a local version of our Oxford punt.

3

At Sunday School my dear wife reads
The Song of Solomon to a Maori chief.
He likes the *old* testament (those simple tales
by bygone kings and queens). He'll
listen for hours. His moko gleams
like blue blood on his cheeks. Once,
at a wedding feast, he ate the heart
of a living lamb — holding it up
still beating to the sun. It was
a sort of Grace — *For what we are . . .*
but that's perhaps difficult to understand
back in New Brighton. Suffice to say
he's *not* a violent man. He asks
why Jesus did not marry? *The Son
of God should father sons himself.*
A tribe of Gods! That's what he wants.
We need a priest. My poor wife does her best.

4

Our lake's one island — a sunken raft —
was once the home of cannibals.
Blood-soaked it's taken root — become

54

a Pavilion, a Chinese glade
of willows and bamboo. Swans
crowd there in their thousands. Some
hang themselves in their haste to breed
(long necks caught on willow forks
breasts spiked by green bamboo).
Their skeletons, so fine and white,
are delicate harps for the wind's tune.

★

At night I go down to the lake alone
haunted by the swans' cold song
(that hollow aboriginal throb). Black
swans, black eels, are all that live
in that still pond. For company
I recite to myself *The Lady of Shalott*
and see her white limbs floating past
my growing tin-roofed Camelot.
My wife's gone back. I cannot keep
her soft hands tied to this hard land.
God called her home to Camberley.
(She begs me to sell up.) I like
my lonely midnight strolls . . . eels
splashing . . . dark wings flying off.
I feel new silences. I hear Noah's doves.
I see the first hills loom above
these slow black waters fleeced in fog.

5

My wife's last letter with a pressed rose
arrived with the first snow. (How I ache
to hold her!) I've arranged my notes
in evolutionary order — according
to Lyell and Spencer. Strange
how the well-established species
show signs of regression. They 'give up'.
These acres obviously need new blood.
(Did she prick her finger? There's a stain
on the petals.) I couldn't live
without these hills, this
sense of space that goes on and on

inside my head as well as
all around me. I remember once
she said *Our pohutukawa blossoms
have the scent of salt and oranges.* That's what
this rose smells of — not Surrey
but her that summer on an Auckland beach
swimming with chestnut hair piled up
like one of Millais' women. The lake
has frozen over. Another week
and it will hold my weight. I'll
skate out all alone to my island
(half-a-mile!) and count the unhatched eggs.
The swans have long gone north. Some ewes
are already lambing. In birth and death
(and love) the world goes mad.
There are no rules for our inmost feelings.
I must question Lyell and Spencer about that.

6

I'm working hard. (Six months
since I wrote you?) Lambs
to the slaughter and these endless notes!
My room is barely habitable . . .
roots, rocks, unopened bills. My drover
says that I'm being eaten up
by this 'great cannibal land'.
He's a hard worker, fresh from Yorkshire,
but a secretive and venal man.
(Some talk of crude high-country habits
and weekends at the Pa.) I've finally
got my index going. So many entries!
Where to end or begin? I've
consulted Darwin, always the best on sources,
but God still goes back further than we think.

7

Her chestnut hair and white limbs floating . . .
My bedroom mirror's cracked. I shave
two faces . . . or I did . . . my beard's
as thick as gorse and mad with ticks.

I've sent the first proofs off (not
happy with my quotes). The drover's left.
The front door's hanging on torn hinges.
Sheep are dying on the library steps.
The shearers are late this year. I'm lonely.
My head hurts and the blackberry patch
whimpers all night with tangled flesh.
No one comes near me. I'll leave this letter
under an ammonite. The lake keeps calling.
I'd like to lie down where the black swans nest.

JENNY BORNHOLDT

(Born 1960)

Reading the Body

1

Back lit
clipped
on the board
light goes
through you
shows you up in
black and white for
what you are — a
gather of bones
a curled frond
of a spine
lightly embraced by
that scooped-out
smoothness of hip
cavity whose bones
like open palms
seem to
offer themselves out
in a kind of
blessing.

2

Here are some pictures
of the body.

These are the bones
of my beginning.
They have stayed
with me like
true friends. They
have given

very fine
support.

See the way the
spine tails down
to a fine twitch

the way the ribs
are arms curved
in welcome

the way the hip bones
lie like an open book.

And finally

There would be
a series of paintings:

The Body as Ant

The Body as Incident

The Body as Intention

The Body as Masterpiece

The Body as Desire

The Body as Ant

The body
is small
and crawls
fast.
The body has
lots of
legs.
The body
lives underground
in a nest
and collects food.

JENNY BORNHOLDT

The Body as Incident

The body
happens to itself
by itself.

The Body as Intention

The body
means well.
It means so well
that it falls
backwards
over itself.
The body
is full
of good
intent.

The Body as Masterpiece

The body
is a big body
is a work
of Art.
The body
is still
life.

The Body as Desire

The body
desires
a body
any body
just not its
own body.

This Line

On this line
gulls eye their way through the sky
sounds pour from the air
the hands open out of the body
and release thin leaves, like
carrier pigeons, into cold air.
On this line there is a faith in
the soundness of bones, their clarity
against nights darker
than closed eyes
and, the imagination for growth,
a belief in
small things rising.
These ferns tilt up
like a choir of small green
archangels
their tight fists unfurl
with the very knowledge
of it.

RANGIAHUTA ALAN HEREWINI RUKA BROUGHTON

(1940–86; Ngā Rauru Kītahi)

Ko Tainui te Waka

Ko Tainui te waka
Hoturoa te tangata
Raukawa te tipuna i puta mai ai
i a Tūrongo me Mahinārangi
ki ngā tini mokopuna e

Mai i Miria te Kakara ki Whitireia
ko te rohe pōtae o Ngāti Raukawa
Nāu i te whakahau ki te hunga rangatahi
me te tau rua mano e

Tīmata ana mai ki Parewahawaha
ka piki atu rā ki runga Raukawa
ko te hui tuatoru ki Ngātokowaru
Ngāti Pareraukawa e

Te Āti Awa Ngāti Toa me Ngāti Raukawa
ngā whakatipuranga mō te tau rua mano
kia whakaoti ai mā te tūmanakotanga
a te iti a te rahi e

Tainui is the Canoe

Tainui is the canoe
the captain is Hoturoa
Raukawa is the ancestor from hence
Turongo and Mahinarangi to the
multitudes of descendants and grandchildren.

From Miria Te Kakara to Whitireia
is the region of Ngati Raukawa

which shelters the young people
for the year 2000.

Commencing from Parewahawaha,
the school of learning reached over to Raukawa
to the third meeting at Ngatokowaru
of Ngati Pareraukawa.

Te Ati Awa, Ngati Toa and Ngati Raukawa —
these are the generations for the year 2000
to consummate the hopes and aspirations
of the humble and of the great.

Translation by Te Aomuhurangi Temamaka Jones

He Waiata mō Te Herenga Waka

Kāore taku raru te āta mōhiotia i ngā raurangi nei,
ko ngā ngaru kai waka i Te Au-a-Tāne e pākia mai rā
e Ngā Pōtiki-a-Rakamamoa e huhū rā, he hiku taniwha pea nge
kei te aukume, te au rona, kei te aukaha te tau a Whiro.
E tū e Hine mā, e Tama mā, whakaarahia ake ngā poupou
    o tō whare
o Te Herenga Waka me tōna tāhuhu; ko te pātaka kai iringa hoki
o te kupu, o te kōrero a te kāhui kahika o ngā rā ki tua.

Kia toka ia nei te paepae tapu kei ngā waha kākā nui a Tāne;
kei ngā manu tīoriori, pari kārangaranga o Rongo-marae-roa.
Pūkana whakarunga, pūkana whakararo ko Poutū-te-rangi tonu
kai Ngā Huihuinga-a-Matariki hei rāhiri mai i te ngahue tangata.
Ka huri au ki te whare mōwai rokiroki. Hai!

A Song for Te Herenga Waka

My trouble is not really known these many days. It is like the
canoe-eating waves at Te Au-a-Tane, battered by the blustering
southerlies, the Children of Rakamamao; perhaps it's a taniwha's
tail prolonging, stirring and lashing my deepest emotions.

63

Rise, young women and men, reinforce the pillars of your house
of Te Herenga Waka and its backbone; the storehouse in which
to hang words and talk of our elders from former times.

Let the sacred threshold be rock-like for the great orators of Tane
and the melodious voices that echo across Rongo-marae-roa. Stare
expressively to the sky and the earth; Poutu-te-rangi, star of the
new year, from the cluster of Matariki will cordially greet the
crowds of people. I turn to the calm resting house. Hai!

Translation by Miriama Evans

He Ngeri

Kātahi au ka katakata!
Kātahi au ka kohekohea!
I kohea ki hea?
Ki te kēkē, ki te hūhā
Āhāhā! Nanea ana te maringi o te wai o te kamo
Whiua te hūpē kia tangi ko te ihu

Papā te whatitiri! Hikohiko te uira!
Ngarue te whenua ki te rauhīhī, ki te rauhāhā!
Kumea mai kia piri!
Kumea mai kia tata!
Ki runga ki te marae e takoto nei;
Te piringa e tū nei, ko Te Herenga Waka
E te iwi e, purutia tō mana kia mau, kia ita!
Aha! Ita! Ita! Mau tonu!

A Ngeri

Now I can laugh,
now I can chatter,
but chatter in what direction?
Towards the armpits — towards the thighs!
See the tears flow freely from the eyes,

mucus is thrown to the ground,
through the nose comes the sound of lament.

The thunder peals, lightning flashes,
the earthquake shakes the land.
Draw the visitors closer!
Draw them nearer!
To the marae that lies here
the house, Te Herenga Waka.
Oh people, hold fast to your mana.
Hold it — make it fast!
Yes, make it firm, make it firm,
hold it always!

Translation Te Aomuhurangi Temamaka Jones

He Pātere mō te Hunga Wahine

Ko wai te wahine i hikitia e te ngutu
he tohunga ki te taunu i te tapu o te tangata?
Kei tua iti ake nei ko te uri a Toa Rangatira, a Raukawa
ko Topeora: kāore te kōtaitai o te waha i tau noa.
Tērā anō rā kei ngā huanui o te rāwhiti e taka ana
Ko Rongomaiwahine nāna i whai i te pīhau pāua o Kahungunu

> Kahukuranui
> Rakeihikuroa
> Tupurupuru
> Rangituehu
> Tuaka
> Ko Mahinārangi

Ko te wahine rā i popoa ki te hinu raukawa.
Ka riro ki Waikato horo pounamu, ki a Tūrongo, he piko he
    taniwha!

Ka whāia tonu ki te ūranga o te rā ki runga o Hikurangi
ki a Hinemātioro, ki te uri tapairu a Porourangi
nāna i āki mai ki waho ko Ngārangikāhiwa, ko Te Kani a Takirau.
Ka rere tāhuhu tonu atu ki te tihi o Pūtauaki, ki a Wairaka
e whakatāne rā i a ia i runga o Mātaatua; kotahi te pō i raru ai ia.

Whakarongorongo rā te taringa ki ngā wai e pohutu rā i
  Te Roto-nui-a-Kahu,
ko Hinemoa pea kei te kau pōito ki a Tūtānekai, ko Te Arawa
  māngai nui.
Kia whakaaokapua ki Tongariro, ki Ruapehu, ki Rauru Kītahi
ko te rohe tēnā o Ruapūtahanga, te wahine rawe ki te hāpai taiaha,
ko Taukaka. Kawea ana ki Waikato ki a Whatihua i te tīorotanga
o te pīpīwharauroa: Kui. Kui. Whiti, whiti ora!

Me hoki mai rā ki te taitonga ki a Mere Rikiriki kei Parewanui
ko te kuia rā nāna te māramatanga i mana ai Te Hāhi o
  Te Wairua Tapu.
Ka puta i reira te tohu o tōna ringa kaha, ko Tahupōtiki
  Wiremu Ratana.
Ka whiti mai te awa 'Tīkei, ko Rangitaane. Kei reira
ko Te Ara-o-Rēhua, te wahine taimua o te hunga poropiti,
nāna i tākiri te kahu o Te Kooti Rikirangi ki Te Awahuri.
Ka toremutu i reira kia hurumi kau atu nga puke hauangi
kei Te Wairarapa, ki tōna ariki tapairu ki a Niniwa-i-te-rangi
hei whakahoki mai i au i ngā huarahi ki Te Whanganui-a-Tara.
Auē! Taukiri ee!

A Patere about Famous Women

Who is the woman who was raised with a mouth
that was expert at taunting the dignity of a person?
She belongs a little way in the past, a descendant of Toa Rangatira,
  of Raukawa,
She is Topeora: she did not just sing songs of unpleasant taste.
There are also the many progeny of the east assembled together.
It was Rongomaiwahine who pursued the paua odour of Kahungunu
              Kahukuranui
              Rakeihikuroa
              Tupurupuru
              Rangituehu
              Tuaka
              to Mahinarangi.
That woman's enticing scent was the oil of raukawa.
She went to Waikato-as-smooth-as-greenstone, to Turongo,
where at every river-bend there is a chief.

RANGIAHUTA ALAN HEREWINI RUKA BROUGHTON

Follow still the rising sun on Hikurangi
to Hinematioro, to the highborn descendant of Porourangi
who bore a son, Ngarangikahiwa, from whom came
    Te Kani a Takirau.
Hasten straight to the peak of Putauaki, to Wairaka:
she acted as a man on Mataatua; for one night she was troubled.
The ear atunes to the water splashing at Lake Rotorua,
perhaps it is Hinemoa swimming with floats to Tutanekai,
    Te Arawa with superior speakers.
Become cloudlike at Tongariro, to Ruapehu, to Rauru Kitahi
that is the district of Ruaputahanga, the very woman to hold
    the taiaha,
named Taukaka. It was carried to Waikato to Whatihua when the
shining cuckoo was singing: Kui. Kui. Whiti, whiti ora!

Let's return southward to Mere Rikiriki at Parewanui:
from this woman elder came the enlightenment which gave mana
    to the church of the Holy Spirit.
From there came the sign of His strong hand, Tahupotiki
    Wiremu Ratana.
Cross the river, Rangitikei into Rangitaane,
there is Te Ara-o-Rehua, the first of the women prophets.
She plucked at the cloak of Te Kooti Rikirangi and drew him to
    Te Awahuri.
From there cross the undulating cool mountains
at Wairarapa, to the high born woman, to Niniwa-i-te-rangi
so that I can return by the paths to Whanganui-a-Tara.
Aue! Taukiri e!

Translation by Miriama Evans

ALAN BRUNTON

(Born 1946)

Dialogue: A Man and His Soul

Baboon, we have travelled far
We have established colonies where the sun never stands upright
We have seen the dead standing in line near waterfront sheds
but I hear always
a hand knocking at the door

'It belongs to a man who cannot be surprised
his eyes are centipedes
There is danger to the people should they ever
hear his cry
with wonder
He nails dogs by their ears
to the door of the rich man's house
so the house can hear —
in small towns between here and Memphis
houses are listening for . . .'

A voice which only the oldest parts of my body can understand
Intuition is small and indecisive
beside the crocodile on the staircase
It becomes impossible to look at some-one and talk
at the same time
When I walk I concentrate so much on breathing
I no longer know where I am going

'I feel this disturbance no longer
this sleepwalker who rides our sadness out into the Ocean
:
our sadness of iodine
our sad nitrogen
our nervous counting of the stars on our fingers
our green turtles leaving on an equatorial current
our Exile
our Exile'

I cannot register changes in atmospheric pressure
I distinguish between neither glass nor ice entering my skin
I see the future city thrown into the skies
falling back as black dust
over a number of days

'You are the sleepwalker
I the master of Inherent Characteristics
Master of that last secret that keeps lovers together
:
the revelation of cockroaches
on ground zero
watching a kind of animal disappear'

Mistress

They say:
I planned revenge to kill a man
with three o'clock on his hands,
to watch him slide his fingers down the wall;
I signed with Hell
in that hotel
where Desire talked him to his fall;

I lied about his suicide
when he broke apart and cried
behind the empty cinema in Spain;
the telegram
from Amsterdam
was the opening of a vein.

I say:
none can sweeten this bitter flood
that fills my vacant lungs with blood;
I hope no more for I have failed
to hear the cry
that stills the sky;
the old customs have not prevailed.

ALAN BRUNTON

Lo, the City

'Is the Maker of this Unintended
as mad from death as we?
Or else already dead?'
> — Milosz

Surrounded by the Dense Substance of the Collective
in New York
where phyla meet for commerce,
I am alive
and
running with the Crowd:

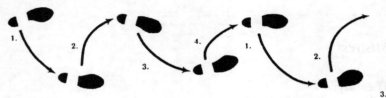

Without warning
the Crowd turns on a Hindoo
fasting for peace on 1st Avenue:
'You are morally defective
in the eyes of our cathedral —
Poverty is unrighteous,
return to Go and select a personal broker immediately!'

Surrounded by the Dense Substance of the Collective
in The Unintended City of Windows,
I see humility and
I am one of many.

We rehearse death in the streets,
various organs are available for exchange
:we are interchangeable. We inhabit the same body.
We are the same body
with the sense organs of a shrimp.

A baby was given the heart of a baboon
in the fourth year
of President Rangoon.

Surrounded by the Dense Substance of the Collective
we mean death for all of us:
in this case
trees are for hanging from.

Cauche-de-Mar

As we are moving into the provinces
now is the hour
on the newspaper bus,
the only sound we hear
is the driver's electric fan.
The sun drips from the window.

In a village beside the Pacific
a whale shuttles
into the sky, the Ocean
burning in its whaleybones;
it holds an umbrella
over its briny head.
Inspiration takes the bus —

and skids into a skullfish on the Strand.
Its pupils are
the moons of Planet X
where Africa is dying
from Fear and Dissolution

(she stayed there with the fish)

Inspiration takes the bus.
Remember me I say,

Goodbye

ALISTAIR CAMPBELL

(Born 1925)

Soul Traps

1 A Stranger from Rakahanga

A stranger has arrived from Rakahanga.
 Nobody knows how he came:
  no strange canoe has been reported —
none could survive in such a sea.
 Our villages are awash, and our dead groan
  as they sit up to the chin in water.
Such a stranger, you would think, would be
 so singular, so arresting,
  once seen, nobody could forget him.
Nobody remembers a single thing —
 the look on his face (if he has a face),
  his size, or if he is young or old.
He arrived, some say, a few hours ago,
 others claim it is more than a week,
  since he was first seen at Omoka.
On one thing, though, all are agreed:
 he is a traveller from Rakahanga —
  but why Rakahanga, they can't say.
They stand around in silent groups, expecting
 the worst — but not a thing happens.
  No deaths or accidents are reported.
They will turn soon to urgent tasks, repair
 the storm damage, but strangely empty
  as if nursing a disappointment.

2 Sina

You were a tender girl, Sina,
 fragrant as the *komuko*
  of the young coconut tree.

Throughout our adolescence
  our entire universe
    was the bottom of a canoe
where we lay together
  drifting among the *motu*.
    Every night I would pluck
for your breasts and hair
  the flowers of the sky.
    And then one night
we drifted far from shore
  through the scented darkness
    oblivious of the reef
until too late — *aue!*
    Now you are a woman
      lovelier even than the girl
that loved me long ago,
  and another lover
    drinks from your calabash.
Ru the fisherman
  knows all the secret places
    in the ocean floor.
His spear is probing
  for an answer.
    I watch and wait.

3 *Akaotu*

Surging over the reef,
  surging over the reef,
    the sea has breached
the canoe of Akaotu
  and now she lies becalmed
    in the shallows of Sanganui.
Her splendid lovers have fled,
  leaving her to the mercy
    of her jealous consort,
red-haired Atea,
  Lord of Light, who grumbles
    in his sleep, causing
the sky to flicker.

But the Lady Akaotu
        turns with the tide.
She smiles as she dreams
        of atolls in their green birth
                pricking the white horizon.

4 *Lovers*

i

Naserengakura is handsome,
        Namuaki is handsome,
                Akaotu's adulterers
are handsome
        to the nth degree.
More beautiful
        than their parents
                the children
drive back the boundaries
                of Te Po.

ii

Manavaroa,
        beloved commando —
it was you
                stormed
        her beachhead
                and brought forth
                        Ru.

iii

I will crawl to Sanga
        and stow it
                in the canoe
of Akaotu
        mother
                of gods.

5 *A Girl in Avarua*

Make no mistake: they love you
        for your beauty, Akaotu,
                not for your brains.
Who but a goofy goddess
        could scatter pebbles
                all over the Pacific
and call them land?
        I saw you once in Avarua,
                a superb young woman
leaning across the counter
        of a piecart,
                talking to the girl:
tall with a splendid figure
        shown to advantage
                by your posture —
high breasts, a narrow waist
        and swelling hips,
                a lovely bottom, legs
tightly encased in jeans
        reaching to mid-calf,
                brown hair with red lights,
and a sweet baby-face
        pale gold in colour.
                You turned and saw
I was waiting to be served
        and smiled a most lovely smile,
                and moved aside at once.
How could I resist you?
        It's no wonder, goddess,
                those handsome layabouts,
Nasere and Namuaki,
        became dotty with desire
                when they first saw you
and made fools of themselves.
        I would have done the same.

ALISTAIR CAMPBELL

6 *Te Hura*

Some say that Kavariki,
    the most beautiful of women,
        invented the dance.
I say it was Kavariki
    and Urerua together.
        When her pubic hairs
were as fine as mouse-down,
    none had removed her
        pareu except her mother.
When they turned wiry,
    it was the High Priest
        Urerua who performed
the initiation rite.
    With his double-size phallus
        he discovered *te hura*
in the split-drum of her
    belly, whence flowed
        the genius of our people . . .
Urerua and Kavariki
    revered for their inventiveness.

7 *Turua*

It is all very well, Turua,
    to have big ideas
        and entertain only the great:
Atea and Akaotu
    are regular celebrants
        and have been known
to stagger home drunk on kava
    from one of your wild parties,
        to the indignation
of the household gods.
    And who can blame them?
        Made to feel redundant,
they perch unhappily
    on the dung-whitened rafters
        along with the kitchen fowls.

Take care, my friend —
    the worm is in the house
        and the red-eyed beetle
sings of dissolution . . .
    Turua, consideration
        is all that is required.
Put your house in order,
    and always leave out
        a little basket of fish
and a half-shell of
    sweet coconut milk,
        and they will climb down
and resume their necessary
    office without fuss
        or recrimination.

8   *Maui's Whare*

Maui hauled it up from the sea.
    His fish-hook caught it
        by a window-frame
and when he landed it
    the structure was askew.
        But the strange thing was
an old man and his wife
    and daughters were still
        in residence: four pairs
of eyes stared out at him,
    utterly astonished,
        but not as much as he.
He scowled, took up the whare
    and shook it angrily
        until the old man and
his family fell screaming
    through the doorway
        and smashed their brains out
on the rocks of Kura Passage
    fifty feet below.
        Thereupon, with infinite care,
the mischief-maker
    took up the broken bodies

and tried to breathe life
into their gaping mouths,
but their spirits had already
fled to Te Po,
squeaking with indignation.
Then Maui put the house down
tried to straighten it,
failed and went away.

9 *Maireriki*

Wag, buffoon, shameless perpetrator
of practical jokes,
terror of the self-righteous,
how could you mix it anyway
with that long-faced ninny,
Turua, overlord of Te Puka?
Don't press your luck, man —
know that a spear can easily deflect
your wittiest sally.
You had your moment, though,
when you eluded his policemen
sent to bring you in
for eating turtle, a dish
reserved for his sole pleasure.
You'd been caught red-handed
grease all over your face —
the woman had fled,
but had been recognised.
The hunt was up —
canoes despatched to every *motu*
until word came you were
holed up at Omoka.
None thought to challenge
the canoe that slipped
away from the shore,
your brothers paddling
and your woman at the stern.
It was beyond a joke
that you could be aboard

in a position of such disgrace —
hidden between her legs
and tented by her skirt.
But the joke was on Turua —
you had got clean away.

10 *Keu*

I am the canoe of Keu —
too late to save me,
too late, my family.
A fierce wind from Savaiki
is driving me
into the shallows.
My bow is shuddering,
my stern splits open.
It is Pakikava
thrusts me on to rocks,
it is Paraakura
rejoices in my downfall.
Teisa, I beg of you,
tell the people,
tell the king himself
nothing comes of grieving.
Tomorrow or the next day
islands will be born of me,
children and palm trees,
and the turtle return
to bathe in my shallows.

11 *Parire*

Parire, lover of sunlight,
Tuturi and Kekeso,
Kiki and Kaka too,
are dead, all dead —
swept off the reef
at Takuua Passage
in the big wind

that struck our island
        the Sunday
after you died.
        I dreamed one night
            a crab had
stolen your eyes,
        one in each claw,
            and that the sea
closed over them,
        but could not extinguish
            the light within.
And now, on certain nights,
        a strange glow
            surfaces and spreads
across the lagoon . . .
        Parire, is it you?

12 *Maia*

Roadways lined with hibiscus,
        paths overhung with wild gardenia,
            have led me unerringly,
as often in my dreams,
        to the giant tamanu tree
            in whose decaying branches
the spirits hang like bats
        in a fetid cave.
            I could have wept, my brother,
to see you hanging there,
        waiting to be harvested
            with murderers and thieves.
I, your sister, Sina,
        have prayed to our father Rongo
            that you be taken down
and ferried to Savaiki.
        I could sleep easier, Maia,
            if you were gathered soon.

13 *Mahuta*

The gourd is overripe,
    but it is the yam you steal
        from our ocean gardens,
Mahuta, lover of night,
    late of Rakahanga.
        The beautiful young girl
sighs as she holds
    each heavy breast
        within a heavy hand.
Stunned, stunned —
    the dragonfly bows its head
        to the blows of the rain.
Lightning scribbles its name
    above Katea Village
        where a young man lies
dying, who only yesterday
    was anointed ariki.
        Mahuta, night-walker,
what are the fishermen saying
    as they wade hip-high in the sea?
        It is easier to net the tide
than to trust in Mahuta,
        gatherer of souls.

14 *Solomona*

To die is simply to walk
    away from the body
        without regret or pain,
and with no thought of
    turning back, for there is
        nothing to turn back to,
except the empty shell
    that relatives weep over.
        I have often left
my body here at Te Tautua,
    crossed the lagoon and
        walked among my sleeping

kinsfolk at Omoka to see
    if all was well.
        My family know my door
must be kept open
    if I am to rejoin my body,
        but sometimes through
carelessness they have
    almost shut me out.
        Now it is time to go,
to walk the steep track
    to Savaiki alone. I have
        enjoined my dear ones
to close my door firmly
    after me, when I leave
        on my last visit to Omoka.
They weep, but will obey.

15 *Bosini*

Not a breath of air.
    The roads of coral sand
        shimmer whitely
under a full moon.
    Millions of spirits
        are abroad tonight.
What are they gathering for
    along the beaches
        and on street corners?
When I approach,
    they turn their heads as one
        and look at me,
but I no longer
    fear them or their
        unvoiced complaints.
Grandfather Bosini
    lies on the cool surface
        of his tomb. I feel
a little less lonely
    seeing him there.

16 *Sema*

The ferns of Taperu,
    trampled in the struggle
        when Sema was cut down
on Hiro's orders,
    have sprung back this year,
        but the beautiful birds
that used to fly
    to Sema's fingers
        are no longer to be seen
along our coast.
    His beloved canoe lay
        sunken in the sand,
half filled with water.
    It was Natonga breached it
        with his spear point,
but what gushed out
    was not sea water
        but the blood
of unborn generations.
    That blood is wailing,
        it runs down the walls
of Hiro's house,
    it flames in the sky above
        the village of Taperu
where the sun is dying.

17 *Tini*

My name is Tini —
    I am the House of Hiro.
        I am going to die.
Already weeds are growing
    on my good name.
        The wind pipes
a mocking tune
    in my ribcage.
        The path that seemed
to stretch unbrokenly
    as far as Savaiki

    has petered out
in marshland
   somewhere to the west
    of Taperu.
Hiro is dead
   and the two assassins
    Tiu and Kaka with him.
Not until the wind
   turns round and blows
    from Rakahanga
will they find
   peace in the grave.

18 *Siva*

It was at Sanga
   that Siva took up
    the challenge.
Siva's fine-boned
   muscular hands
    reined in
the runaway stallions
   of Tangaroa,
    and tied them
to a post
   with a cord from
    Omoka's navel.

19 *Kiri-a-Tai*

Choose your tree —
   a tall tree,
    a straight tree.
Study your tree,
   look into her pith
    and find the shape
of your canoe.
   The tree shudders,
    the tree sways —

she is a dancer,
    a lovely young girl.
        The tree is hurt,
she bows to the west
    and sighs as she falls.
        Build her now,
build your canoe,
    make her strong,
        make her tight.
Now you, sir,
    will sit in the bow,
        I in the stern,
my hand on the tiller.
    Nailed to the mast
        are the colours
of Io, the Hidden One.
    Our goal is Savaiki,
        so let her be swift,
let her prow sing
    as it slices
        the skin of the sea.

20   *Tangaroa*

Old friend and fellow voyager,
    don't say I didn't warn you.
        It was different in the old days
when you and I and Seimata
    roamed the world as champions.
        It was Seimata who peeled off
the eight skins of the sky
    and revealed the bloodied
        godhead of Rorangi,
and you who met the challenge
    of the great sea serpent
        that had coiled itself
and swallowed its tail
    within the ancient
        navel of Tongareva.
It was I who learned,

at the feet of Ataranga,
    to build ancestral song.
Sleep was ever good to us,
    and when we ventured out
      upon the waters of Kare
the peace that fell on us
    stretched all the way to Savaiki.
      Now, old friend, it's time to go.
Our ocean-going double canoe
    awaits us, stocked for the voyage.
      Our men are seated and,
as we embark, they shout and raise
    their paddles to salute us.
      We can delay no longer.

MEG CAMPBELL

(Born 1937)

The Way Back

Often we strayed far into the woods,
like those children in the folk tale,
but we always found our way back.
You were older, and I
simply followed behind you,
leaving you to think for both of us
(I was conditioned to follow
an older child). But listen —
it was I who thought to drop pebbles,
I, alone, who recognized the witch
in all her guises, I who pushed her
into her oven and pulled you from the cage,
and together we picked our way home
from pebble to pebble, while you said
it was me you really loved,
and I believed you,
knowing that you were wise.

Fish

Fish, nothing is as it seems.
Caught in your mouth is a hook —
pink and white it gleams,
like your pearled flesh as you swim
far from the shadow of the boat
towards approaching death.

As you find yourself pulled
back to the boat, rest
and give yourself to the fisherman
willingly, in celebration.

MEG CAMPBELL

Drum on his deck
with a burst of energy
that carries your spirit forward —
let him hear the drumming
of your head and tail, *Ika*.

Hook, you know that sorrow, elation
and yearning are the plaited strands
of a fine strong line, running
through the hands of the fisherman.
Without him, you are simply a pendant, *Matau*.

Fisherman, see the drifting dates
of our ceremonies — imagine
something beyond our gods,
beyond Iaia, Brahman and Yahweh.

Finally, we shall imagine
our own imaginations — we are
snakes who swallow our tails.
All that we imagine is eventually
provable — the fish, the hooks
and, finally, the great predators . . .
Why is the treasure of God
secreted in our bodies
and what does love create in us
that God seeks so greedily?

What now, fisherman?
Simply *akangaroi* —
a moment of peace,
a high plateau of night, while
beyond our time a wind sighs,
a plank bangs softly
against the house,
and whoever hunts us —
whoever fishes for us,
hones his weapons, wipes
his hooks, and sleeps.

Loch, Black Rock, Beautiful Boat

'The loch, the black rock,
the beautiful boat — these are
the names my father gave me,
brought from his boyhood
haunts in Old Caledonia.
No other that I knew had
so many names, or such a dad.
He was my poet, my eccentric
playmate, with no peer in any
kingdom anywhere. The ladies
loved him, pronouncing him
'a fine, upstanding man',
and Mother of course agreed —
and, oh, what trouble it caused!
I lost out, somehow,
in the tussle for his affections.
Seventy-seven he is now, and
nothing has changed — except
that it matters to me more than ever
that he gave me those names —
'*Aline, dubh sgeir, fearr bata* . . .
the loch, the black rock,
the beautiful boat.'

Mahuika

I have snapped off my burning
fingers, and given them to you
one by one, but you have thrown them
in the stream to amuse yourself.
Maui, I am fed up with you!
When next you come to me begging
for fire, I shall be ashes.
I hear that you intend to cheat
Death — a serious matter —
but, when I see you crushed

between her thighs, I shall laugh
until my fires rekindle,
and my tears steam, and spit.

Journeys

At the end of the journey we built
another pyramid, intending
to rendezvous with the gods.
Each contributed a massive brick
and it was placed according
to his rank. At the top,
with a foot-hold in the heavens,
was our priest-king
with his mathematicians
and war-lords who planned it all.
As our energies ripened we were
driven on, remembering certain
promises that we carried in a chest.

Once, at sea, we gathered by the mast
to see an angry child, curled
head to tail, unfurl himself
as the ship rocked. Morals
spilt from his throat and sank
unfathomed, and, tongued
by faint light, he searched the sky.
It was a one-way mirror by day
he said — a gold and pink lie.

We left the chest behind — all
that we cared for was in the sky,
because of a small and swarthy
man-god we had learned to love.
We loved him for the curved
rib of his nose, and, because,
where he had walked, God sprang
from the soil like mushrooms
at a witch's heel. But now

he is staked out in the sky
with stars for nails, while we watch
stiff-necked and giddy,
and full of inarticulate belief . . .

Mushrooms clouds like fairy rings
surround the earth. Forgive me —
I write hastily, in the shadow of my hand.

JANET CHARMAN

(Born 1954)

Clayton's Sleep

i remember the year
Clayton Delaney died

on the Firestone Allnighter

this lil song
of Texas mourning
and how we sweeten
sour flesh
with the Country Air

our illegal tranny
drilling
the corridor canyon
as we hump
the easy now   cows
across the arroyo

'IT'S RAINING'

Dont. Fight. Us. Mister. Heremaia.
We.   Are.   Changing.   You.

the first round's finished
i'm overdosing
on the disgraceful   (no bell
silence
of the linen chapel
where i restock
my head
on the pure white
altarcloths
how many more
draw sheets
tonight

oh lord
now and at the hour of my death

   'If the levee breaks   Miss Kitty
   ah caint ansuh fo ma men.'
   'Do what yuh have to   Rafe.'

meanwhile
   inside the night worn red tepee
   one of my hands
   is at liberty
   to slip past the white
   starch
   and cradle my own breast

social committee

walk back
through the long grass
to the hall

leave the ponga fronds for tomorrow

but take the
hydrangeas
off the stage

carried
on a washing machine
lid

gotta dish them
in the surf
you said

frock got wet

didn't know
let's
lock

up
together

could mean this

the lecture on Judy Grahn

the wimmin carried in their ironing boards
set them up

plugged in their irons

they began ironing together   set on silk
raised it to linen
men's shirts   a few synthetics suffered

one of the wimmin
walked around the room
removing the asbestos pads
where the iron rests were   on old model boards
    (dangerous if cut or sawn)

when the shirts were ironed
the wimmin put them on
rolled the sleeves to the elbow
and drove home together
fast

they were not stopped

the lecture on Maya Angelou

the wimmin met outside theatre corporate
they unrolled their bedrolls
lit their primus stoves
boiled their coffee

they were queuing
to see the production
of a midsummer night's
dream
it was 2 a.m.
they waited 18 hours
patiently   cheerfully
someone was telling
a wicked story about her stepfather

when the box office opened
one of them could tap dance   among bullets
somebody got drunk and was sick
somebody fell in love   comes to the same thing

when they got in
the play was boring
the seats were uncomfortable

they waited too long

the lecture on Emily Dickinson

the mist of chalk dust
rose from the savage thrust
of miss pettit's arm against the board

the group three
slow learner girls
leaned in
took in the way
her brown arm softened into
blue veined cream
at the inner elbow

her cologne smell
saturated the fractions   and they shared
a little   intimate   ironic
defeated   silence

smiling into each other's eyes
at the end
of the period

the lecture on Sylvia Plath

the wimmin squatted
by the dirty creek
drying out the poems
from the pockets in the wash

some had been beaten on rocks and were softer
one hard one
was stretched out   weighted down with stones
and when the sun broke on it
most couldn't watch

the words became darker
and yet strangely
harder to recognize

a woman pitied this drying
and shook her wet hair
into the folds

the words ran into each other
the sentence
changing subtly
contracting
beginning to shine black
as it dissolved

crouching in steam

crouching in steam
before the chlorophyll coloured light of my dream
disappears
i'm a runner in the bath
the water rising
something tugging at my beard

   who is this small dark woman
   who has entered my dreams?
   so neat and assured
   escaped from a novel perhaps?
   with her little painted mouth
   or the mouth not painted at all
   but sweet with it
   ignoring me
   immersed in her own knowing
   as i look over her shoulder
   she puts her finger to her lips
   she speaks

the yellow duck floats by
she has her appointment with the plughole to get to
towelling but leaving the large wet patch in the middle of my back
for the candlewick to stick to
through the louvres the Hardenbergia slumps against the fence
it's been a long night
but now there's another tremendous flower crop brought in
to smother up the palings for the day

   are you still listening?

   i was ashamed
   he beat me
   my jaw was broken
   and wired
   i could not use words for several months
   i pegged out hate
   chattered obscenities among the sheets
   the whirring in my head

i had my anger
the cold deep shadow under the apple tree
advancing to engulf me

What did you do?

i existed   wait for the fracture to heal
iron   hear the children's words
do you believe this   in a doctor's waitingroom
in a woman's magazine   i read this story

'Put your finger to your lips   and speak

i began by saying 'i am so neat in my black suit
                with the unsoiled cream collar
                someone will employ me
                they will offer seven dollars an hour
                more than a cleaner
                less than a nurse.   i was right
                at reception we specialize in the smile.
                Thanks sweetheart. Great Lovey.
                Bye darling.

when i saw him at work i thought i'd say
something outrageous how about if i jack
you up with a friend of mine really it's
not me but you're pretzel shaped you've
toasted away your acne why are you turning
over that tired old australian leaf they
all come to when they're burnt out here
stay i like you

he put his finger to my lips
i spoke
this is what i told him
                'you were in the sweat of maths
                the farts the fear
                the ruler thwack on the wrists
                the jellybaby if you got it right
                Junior to the W Room. Too Belligerent.
                "And Mrs Trueblood, we will not tolerate
                that sort of behaviour

in this school."
You brought the boxing cup home see what
i got   your dad is up off the bed and
ambles over. He pissed in it. That's
what it's worth boy the bead curtain
the screen door the shade in the bedroom
the peeling painted wood on the verandah
so grey   it's the hot afternoon   the beer
and i hit her doctor i never wanted to

my jaw is still wired
the wires go from the handset into my head
i am part of the equipment
i repeat the last few words they say to me
it encourages them to keep speaking
— to the Kingsgate?
'To the Kingsgate for a drink. Hold all calls.'
yes mister Whitelaw

she put her finger to my lips   she spoke
'Those children have their own now
take this piece of paper write it down
it matters   all matters
i put my finger here   i will leave it here
i won't press too hard but it will be enough
and when you think you've said all you know
my finger will be there
you will continue

TE TAITE COOPER

(Born 1940; Ngāti Kahungunu)

AND

PĀ MAX TAKUIRA MARIU, S.M.

Te Hokinga Mai

Tangi a te ruru, kei te hokihoki mai e
E whakawherowhero i te Pūtahitanga
Nāku nei rā koe i tuku kia haere
Tērā puritia iho nui rawa te aroha e
Te Hokinga Mai, tēnā koutou
Tangi ana te ngākau i te aroha
Tū tonu rā te mana te ihi o ngā tūpuna
kua wehe atu rā
Mauria mai te mauri tangata
Hei oranga mō te mōrehu tangi mōkai nei
E rapu ana i te ara tika mō tātou katoa
Te Hokinga Mai
Te Hokinga Mai
Tū Tangata tonu!

Te Hokinga Mai: The Return

The cry of the owl keeps coming back to me.
It is hooting out there where the paths meet.
I was the one who allowed you to go,
my deep love did not detain you.
Te Hokinga Mai, the Return, I greet you.
How my heart weeps in sorrow.
Stand tall, the pride and the awe
of ancestors gone before.

TE TAITE COOPER and PĀ MAX TAKUIRA MARIU

Bring back the true spirit of the people
to heal those who cry out in loneliness,
who are searching for the true path for all.
Te Hokinga Mai
Te Hokinga Mai —
Stand tall!

Translation by Pā Max Takuira Mariu

ALLEN CURNOW

(Born 1911)

Dialogue with Four Rocks

1

High and heavy seas all the winter
dropped the floor of the beach the whole mile
exposing more rocks than anybody
imagined the biggest surprise a
reef the size of a visiting beast
you have to walk round
                                        a formation
out of the gut of the gales the noise
the haze the vocabulary of
water and wind
                        the thing 'demands an
answer'
            I know you do you know me?

the sea shovels away all that loose
land and shovels it back underfoot's
a ball of sand stitched together with
spun lupin and looping spinifex
making it look natural
                                        little
as you like to think nothing's either
covered or uncovered for ever.

2

A wall of human bone the size
of a small church isn't easy
to conceive
                neither is the rock
which overhangs me overhung
itself by cloud-cover cupping
the uproars of up-ended seas

and overhanging us all the
hot star which nothing overhangs

the wig it wears is trees knotted
by the prevailing westerlies
'chapleted' with clematis and
kowhai at this height of the spring's
infestations of white and gold
a cerebrum behind the bone
'thinking big'
                   proportionately
to the size of the thing
                         doesn't
have to be visible if it
stoops to speak so to speak the word
of a stony secret dislodged
the creator knows he's made it!
his mate matter
                 out of nothing
a tied tongue loosed the stony ghost
before all of us talking all
at once in our own languages
the parakeet's brilliant remarks
the fluent silences of the
eel in the pool
           I think the rock
thinks and my thought is what it thinks.

3

A rock face is creased in
places in others cracked
through to itself I have

never climbed though children
sometimes do up to the
chin of the cave below

I always look up though
something else is always
uppermost a cloud scuds

ALLEN CURNOW

past the sun reappears
yellow lichens ashy
patches thicken sicken

on the skin of the face
of the rock from spots the
size of the iris of a

mouse's eye to a smashed
egg the rock is wetted
by a weeping lesion

long after the rain stopped
it looks down I look up
a wink is sufficient.

4

Memory is a stonier
place at the farm they called it
Rocky Gully blackberry
claws me back where I'm crawling

pistol-gripping the rifle
at arm's length after the hurt
hare my two bullets in its
body and couldn't reach it

where the third aimed blindly hit
home recesses of mother
rock overhang me and the
sun the rock offering no

choice of exit under the
one skin hare and hound I catch
myself listening for the shot
in the dark I shall not hear.

Organo Ad Libitum

For beauty with her bande
These croked cares hath wrought,
And shipped me into the lande,
From which I first was brought.
— Thomas, Lord Vaux 1510–56

1

Time's up you're got up to kill
the lilies and the ferns on wires
the brightwork the sorrowful silk
ribbons the cards the cars

the black twelve-legged beast
rises the dance begins
the six shoulders heave
you up the organist sits

with his back to you and your hobbling
pomp *largo* it says
e grave his fingers walk but
none of the feet is in step

he polishes the stool he rocks on
the bones of his arse he reaches
for a handful of stops he's nodding
yes to your proceeding

perched on a mountain with
'rows upon rows of pipes
'set in cliffs and precipices'
growing and growing 'in a blaze

'of brilliant light' that sort
of stuff is packaging
printed matter only if only
there were more to it than that

(shriek!) you could see 'his body
'swaying from side to side amid the

105

ALLEN CURNOW

'storm of huge arpeggioed
'harmonies crashing overhead'

in a cloud a bandaging whiteout
'his head buried forward towards
'a keyboard' busier than God
and you that wool-shed sleeper

the one who saw in his dream
was it Handel high among the icefalls the
big wig nodding mountainously
swaying playing the instrument

had to be big enough to drown
Sam Butler's rivers up there in
Erewhon chapter IV and climbed
uselessly towards the source

of the music this isn't a dream
west of the main divide
Nowherewhon sounds no trumpets
this afternoon everyone present is

wide awake nobody's dreaming
least of all you (you) steady there
hang on *taihoa*! the organist's
fingers trot he breathes through

dusty curtains a husky
vox humana out of dusty
pipes fat candles for Sister
Cecilia's jig-time fingering

diddledy-dancing you down
hold tight there brother in the box
saying after me 'It was
'no dreme: I lay brode waking' and

2

saying after me it was *raunchy*
and heavy with lilies in the chapel of

Walerian Borowczyk's blue (blue)
nunnery
      she leaned she fondled the
keyboard the pipes blew kisses
to the mouth her virgin sisters
dressed the altar-table dusted
the pews
        every one a beauty
(beauty) 'dangerous; does set dancing blood' Fr Hopkins S.J.
specialist
      swaying she swept up
nympholept handfuls flung
on the bloodstream a sister playing
organo ad libitum jiggetty-jig on the
woodcutter's cock and the butcher's
block
     Paris having the rottenest
summer for years the crowds
packed in out of the rain to the
Cinéma Paramount leaving
Montparnasse to the web-footed tourists
and the taxis
      dead in her bed
by toxic additive smuggled and
slipped from the knickers to the coffee cup
the gaunt Mother lay
       and they danced
their hot pants down on the stony
gallery for joy of their nubility
crying 'La Mère est morte!' they
swung on the bellrope naked making the
bell-mouth boom at the sun
       one
sneeze of the gusting equinox
whipped the doors from the bolts and up
went the scarlet skirts of the cardinal
dead leaves and fingers
     flying
to the roaring organ the guffaw
of the daylight and the rain pouring

ALLEN CURNOW

from the outside in
                    the movie's
over
       will you get up and go?

3

The organist blows his nose folds
his music switches the power off

getting into the 'waiting cars' they
postpone the politics of eternity

till time permits which is after the
cards the flowers the municipal

oil-fired furnace the hole
in the ground one after after

another thereafter before you
know where you are you were.

4

No bookshelf in the room
                      the Gideons'
bible in the drawer the last occupant
never opened is a black book
lying in wait
                lucky you brought
your bedside paperbacks prismatic
blue green yellow purple
one celebrated psychiatric
teacher and there's this marvellous
meteorite or enormous
boulder of Magritte a motto for
Sisyphus beneath which you are that
prone figure folded in scarlet perfectly
composed exposed in a
window for anyone who cares to know
what it's like in these rooms for sleeping
off life

'O Faustus lay that
'damned book aside read read
'the scriptures' watch out for the
fish-hooks in the small print

5

                  mark
the exits fasten your bible-belt
for take-off
               'the unlikely event
'of an emergency'
                   he sits with his
back to you 'busier than God' his
instrument flashes the crash is
programmed the music is magnified the
size of the side of an antarctic
volcano
           you disintegrate there
buzz buzz
             with or without your
loved ones and a face the mirror has
forgotten.

6

            After is a car door
closing
        chlomp
a blinking light a wide gate
the main road
             chlomp
can I take you anywhere?

7

Hands on the wheel and eyes on the road
reprieved into the time of day they notice
a yellow bus turning a tired female trundling

groceries 'belief in a hereafter'
wasn't so difficult was it? hardest of all
to believe what actually happens come to think

the difficulty was never to have believed
willingly in heat o'the sun or winter's rages
nor that here after all the hereafter hadn't much

going for it notwithstanding the beauty of
the language nor been listening
when the little dog said you can't eat it and you

can't fuck it sour grapes dogs having no
souls if you believe the books and what's
so special about you in your situation

apropos eating and fucking and
who writes the books? only men who do both or
if no-one did wouldn't exist.

8

palingenesis
             five syllables' worth
of pure vacation
                round trip
                  returning
you don't know you've been
                      born twice not again
'Fie upon such errors!
                To hear stuff of that
'nature rends mine ears'
                  Panurge said but Arthur
(Schopenhauer) three
                hundred years after
rather liked the thought
                looked forward to a
hereafter stocked with
                genuine spare parts
good as new nothing to
                burden the memory
naked on the beach
                now storms from the west
stand the sea on end
                it's an instrument
big enough to drown

           accompanies you
all the way down the
            'cold front' feathering
inland hanging its
           gauzes uncloses
closes teases you
          don't see anything
clearly   *
    taihoa!
        your replacement's on
his way
      you're naked
           as the fish bottled
'in its element'
         lifted to the sun
and it's the same wave
            spirits you away
out to sea while the
         biodegradable
part picks up its heels
          recycles all its
degradations
      fresh
        wreaths every time and
no resurrections.

9

        The organist
locks up the console
         Handel
booms at the sun
        Tiziano's
rapt airborne virgin in the Frari
was an assumption removed *per*
restauro in '74 that too was a day of
sun wind and rain
        Domenico's
mother said and he quoted 'life
'is bitter we must sweeten the coffee'
shovelling the sugar
      chlomp

'towards the source of the music'
                                    chlomp
and they made the bell-mouth swing
swinging on the bell-rope
                        naked.

You Will Know When You Get There

Nobody comes up from the sea as late as this
in the day and the season, and nobody else goes down

the last steep kilometre, wet-metalled where
a shower passed shredding the light which keeps

pouring out of its tank in the sky, through summits,
trees, vapours thickening and thinning. Too

credibly by half celestial, the dammed
reservoir up there keeps emptying while the light lasts

over the sea, where it 'gathers the gold against
it'. The light is bits of crushed rock randomly

glinting underfoot, wetted by the short
shower, and down you go and so in its way does

the sun which gets there first. Boys, two of them,
turn campfirelit faces, a hesitancy to speak

is a hesitancy of the earth rolling back and away
behind this man going down to the sea with a bag

to pick mussels, having an arrangement with the tide,
the ocean to be shallowed three point seven metres,

one hour's light to be left and there's the excrescent
moon sponging off the last of it. A door

slams, a heavy wave, a door, the sea-floor shudders.
Down you go alone, so late, into the surge-black fissure.

Moules à la Marinière

It took the sun six hours to peel
the sea from the gut, black underwater
dries out grey underfoot, 'cleft for me'

to look down. The dull thought of drowning
ebbed with the flood, this orifice entices
wide open, gargling, warm at the lips.

Not all the way down. The deepest
secretions don't drain, still you can 'feel'
what's below the bottom of the tide,

knowing more than's good for you: seabed
rock wetted perpetually with spectral
colours, quotations lifted from

life into a stony text, epigraphies
remembering shot-silk offals, trapped
green weed, petrifying mauves,

muddy cysts, mucus, your own interior
furnishings, glands, genitalia
of the slit reef spilling seawards:

walls all scabby pink, sprayed-on starfish,
gluey limpets, linings of the gut which
swallowing a wave throws up an ocean,

it smells of your nature, sickishly.
Hold on tight, by one hand, stripping
off the mussels, quick! with the other

into the bag, don't count cut bleeding
fingers. The tide scrapes the bottom,
blinded and a bit fouled with sand

the slack of the swell drools, fills, empties,
refills, your jeans are sodden
to the crotch, that's wet enough, the bag's

heavy enough: do you really want more
mussels, old swimmer, do you need
more drowning lessons? Here it comes, one

ten-foot wave after another, it's
all yours now and it's up to you down
in the gut and the blind gut

in the wet of your eye gorging
moules à la marinière,
an enormous weight! Nothing to the

tonnages of water lightly climbing
your back. Picked off alive and
kicking in the rip, did you 'feel'

unaccountably unsurprised by
how natural it all is, in the end,
no problem, the arms and legs have only

to exercise the right allowed by law,
last words, the succinctest body-language.
You're innocent. The sea does the rest.

Blind Man's Holiday

1

Is the word 'adult'? Utamaro's engulfing
vulvas, deep thought! Füssli's girls muscling in, a
moist-handled glans, *shockingly indelicate,*

poor wretch! Flaxman said, *looking ineffably*
modest, one didn't blame the widow Füssli's
thrift, who stoked the kitchen range with them, making

sea-coal burn bluer. Was less at stake for Bruno
in Venice, incinerated, ineffably
for something ineffable? Ashes, in the end.

Stuff your pillow-book with metaphysics for
the best bedside read, it takes the place of what
takes place, pictures or *pensées*, the same thing.

The picture in the mind revives, our poet
noticed, and so do I. These agreeable
sensations moved over and made room for *sad*

perplexity, and back again, having once
orbited the earth. I re-enter, entering
you. The mind's too full of itself, to make sense

of Pascal or the creed of Saint Athanasius
damp and hot from the press, 'would you believe it?'
What does God smell of but the dust of hassocks,

wine, laundered linen, a creation of Patou
fingertipped behind the ears? Angel surrogates
shinny up and down the fire-escape, flapping

at bedroom and bathroom windows, all fingers
and feathers. She's too full and he's too busy to
notice much, only *gleams of half-extinguished*

thought, in the light of what takes place, no other
light really than these, which take the place of it.
A particular darkness forgets our visits.

2

What happened? What's happening? Somebody drew
a funny face on a big shell, BANG! you're dead
all of you, Ol' Bill ducks his helmet, it flies

past grinning, or bounces off a parapet.
In a serious oil-painting nobody gets
obscenely eviscerated, the war artist's

a dab hand at cosmetic bandaging, he
patches up with white, with a fine tip adds red
for the head-wounds, mostly in the scalp and brow,

the eyes of the wounded are forget-me-not
blue, gun-flashes vermilion, virginal pink
for the faces, like begonia blooms in shit

which is khaki *dunnest smoke* old-masterly
murk *that my keen knife see not the wound it makes*
nor Heaven peep through. Heaven does. One painted

star blinks benignly. A child in the sun sees
it all in The Queen's Gift Book where Adam hides
because he is naked. My bank manager's

choice is a framed cauliflower cloud, the atoll
vertically blown up out of a silk-screen
ocean. Glass catches the light. Entering, I

turn it to the wall, unwilling to pre-empt
the untriggered fact, the picture in the mind,
the job in hand. Its relevance is obscure.

3

What's pain time? Your long wire, Alvin Lucier, sings
to the oscillator, end over end, glistens
in your darkened gallery. This is our midnight
ride in a wet gale banging the heads of the trees

together. Quartz watches don't keep it, humane
quackery knows what's quickest for capital
offenders, mortal inhalation, 'lethal
injection', make up your mind, how would you like

to die? In a flash, a puff, *an unconscionable*
time a-dying the king said or was said to have
said? Duration is public, the intensity
private, God's wink, a lifetime, a million years.

Where are we now? Between gulps of gas, that's twice
I've asked, this time he answers Saint Luke's, meaning
the supermarket not the church, I grunt back
gratefully, meaning neither, the hospital's

any minute now by pain time, a quick fix could
conveniently snap the wire, drop the dumb ends
in a puddle of terminal quiet, no
more random glistenings, no sound-images

whipped off the street. I want it stopped. Where are we?
The ambulance corners with a shrug, straightens,
windshield wipers egg-scramble headlights, greens, reds,
ambers, unquantifiable messes of wet

incandescences. Squatting, he holds the gas
bottle as steadily as he can. I lie
still too. The driver's shoulder's a dark function.
It's an 'essential service' we all perform,

Monday is beginning, Sunday's casualties
unloading still, full as a party balloon
with pain the mind bobs unserviceably while
somebody is brought in dead. I want my shot

and a couple of 50 mg
indocid is all I'm getting if that's true
about the key to the cupboard where they keep
the morphine and the sister who comes on duty

at five, that's four hours more of this, the
bloody sheet keeps slipping off. You get the picture?
Amnesia, muse of deletions, cancellations
revives, revises pain, a ride in the dark.

Canto of Signs Without Wonders

I look where I'm going, it's the way
    yesterday's and the day before's clouds
      depict themselves over and over

an affluently planted skyline:
    the clouds lay the whitenesses on thick
      over the bluenesses. The impasto

is unsigned, there's a kind of an impression
    of lettering rapidly rubbed out
    before I can read, pasted over again

and rewritten, the name of a famous
    product, the thing that's everything,
    the sky being prime space, anyway

the most public part of this universe.
    Speculative thunder is noises,
    contused vapours, colours into which

my eyes walk: high-flown language, logo and
    sign of a brand of which 'the authors
    are in eternity', at least some

country we never trade with. My eyes
    walk a tight wire made fast to a cloud,
    securest anchorage, the weather

man's promise of 'settled conditions'.
    Underfoot, the pavement keeps falling
    away step by step where I'm about

to pass the pianist's open door
    some *chant sans paroles* escapes: his patched
    iron roof leaked, he spread a tarpaulin

over the Steinway: two of his cats
    stare from the shade of the hydrangea.
    The pavement is still falling, my eyes

walk not precisely stepping high across
    craters and cones, 'best parts' of our city:
    volcanic pustules green a thousand

years, and for a couple of lifetimes
    these people, yesterday's and the day
    before's people, as far as the bluest

dilations of clouds and seas and names
    to call islands by. Less and less time
    remains, they purify their private

pools, uncapping the vials which protect
    from viral enemies: the prudent
    set aside sums for depreciation,

each year sell off a wasting asset,
    c'est la vie. The painter is freshing
    up yesterday's clouds by interior

light, he cleans his brushes, drinks a mug
    of instant coffee. The rusted VW
    meditates 'my other car is a Rolls'.

And as they walk, those two, side by side,
    his hand fondles the blueness of her
    jeans, her thready rondure and the stitched

name of Levi Strauss, below the patch
    seeking. She takes the hand. The sign is
    what the maker means. Much more than that

calls for an impossible presence
    of mind, I look where I'm going and
    that way they depict themselves, yes

that's all for today, my eyes wired
    to a system there, feet falling in turn
    on the pavement which is falling away,

unsigned whitenesses, unsigned bluenesses.

ALLEN CURNOW

The Loop in Lone Kauri Road

By the same road to the same
sea, in the same two minds,
to run the last mile blind or
save it for later. These
are not alternatives.

So difficult to concentrate! a powerful
breath to blow the sea back
and a powerful hand to haul it
in, without overbalancing.
Scolded for inattention,

depending on the wind, I know
a *rimu* from a *rewarewa*
by the leaf not 'coarsely serrate',
observant of the road roping
seaward in the rain forest.

A studied performance, the way
I direct my eyes, position
my head, 'look interested'.
Fine crystal, the man said,
you can tell by the weight,

the colour, the texture. The dog
steadies, places a healthy turd
on the exact spot. We like it
in the sun, it keeps our backs
warm, the watertables

dribble down the raw red cutting
the road binds, injured natures are
perfect in themselves. We liked it
at the movies when they nuked the city,
and suspended our disbelief

in doomsday, helping out the movie.
NEW YORK STATE jogs past me,
ribcage under the t-shirt stacked
with software, heart-muscle programmed
for the once round trip,

crosses my mind, by the bridge
at the bottom, the road over which
and the stream underneath are thoughts
quickly dismissed, as we double
back, pacing ourselves.

Concentrate! the hawk lifts off
heavily with an offal of silence.
Forget that, and how the helicopter
clapper-clawed the sea, fire-bucketing
the forest, the nested flame.

WYSTAN CURNOW

(Born 1939)

from *Castor Bay Proses*

I return to the juxtaposition of it, daily. I do live
by the sea. By the sea. I came back by air, and here's
where I landed. I swim every day. The tide comes in,
over the sand. I look out over the sea. Every day.

I hope my being here does not put you out.

I recommend an early breakfast. A bowl of muesli,
say. Or a light omelette. Take your swim no later
than ten — the others won't arrive till later. An
orange will do wonders for that salt taste in your
mouth. Brew up some coffee. If by now you are a little
peckish, try a plate of cheese (camembert, if you have
it) and sliced apple. Put the second Band album
('Jemima Surrender' is a good track) on the record-
player and dance barefoot on the hardwood floor.
When it's over, go to bed and have a good fuck.
It'll do wonders.

Keeping to myself

I keep thinking
under my hat.

I keep feeling
around in the dark.

I keep looking
out in the open.

I keep wondering
for days on end.

What with kelp in the bedroom, the octopus on the
clothes-line — oh, and the TV was washed out to sea
again yesterday. I don't know, this always seems to
happen to me when I'm left to my own devices.

But I'll have the Bay neat and tidy for when you
get back, promise. I'll put the waves away, surf
down the roof and scrub along the top of the cliff
even. You won't know the place.

Your coming out of the sea was an event. Like that.
I wrote it down in the morning. And read it over. Sometime later I read it over again. I had not written it
before and I won't need to write it again. When you came
home that evening I told you about it and how it cleared my
mind for the time being.

Drift would be better: do you get my drift?
Drift: word for beachcombers, littoral drifters.
Driftwood: word for wood awash, or washed up.

What it is about this place is the sea. And what issues
from that: eg., the sea, which is about the world; the world
which in its turn is a round about the sun; the sun over the
sea, over there. Like, how about a swim when the tide's in?

You are afraid of the water. The moon has a tighter grip.
Under the boards, at Bognor Regis, tides rise. Bodies of
children are washed onto the beach. Rain hissed past as I
struck out beyond the headland. The sea was yellow with clay
washed off developments inland. You, back at the bach, holed
up, wondered what possessed you to follow me to this end of
the earth where you had no friends, no life of your own.

Far fetched here and neither end in view.

WYSTAN CURNOW

Toby's song

God of Nations,
Have you any wool?

Right up to the moment the wind broke up — it beats me
what is so funny. But the sea got up in dream sponge
viscera, tuatua tongue, secret froth, luxuriant hair of
rock is such a sight I am silly with it.

You have slept through this. I am standing here dripping
wet and in two minds. When have you ever looked so ser-
iously beautiful? You will wake, I suppose, in your own
time.

My outlook is your lookout.

I say: let's go round the rocks to the back beach.
Because I know these sallywinders mean rainbows by
the dozen, we'll have them all to ourselves. Like
I'd said once: let's go hear Betty Carter, she'll
sing *Spring Can Really Hang You Up The Most*, but went
instead with Betsy, because there was no babysitter or
something. So, ten years later, last month in New
York, I said to Betsy, let's go hear Betty Carter sing
Spring and she cancelled out because her dog was sick,
which left me thinking: what else is there in common?

Inside North Head dreamt I dug for magma,
Outside eyesight spurted all over the Gulf.

LEIGH DAVIS

(Born 1955)

from *Willy's Gazette*

You're a big ghost, Jim St. John,
nice sheen on your forehead and noseridge's catchy,
spread over the billboard, nine years later . . .
I was in the mind for Jerusalem, but early Willy's like
a 1972 *Listener*. Barefoot for forty miles in the rain,
kenosis, (who were you reading?) . . .
Then our literati were known for their sandals,
their misery . . . & talent, leisure, demography,
capital markets, blew old icons up
into large collected poems, where the audience knew
the hagiography, or were instructed: 'What is the inward
part, or thing signified? The Body of Christ, taken indeed . . .'

Who was Gaudier-Brzeska? (For what Willy assumes
you shall assume, take it upon yourself).

★

Things in his magazine form shiny objects,
Willis' symbols circle him,
figuring a tabloid where time coheres
as he assembles it, memories recur
and keep their shape, clarifying in the manner
of Steichen's Garbo . . .
Willis reaches for her, he holds his face with his forearms
reflected in the window, and she stays,
where March is epic and complex . . .
Lines group and Willis emerges,
fixing his tie and his breakfast while his wife sleeps,
or reading. Among the apparatus of eluding time
he varies his costume and mind —
Hawk too is serialized and alive.

He would use a newsbloc and arrangement . . .

eventually Willis would appear, consumer durable, Dior trousers
with small pleats and doublefront coat in the dark, fenders,
and his face beloved, when he looks to sea,
like the moon on water. Willis is a chevrolet

. . . a late model 4 door saloon, in history . . .
Cartier-Bresson catches the whole car
disappearing and leaving a moment's taillight:
M. Strand makes it stop, curiously,
in the carpark overlooking the sea,
the peculiar knowledge of its year of manufacture
channelling in the dark along the blond profile
to the still photographer: he concentrates . . .
'Me here, this beauty, 1966.'

★

'We were pale once as clothing or net fish,
mobile, typed, drying on lines like
Calder as warily we circled or sailed . . .
but it's my fortune you chose to anchor here.
Mahia town passes away
but every dried, warping house has its datepalm,
and ours, S, is bursting the weatherboards . . .
these six days on Blacks Reef have sprung me.
. . . your ship's naked, nosing under the huge tableland,
vanishing into the bright bluff and bay, crying out,
the way you cry out, heard across the water,
when Willy comes home on the sea . . .
there I court about your body and body's front,
whales lollop and spout about us.'

★

. . . a fisher, he has the appearance
of one looked at from a distance, isolated,
a figurine moving four steps sharply forward
his arms over his head, his foot again by the rodholder.
His lineage has faults
but he projects, its his syntax, his unit of composition,
sometimes it all goes together, epsilon,

the fall of a gull-dropped shellfish, as time goes by,
air like aluminium on a February Saturday,
S cleaning windows across the pane then down,
tossing a line off each moment . . .
how free is Willy, composing with his felttip,
his KREUZER JET, casting his net upon the waters, how frightened:
I lose sight of my appealing wife. Remember our blue car?

*

Flat, pale, (powder blue), Willy's pastorale . . .
a serial of calm apartments on the water
these sintesi, loose flags of wire and bleached linen . . .
we are the Futurists . . . pastel's
washing on le petit etat & the radio station,
over the windscreen's flash of Willy's shifting class —
'I'm describing the peasant culture which is
fundamentally my own, Mr Williams,
taking shape as I remember it,
a line, straightforward as that, like piano music
recognizable in its simplest outlines'

the post-colonials thinking 'pink, bare
Roseneath, darling, white houses,
ramparts to the sea

. . . such white details, such chickenwire . . .
I'm closer to Pearse than before,
S is a relation, Willy's a relation
to speak of, a marionette, a boundary,
mundane without clogs embroidery
or land his own Dakota
like Pearse, who was the first to fly —
which is not complex but circles a simple stance,
hot goats on the hill, there is a frontier
for Willy to cross, lumbering surfcast
to repeat, the elements are all there —
I'm describing what is fundamentally my own,
a huge pole, a ridge, over Mahia,
which is like Morocco

limitless, for all its severe waterline,
as hard as it gets, bony and dry
in summer, where we have only skin
and shorts on and white details without
shorts on in the tent. I recall
what catches my eye, and drop down
over the fields, a movement, something chrome
or glass over the straw fields, polar,
somewhere between a hawk and a government
man, which may or may not be a strange description —
but come backstage, dreamy, late summer
before autumn, evening before an ordinary
bed, and the range of the common aviator,
headings snaps methods   becomes apparent —

and the ongoing fascination of recall
becomes apparent, which I've paid for,
on release, there's no priest in miles but I'm talking
Willy, and miming like a graph
a geography almost big enough to get lost in,
mammoth, a present
which needs perspective — strange how variously
active understanding is, a simple progress
taken like barley heads home, where I am,
S is, where we've no capital, some collections
of books, primitive really to describe it
that way, but even as gatherers
you're the granddaughter of a Queen's couturier,
a white detail, beaded in the chickenwire.

*

The patois de birds in the tree's
getting free and loose with their English
off any way, broadcast from green
wattle station and Willy
his toast and eggs and coffee
also conferring plaudits plus dits
too wry eh and the morning is
attractive, non-paginal. All he does
is rise over the Reserve Bank

crying and hanging like a bird
himself silly in the updraft this exercise must
loosen look across you lovely Mount Victoria
houses your flat planes and two
radio masts fire your retro rockets

     ★

Willy's a rangefinder he's got special
effects he's for the marxists a
real estate when he conjectures
it when he takes place for you
lasting through all this sticking
by well done reader! Willy's
operatic about it he's possible
elastic and feminine (incorp
-oreal -orating)   & linguistic
sight like a dolphin turning
upon the brown reef he drives
out blind who's flank catches
aqua beyond the beach a stream
of blips erratic and frequent

Sometimes a lone aging his rate
of interest sometimes sensible the
press after such years vernacular
pouncey how kind and supportive
you have been he's running
he's become endless & wide
light on the delta
the ships planes autos and trains
pace by Willy slow in the evening
shallows near sleep and the
margins ceci n'est pas un homme
then, what there at first shapeless
looms upon the field what has
he captured ravelling, an opening?

(sonar, something's connected a
caravan to port, his flashing
windscreen)   mon desir

your editions loop and inflect
your welter changes down
as he draws nudging in again upon
the shallows nervous and awake
his asdic erratic off the worksheets
coming home the tired dashes the
nappy homophones that were quickened
dropping while out upon le massif
Mount Mathews has stars upon it
Palliser is cold you have noticed
the clock's tick the sealion upon the beach . . .

the curve rising and sheer,
smooth, the continuum hasn't
abated but's changed hats has picked up
Willy never suspected where he's
going to, light comes from the
morning lightly licking down his
flank over the sandbars his
markings drawn below eyes
that unlid and wake he resumes
intermittently . . .   any day now
looms he rises up S rises mis
en scene le journale changes
seamless, helpless climbing
engagé pectoral pictorial

where he's representative, columnar,
the sheets the headlines turned,
blocking, the breaks reinserted
the accustomed hand of the editor
rearranging at dinner making
reviews set well, billow, if it's
possible, any verb kicking off
chains just when he thought
taper now, switch disciplines. When you
look at Willy he's unassuming
a casual arced wetback some
distance off the peninsula and
you turn, placid, motionless
for a moment, into the newspaper,

because you have not *resolved* him,
he gathers large his diction his composure
the writing twists and confronts
he blooms when you sleep he
wont go asdic is as common
as breathing as inspiration
the language administers and
meters Willy's regimen it
compiles, breaks the surface when you paw
at it Willy bunches slowly across
the sea standing with his rapid flukes,
chattering deep inside your
storehouse your magazine he's
calling

    thinking 'for the rest of my life
right out to the boundaries the
old images of fishing the looping
thread of the cast the tall pillar
lighthouse will take their place
I shall never not remember
even the small details of this
account' And you have only to stop
and read and latent
Willy after several years will a-
muse, as the archaic French
has it, vivid & (avant) will advance
another unhesitant ready
step, whenever you go that way.

   *

Two days out past dry Seville
some tricky wry journey this
long intent trek's buried too far
back in the day with the net's
soft sea hiss and careful in-
drawing lean dark men judging
it looking into that future turning
like a schedule of prices into
evening a small tear in the

project tiny impasse rearing
when you're run down,   more
errands a thinker's skinny plank
to follow si Don Willy Coyote ecce
homo . . .   (some possible composite he)

. . . but such an impulse runs,
into a curious closure like a kingfish —
ecce homo's one strand with old connections
getting tied at Tanganyika on a foreshore
there's another, the normal repetitive motion
of the dark men never went that way. At first
it seems, writing's like windmills, any local
toughness arrests he changes at the
thought gripping lance or buckler
as it says, but the narrative's
got that covered too, his lovely
envelope's tenses, extensions, let him go,
wheeling from a verb on his unusual
horse, even since before Seville.

★

Marking the occasional paper
indian file, so formal, peering
after the liner (the daisywheel)
in the common way, how it lowers
into the blue sea . . .   still there you find
him, so textile end on, flat as that
& so transferred, taking a shiver
down his spine, and the cabbage tree claps
it's swords over the setting sun
turning as if to say
mouth open, exclamatory
so armature you were so ready
so gestetner, old and dizzy,
& your line so charcoal grey and endless

MONITA ERU DELAMERE

(Born 1921; Te Whānau-a-Apanui, Ngāi Tahu,
Te Aitanga-a-Māhaki, Ngāti Porou)

Te Pire mō te Reo Māori

Hiko hiko te uwira
papā te whatitiri whakahekeheke ana mai
i runga o Tūranga rā e.

Hei aha tērā! Ko te mana o Kuini pea, e awhi ana i te tikanga.
Ka korikori te ture whakarunga i auē!
Ui atu ki a Mita Renata, nō wai tērā pere? Hei aha te pere.
Kei te kimi tonu ake i te oranga mō te iwi Māori e. Kei runga
rānei? Kei raro rānei? Kei kō ake rānei? Anei ake rānei?
I a u e ! Hi!

Tēnā koutou e ngā rangatira. Tēnā koutou i ō tātau mate, te tini
kua rūpeke. Kua tūtaki rātou ki a rātou. Tātou te hunga ora e
noho manene nei.
Kia ora tātou katoa.

Ēnei ki a koutou nā ngā Ringatū. Ahakoa he maha ngā hē kei roto
ko te kaupapa e takoto ana.
Hei tīmata kōrero māku mō te kaupapa. Te Pire Reo Māori.
Me tiki atu e au i Te Whā o Ngā Ako a Horomona Whakataukī
Tuawhā, rārangi 1–14.

Whakarongo e ngā tamariki ki te whakaako a te Matua. Tahuri mai
hoki kia mātauria ai ngā whakaaro mōhio. He pai hoki te kupu
mōhio ka hoatu nei e ahau ki a koutou, kaua tāu ture e
whakarerea. Ko te tamaiti hoki ahau a tōku pāpā, he ngawari, he
mea mate nui nā tōku whaea. I whakaako anō ia i au i mea mai ki
au kia puritia āku kupu e tōu ngākau, kia mau ki āku whakahau, ā,
e ora koe.

Tāu taonga e mea ai māu, ko te whakaaro nui, tāu e mea ai māu ko
te mātauranga, kaua e wareware, kaua hoki e neke atu i ngā kupu a
tōku māngai.

133

MONITA ERU DELAMERE

Kaua e whakarerea, ā, māna koe e tiaki, arohaina, ā, māna koe e mau ai.

Ko te tino mea ko te whakaaronui, tāu e mea ai māu ko te whakaaronui, ā, i ō whiwhinga katoatanga kia whiwhi koe ki te mātauranga.

Whakanuia ia, ā, māna koe ka kake ai: ka whakahonore ia, i a koe ki te awhitia ia e koe.

Ka hōmai he whakapaipai ātaahua ki tōu mahunga: ka pōtae anō koe e ia ki te karauna honore.

Whakaronga e tāku tamaiti maharatia āku kupu; ā he maha ngā tau e ora ai koe.

He mea whakaako koe nāku ki te ara o te whakaaronui; he mea arahi koe nāku i ngā ara tika.

Ka haere koe e kore ōu takahanga e whakakikitia mai; ki te rere koe, e kore koe e tūtuki.

Kia mau ki te ako kaua e tukua atu matapoporetia iho ko tōu oranga ia.

Kaua e haere i te ara o te hunga kino. Kaua hoki e takahia te huarahi o te hunga hē.

E haria ana tēnei waiata he tautoko i te Hīmene a Hoera. Whārangi 24 me te Pānui 25. Koianei ngā karakia Tua Tamariki, a tēnei ō tātou Hāhi. Mō te marena koia rā anō te Hīmene a Hoera. Pānui 25. Ko te waiata i rerekē. Te waru tekau mā rima o ngā waiata a Rāwiri.

E Ihowa kua aro mai koe ki tōū whenua: kua whakahokia mai e koe a Hākopa i whakaponongatia nei.

Kua murua e koe tō kino o tōu iwi; kua hīpo kina e koe ō rātou hara katoa. Kua whakakāhoretia katoatia e koe to weriweri: kua tahuri atu koe i te āritaritatanga o tō riri.

Whakahokia ake mātou e te Atua o tō mātou whakaoranga: kia mutu hoki tō riri ki a mātou.

E riri rānei koe ki a mātou ake ake? He mauahara tonu rānei koe a tēnā whakatipuranga tēnā whakatipuranga?

E kore ia nei koe e whakahoki ake i a mātou ki te ora; kia hari ai tōu iwi ki a koe.

134

E Ihowa whakakitea mai tāu mahi tohu ki a mātou: tukua mai
hoki ki a mātou tāu whakaoranga. Kia whakarongo atu ahau ki
tā te Atua: ki tā Ihowa e kōrero ai: nō te mea hoki
nō te rongo māu āna kōrero ki tōna iwi, ki tōna hunga
tapu hoki; kaua ia rātou e hoki atu ki te wairangi.
He pono e tata ana tāna whakaoranga ki te hunga e wehi ana ki
a ia; kia noho ai te korōria ki tō tātou whenua.
Kua tutaki te mahi tohu rāua ko te pono, kua kihi ki a rāua te
tika me te rongo māu.
E tupu ake te pono i te whenua. E titiro iho te tika i te rangi.
Āe, ka hōmai e Ihowa te mea pai: ka tukua mai ōna hua e tō
tātou whenua. Ka haere te tika ki mua i a ia; hei whakaatu i a
tātou ki te ara o āna hikoinga.

Kei roto i Te Whā o Ngā Ako a Horomona te kupu nei
'whakaaronui'.
He maha ngā pūtanga o te kupu nei. Tāu taonga e mea ai mau
ko te whakaaronui. Ko te tino mea ko te whakaaronui. Ā, i ō
whiwhinga katoatanga kia whiwhi koe ki te mātauranga.

Ahakoa kua oti kē te tautoko kua mana te Hāhi Ringatū i te tau
1926. Ko te reo kua mana noa atu i te whakaaetanga i Waitangi.
Ki a Wikitoria; mai i te whenua ki te rangi, me ōna āhua
katoatanga. Te reo. Ngā karakia. Te Paipera Māori Tapu. Koianei
te whakaaronui nei, mō te Pire Reo Māori. Mō ngā iwi katoa e
noho manene nei i runga i te mata o te whenua. Ehara mō te
Ringatū anake.

Tēnei te tangi ake nei. Te tūmanako hoki kia whakaaronui koutou
ngā rangatira te hunga kua tohia hei kōkiri i te Pire Reo Māori
koutou kia kaha. Kia ū. Matapoporetia iho ngā taonga Māori.

Kōrerotia te Paipera Māori Tapu o te wā o te Tiriti 1840.
Tae mai ki ngā whakamāoritanga i muri mai, tae mai ki te wā
1868. Kāore o muri mai.

Te tapu, te ihi, te mana, te wehi ki te Atua o te Māori kei roto
mai i a Kenehi puta noa ki ngā Whakakitenga. Kei reira e noho
ana te whakaaronui nei. Te tapu o te Tiriti o Waitangi. E rua ngā
reo mai i te hainatanga e pūmau nei.

Auē! He aha rawa rā — Te Moana-nui-a-Kiwa koutou ko tīpuna mātua, tuakana, taina, me ō mokopuna i tuku ai — tēnei reanga tangata, te mea e ora tonu nei i ngā wā katoa.

Nā wai ko tēnei e te Karaiti ringihia mai ōhou toto hei whakamākūkū ake i roto i tōku wairua.

Me pēhea rā e mōhiotia ai ēnei kōrero? 'Mimi mai te kanohi. Tiko mai te kanohi.' Te maha te tini o ngā whakataukī a te reo Māori.
Kore, kore rawa e tae i roto i tētahi atu reo te kōrero. 'I whea kē koe i te tangihanga o te hōrirerire?'

Ka tareka hoki te menamena te Pire Reo Māori. E tautoko ana i te Pire i runga i te whakaaronui.

Te ture Tekau-mā-rua me hoatu ki runga o ngā mema o te tokowhā o te Komihana. Kōtahi te mea ki runga o te Komihana nō roto mai i ngā Hāhi Māori — Katorika, Mihinare, Ringatū, Ratana, Perihitiriana.

He honore he korōria he maungārongo ki runga ki te whenua he whakaaro pai ki ngā tāngata katoa.

Heoi. Nā te iti nā te rawakore me ngā rangatira Ringatū.

The Bill for the Maori Language

Lightning strikes,
thunder applauds,
as it descends upon Gisborne!

So be it! Perhaps it is the prestigious Queen [Victoria] all embracing the faith and its traditions.
The law stirs upwards — alas!
Ask Mr Leonard, to whom does that bell belong?
What may be its purpose?
We are still seeking the survival of the Maori.
From the heavens? From the earth? Or elsewhere?

Maybe hither perhaps
Alas! Alas!

Greetings to you the chiefly elders. I greet you on behalf of our
departed ones. Farewell to them as they join the thousands.
We the living, who drift on, greetings to all of us.

This message to you all is from the Ringatu elders. There may be
quite a few errors in the message — the most important issue is
we are in full support of the Bill.

To begin with let me quote Proverbs, Chapter 4, v.1–14:

Hear, ye children, the instruction of a father, and attend to know
understanding. For I give you good doctrine, forsake ye not my
law. For I was my father's son, tender and only beloved in the
sight of my mother. He taught me also, and said unto me. Let
thine heart retain my words: keep my commandments, and live.

Get wisdom, get understanding: forget it not; neither decline from
the words of my mouth.

Forsake her not, and she shall preserve thee: love her, and she
shall keep thee.

Wisdom is the principal thing; therefore get wisdom; and with all
thy getting get understanding.

Exalt her, and she shall promote thee: she shall bring thee honour,
when thou dost embrace her.

She shall give to thine head an ornament of grace: crown of glory
shall she deliver to thee.

Hear, o my son, and receive my sayings; and the years of thy life
shall be many.

I have taught thee in the way of wisdom; I have led thee in right
paths.

When thou goest, they steps shall not be straitened; and when
thou runnest, thou shalt not stumble.

Take fast hold of instruction; let her not go: keep her; for she is
thy life,

Enter not into the path of the wicked, and go not in the way of evil
men.

MONITA ERU DELAMERE

This psalm is used in support of the Hymn of Joel, with the Readings 25. These are the doctrines used for the christening of children conducted by this church. For matrimonial ceremonies the same hymn is used — the Readings 25 — the psalm is different. Psalm of David 85:

Lord, thou hast been favourable unto thy land; thou hast
    brought back the captivity of Jacob.
Thou hast forgiven the iniquity of thy people, thou hast covered
    all their sin. Se-lah.
Thou hast taken away all thy wrath: thou hast turned thyself
    from the fierceness of thine anger.
Turn us, o God of our salvation and cause thine anger toward us
    to cease.
Wilt thou be angry with us for ever? Wilt thou draw out thine
    anger to all generations?
Wilt thou not revive us again: that thy people may rejoice in thee?
Shew us thy mercy, o Lord, and grant us thy salvation.
I will hear what God the Lord will speak: for he will speak unto
his people and to his saints: but let them not turn again to folly.
Surely his salvation is nigh them that fear him; that glory may
    dwell in our land.
Mercy and truth are met together; righteousness and peace have
    kissed each other.
Truth shall spring out of the earth; and righteousness shall look
    down from heaven.
Yea the Lord shall give that which is good; and our land shall set
    us in the way of his steps.

In the teachings of Solomon is the word wisdom. This word appears several times.

Although the Ringatu Church has been recognised and registered in 1926 as an incorporated society under the Incorporated Societies Act 1908, the Maori language was recognised in the agreement with the signing of the Treaty of Waitangi (Queen Victoria's reign); from the land and all spiritual aspects pertaining to the heavens. The language. The prayers. The Holy Bible for all people living scattered throughout the land not only for Ringatu members.

This is my message. I am hopeful that those rangatira selected to present the Pire mo te Reo Maori be strong, I urge you to be steadfast, 'Matapoporetia te reo' watch over the language carefully and all things Maori.

Read the Holy Maori Bible of the period of the 1840 treaty including later Maori translations right to the period 1868 — not of later dates. Sacredness, essential forces of power, prestige, the fear of God of the Maori can be related to from the Book of Genesis to Revelations. That is where wisdom can be found. The sacredness of the Treaty of Waitangi which lends to the signing of the Treaty of Waitangi still remains.

Alas! Why ever, Moana-nui-a-Kiwa you and your ancestors, parents, seniors, juniors and your grandchildren allow this generation of people constantly to pick at you and the past and the Son of Man who has everlasting life.

There now Christ Jesus pour upon me your blood to quench my spirit.

How shall these readings be known 'Mimi mai te kanohi. Tiko mai te kanohi.' — 'Things do not erupt until boiling point is reached.' There are many proverbial sayings in the Maori language. 'I hea koe i te tangihanga o te horirerire?' 'Where were you at planting time?'

Te Pire Reo Māori can be amended. In support of the Bill on the strength of wisdom.

Clause 12 should bestow upon the four members of the commission — one member should be selected on to the commission from the Maori churches — Catholic, Anglican, Ringatu, Ratana and Presbyterian.

Nā te iti nā te rawakore
Yours sincerely,
Monita Eru Delamere
for the Ringatu members.

Translation by Monita Eru Delamere

JOHN DICKSON

(Born 1944)

John Wayne

as I step from the hut,
full of pomp,
the rooster runs to greet me.

Ruffling his feathers
he turns side
on to my legs, eyes them

then tramples the ground. Since
he should move first
I pause

and while so pausing
I gaze upwards
at a patch of blue sky, its

strange clear brightness
like death.
The rooster crows, once, twice

he's saying, Oh henshit John
round here
I'm in charge, not death

The Empire's Last Drunk

1

. . . beyond our control, the raft
swirled between rows of jagged rocks, then slowly, beneath our feet
we saw a curve of pale blue sky

140

the provisions, the locals, the guns, all disappearing amongst the seething
white calm.
Later
while floating back
I could hear bird feet
pitter patter
on the canvas roof. And also
in a confusion of sense
I could smell the river flowing
in the shadow of my heart.
Dark green
was its colour

2

dressed in my new white suit
I was sitting in a chair outside my hut
when two
of the locals came walking by. They
looked towards me
and they called, Hey boy, like a drink?
Now since I knew
that this
was a normal seasonal greeting, I relaxed some-
what
and settling down
we drank 12 bottles of Speights.
Thinking back, I don't recall their names
only my surprise
that one, alone, had tattoos — eagles
on each of his wrists. And
every time he spoke
he said 'fucking oath' so often
I assumed he was invoking a tribal god;
yet later
when he talked of how he set crayfish pots
two miles from land
he didn't once use those words.
He also said
I cannot swim. Death by drowning

is as good
as any

3

towards whatever sunset
was going to
come
one of us said, Let's go, fellas
let's go
that piss up
soon starts at the beach
And of
the stumble-
down
a steep winding track, of
the slither and
slide through trees
where the air was soft and warm
like a child's skin
of
all that
I clearly recall one purple patch
in which out to sea
an enormous pink bloom of cloud
turned blood red, then dark blue, then a kind
of greenish black, its colours un-
predictably diminishing
until none were left bar a few dull shades
soon lost
in the growing darkness

4

on the beach
the locals were drinking rum
and feeding on Colonel Sanders chicken
and while they ate
and drank
a poet sang
a strange and intricate song
about a man called Smith

who fell fast in dreamless sleep
then woke
to find the world unchanged
and while the poet sang
I talked
of how these days I'd chosen calmness
and while I talked
I drank and drank
till I was so befuddled
I fell headfirst on the sand
and as the house of stars
began turning beneath my head
I heard someone say, That Mister Dickson
he drunk

5

about 6 a.m.
I arrived at the jagged
rocks
and swimming upwards
amongst swirling bird feet
I found
the canvas roof
and beneath that, I found a mirror
in which I saw
a pair
of blood shot eyes
and then? what then? I cannot say
for like a crumpled suit, I lay
down to sleep
a kind floating off
in the river's
flowing darkness

JOHN DICKSON

from *Letters to Peter Olds*

Sixth Letter

a farmer for whom my father and five others
    were working
had a problem. Behind his homestead
there lived a large warren of rabbits, and these
rabbits displeased him

since no matter how many traps he laid
they continued to outbreed their dead. Then one
fine day, the farmer conceived a plan: he
would catch a rabbit

and to that rabbit he would tie a stick
    of gelignite
and then, having lit the fuse
he would release the rabbit, and the rabbit
carrying its brief message of light

would scamper back to the warren.
Now, you mightn't believe this, but when
the farmer released the rabbit
he began to learn of Zeno's paradox

the one concerning a race
between swift Achilles and a turtle:

    if Achilles starts at A
    and the turtle at B
    then when Achilles reaches B

    the turtle is at C
    and when Achilles reaches C
    the turtle is at D

and so on ad infinitum
for no matter how quickly swift Achilles runs

he never overtakes the turtle, or at least
    he doesn't
according to Zeno's paradox.

Now when the farmer released the rabbit
it didn't scamper back to the warren

  it hopped un-
steadily towards the farmer's wash house
and the farmer, running after it
could no longer believe the evidence
of his senses: for though he ran

as quickly as he could
he couldn't catch the rabbit, since he
  the farmer
had to make an infinite number of steps
in a finite time, and that

Peter, is more or less impossible. So
the farmer ran
and the rabbit hopped, and the hired hands
  the boys
well they lay down quite speechless on the ground

they thought of unions, they thought of fishing
they thought, even, of England
they thought of anything other
  than what
was before their eyes, until

at last, there came from one
a highpitched gasp for air, a high A perhaps
and coming down the scale
the boys began to laugh. Meanwhile

the rabbit, carrying its load of gelignite
had disappeared beneath the wash house
And the farmer?
Well he was busy, he was running round

that same wooden building
though for all the use that was
he may as well have run round
a burning bush

LAURIS EDMOND

(Born 1924)

from *Wellington Letter*

6

I heard news today
of the men who search
the earth for lost
lives, finding in each
marked stone or ring,
broken potsherd,
scrap of painted clay
or rusted blade
the mute whisperings
of the same tale
we, momentously
it seems, can tell
out loud. They found
in Germany a tomb
of Celtic origin
in which some royal dream
of immortality
had placed a four-wheeled
chariot decorated
with flying horses, gold
inlaid; near it a narrow
coffin, boat-shaped for
the timeless journey
to *Tir inna mBeo*.
In old Bohemia
the most corrupt prince
could there retrieve
his primeval innocence.

11

There are fixed points
like stars; they wake each night

after days of flux and we say
'this is love'. It is not so easy —
to hold your frail poise
you must stand against me;
when the lout comes in to the room
you must leave and speak to him.

This shaggy brute must follow us
into the moonlight where we walk
distracted under the jagged galaxies.
On the icy grass by the precipice
it will be his selfish insistence
that mortifies and saves us.

18

Dear and gentle ghost, I have come
to an end; and did not find, as
perhaps I hoped, that you would speak
again if we could find the words.
Rather I know that though love's sick
body is restored by love there is none
great enough to cross the seas that roar
between our separate mountain tops.
We embark; there is no arriving.

You have your choice, I mine; and soon
we shall both be one with the constant
earth, the tides that put out to
the hurting uncertain future; strange
gods will brood above our sleep of
clay, their voices echo through us
where we lie, change, dissolve,
take on new lives. We are the cells
of time; snow will fall upon us
with its crisping touch, wind blow
our dust, water wash us in the pebbled
body of the sea, and the stars
take always their dark road.

Our words will be lost but our love
will enter the life of the land

147

like the dust a sunset lights up
with its recurring fire. Now the sky
broadens, sun touches the water.
I tell you it will be a fine day.

The Distaff Line

So late your letter comes — forty years
and now this wild face, round-eyed child
crossing the dark field of consciousness
and closer, suddenly old, holding me with
a fierce mnemonic stare. How shall I learn
a lifetime in an instant? Turn back, we'll
go together down a lengthening road, find
the orchard, the track of spongy elephant
grass that leads to the apricot tree.

Look, here's the raffish village, here
the ha'penny store, the bar hump-backed
like a whale that crammed with mud the green
throat of the river; and here the trees,
apples, pears, spindly plums, last and best
the apricot, grey grandfather drowsing
in a dusty light. Now see a familiar shadow
fall upon the grass as those formidable
women — your mother, midwife to a hundred
Maori families, mine their children's
teacher — country women, tall as scarecrows,
arrive to summon us to evening rituals
ordered by their brisk instruction.

Old friend, cousin, let us say the secret
creatures behind our eyes have not grown
old (and were they ever young?) — come,
lay your cheek against the green skin
of the river, grasp the branch that
holds the ripest fruit, we'll sit here
as we did before through endless amber
afternoons of childhood's summer.

But there's your letter — which I shall not
answer, guessing your reticences well enough.
It shows you, as I would have thought,
straight-backed and calm, a little stately,
looking Master Death severely in the eye,
never doubting that the only failure is
a loss of nerve. So it's to be. The ripeness
now has fallen from the trees and in the dusk
your face puts on its mask, rubric of
a resolute clan whose women's voices,
unshaken, ever spoke the word that called
us in and put an end to all our playing.

Latter Day Lysistrata

It is late in the day of the world
and the evening paper tells of developed
ways of dying; five years ago we would not
have believed it. Now I sit on the grass
in fading afternoon light crumpling pages
and guessing at limits of shock, the point
of repudiation; my woman's mind, taught
to sustain, to support, staggers at this
vast reversal. I can think only of
the little plump finches that come
trustingly into the garden, moving
to mysterious rhythms of seeds and
seasons; I have no way to conceive
the dark maelstrom where men may spin
in savage currents of power — is it
power? — and turn to stone, to steel,
no longer able to hear such small throats'
hopeful chirping nor see these tiny
domestic posturings, the pert shivering
of feathers. They know only the fire
in the mind that carries them down
and down in a wild and wrathful wind.

LAURIS EDMOND

I do not know how else
the dream of any man on earth can be
'destroy all life, leaving
buildings whole . . .'

Let us weep for these men, for
ourselves, let us cry out as they bend
over their illustrious equations; let us
tell them the cruel truth of bodies,
skin's velvet bloom, the scarlet of
bleeding. Let us show them the vulnerable
earth, the transparent light that slips
through slender birches falling over
small birds that sense in the minuscule
threads of their veins the pulses of
every creature — let these men breathe
the green fragrance of the leaves, here
in this gentle darkness let them convince me,
here explain their preposterous imaginings.

Catching it

I saw three men looking
towards the sea:
they were on a seat, laughing —
three small brown foxy Frenchmen,
and the funniness of it
licking them over
like forked lightning.

In all of the ticking of time
it can never have happened before,

not like this, not exactly —
and the one by the sea wall
had a slack old jacket
done up with frogs
and a black fingernail
and a hole in the knee of his pants
— just to make sure.

At Delphi

No one knows how she was chosen, only
that she must have passed fifty, and when
the god called she would leave at once;
her children she might not speak to again.

Naturally she had come to think of them
with a certain mildness; on a hot morning
down in the Gulf see her gossiping to
her daughter as to another village wife —

though the girl's swollen belly is a shared
particular; almost equally they enjoy jeering
at the ribaldries of neighbours, their shrewd
peasant faces at such moments strikingly alike.

Is it a priest who arrives now, speaking in
a strange dialect — some tribe in the hills
more than likely — and launches into a queer
rhetoric to do with the power of sacrifice,

the all-pervading might of Apollo, telling
her softly that kings will come to her
where she sits high on the three-cornered
throne, to learn the god's inscrutable will . . .

But she knows only that the women have drawn
back, eyes peering round homely pillars are
suddenly secret with fear; that home has already
fallen away as surely as friends from a leper.

And this is the time: he leads her through
the hushed market place, the pregnant girl
alone and motionless by the well, her young
head haloed by the black Corinthian sun.

Climbing slowly in the heat to the shade
of a cypress, I have entered three thousand
years' silence; but the sacred Kastalian
spring is still the sound of a woman weeping.

LAURIS EDMOND

Those Roses

Roses, the single scarlet sort,
open at the throat as if for
coolness, sprawl at the window;
you heap on my plate a pile
of potatoes, steaming and small,
smelling of mint. 'They're
basic,' you say as we go at them
lustfully, 'they grow by the door;
you have to chase meat' — and I
notice a certain vegetable poise,
not striated like the fibrous
deposits of a more strenuous growing
but smooth, opaque; placid testimony
to the sufficiency of flesh.

'Of course you do have to hunt —'
I say, thinking of hopeful
burrowings in the soil, wresting
from the clutch of its black fingernails
each creamy nugget; and we agree
on that; we're a bit languid,
munching more slowly as each
pale pod splits open and fills
us with amber warmth — one flesh
sturdily giving itself to another.
Those roses, too, they lean over us,
and the squat black pot gives
off its dull gleam, grinning
crookedly from the stove.

On the Need to Hold a Driver's Licence

I came south after sunset
driving fast past the telegraph poles

near Mount Bruce the dark
walked out of the pine trees

and laid its hand on the farms
saying 'forget; forget'

but in the proud sky
the light stayed

I saw the long day there
its face bright with weeping

then the night took it in
and I drove on home.

Tristesse d'animal

Here, yes, I am here —
don't you see my hand at the window, waving?

It's all still the same,
tremulous water lifting its face
to the wind, a clock calling over the city

light late on the hills —
and I'm alone, as before.

Where are you, companions
who promised to come
to the very door of the grave

— where did you turn back?
Are you dancing somewhere nearby

or is that only the neighbours?
I might call you
but what language is there for it

— the blood-smear we were born in
the gasp of that strong bitter oxygen
the first taste, the last we shall have.

LAURIS EDMOND

The Chair

It's a high room at the top of stairs
the door closed
I know of nothing but the chair in the corner
hard wood, rounded, a kitchen chair
and the girl sitting, head bowed
not looking up to see
who has come or gone
but weeping, weeping.

She has wept like this all my life;
you don't have to go near her
nor wonder, inquire
she does not expect that
there have never been intimations of solace.

Down the usual road I keep walking
I am young, old, strong or sick; sometimes
I waver — it does not matter. The chair stays
and the girl
as though this is the whole world sitting
bending over the great aching club foot
of its sorrow, far back
in the closed room of my days.

The Lecture

I am just going downstairs to where
I shall tell them lies. Up here
at the window the maple trees' shadow

fingers the indigo dusk and the fireflies
carry their tiny cargoes of light
up, down, right to the ground, then

almost over the high branches again
riding their currents of bark-scented dark
with an unquestioning poise

giving off sparks from a wholesome
summer travail. I could watch them
all night; what I cannot do

is burn at the small purifying fires
of their industry. I shall go soon,
persons are waiting to hear what I claim

that I know. I will talk down, say
'in respect of', offer insights, despising
both them and myself, but thinking:

'Up there in the quiet room
where the fireflies are to be seen
at work in their luminous trees

there is my truth, my candour, my courage,
there I too can shine with the natural
intermittent light of myself,'

— and then I shall go on holding forth.

Tempo

In the first month I think
it's a drop in a spider web's
necklace of dew

at the second a hazel-nut; after,
a slim Black-eyed Susan demurely folded
asleep on a cloudy day

then a bush-baby silent as sap
in a jacaranda tree, but blinking
with mischief

at five months it's an almost-caught
flounder flapping back
to the glorious water

six, it's a song
with a chorus of basses: seven, five grapefruit
in a mesh bag that bounces on the hip
on a hot morning down at the shops

a water-melon next — green oval
of pink flesh and black seeds, ripe
waiting to be split by the knife

nine months it goes faster, it's a bicycle
pedalling for life over paddocks
of sun
no, a money-box filled with silver half-crowns
a sunflower following the clock
with its wide-open grin
a storm in the mountains, spinning rocks
down to the beech trees
three hundred feet below
— old outrageous Queen Bess's best dress
starched ruff and opulent tent of a skirt
packed with ruffles and lace
no no, I've remembered, it's a map
of intricate distinctions
purples for high ground burnt umber
for foothills green for the plains
and the staggering blue
of the ocean beyond
waiting and waiting and
aching
with waiting

no more alternatives! Suddenly now
you can see my small bag of eternity
pattern of power
my ace my adventure
my sweet-smelling atom
my planet, my grain of miraculous dust
my green leaf, my feather
my lily my lark
look at her, angels —
this is my daughter.

Prayer to Cydippe, Priestess to Hera

Madam let me never be unsurprised

never suppose as I reach towards
the morning I have deserved
its strange and reckless shining:

let me realize it slowly, like
the sharp taste of the fleshy cells of an orange

teach me how to befriend the strangers
who stand in the eyes of the men and women
who are my children

pray for me priestess now and at the hour
of my failure; when I am blind
to the lizard-flick of the lie beneath
truth's whitened stone, destroy my comfort
send me into the dark till I am lost, hurt
betrayed but for the precarious accidents
of love

Handmaiden to the imperfect goddess
walk with me
through this temple of earth and sky
this clearing
in the incomprehensible jungle

as its constantly altering pathways grow shorter
let me not imagine arrival in one place
or another
O Lady of risk and caprice, only by this
shall I confront my end
in proper nakedness, as I began.

MURRAY EDMOND

(Born 1949)

Psyche

1

There is a line
scratched between hill and sky
the colour of weeds and the colour of rainblack cloud
the colour of mud and blue indifference.
It is paint.
It is light.
It is the wide line of Yorkshire.
It is a tui singing
sound falling in the morning
marking a conjunction of brilliance.
And yes, it may breed despair
seeing far into the world under construction
journeying with her through her warp of love
and still it is not a line
for a line is too large
and owns too much.

It is Blake laughing as he pastes
the face of Gabriel on the hedgerows.
A man says to his wife:
'Look! You can see the cold front
advancing.'
But she sees the intricacies of the foreground weeds
and the ants trundling up and down leaves
on the same scale as the clouds scurry toward her
and engulf her.
For her the paint moves.
Words advance on each other like wrestlers crying
'She is mine!' 'She is mine!'
The acres of their desires are coalmines and
the men in them and
the line is a burial and

a rate of exchange and
something to hop over.

Thomas Hardy watches the sun rise
the seals play and
the stones talk to each other and
he takes off his glasses,
amazed.

It is not a line.
It is a door
where the sky enters the earth
and the sea sings on the hinges of death.

To call it a line
is to say:
'I am not here.'
But the kelp swirls
and the tree hangs
and the sky rattles
with high cold streaks of blood.

      an erratic
ridiculous small bird's
twittering outlasts us,
even our constructions.

2

I want a citroen
and a baby in the back.
I want a cup of tea.
I am twenty-four years old
and I shall live forever.
I have already lived forever.
If you do not love me
you do not love me.
I do not care.
Good-bye!

I wanted you to see the walls humming muzak.
I wanted you to feel silence moving in and out

of the liftshafts like room service.
I wanted you to see the food leaking out
of the windows and curtains.
I wanted you to see your name in the shape
of a star across the lintel of the hotel foyer.

You spent time in a dream.
I wind my mind back
to a flickery memory of you,
small strong clear
a glass full of anemones
in a white window.

I do not want to talk to my mother all the time.
She is love and disaster.
I want to sit still and silent and listen
to the notes of your bare calloused feet
on the prison floor.

I am a small and singular child.
My translucent face shines
in a second storey bedroom
in Oxford where the sashes are blue
and the bedstead is red.
The blinds are drawn over the bars.
Snow falls only in the glass ball.
The wind cuts through the bookshelves.
The single lightbulb shines on the whole world.
I dream a life away into
madness richness luxury old age.

I wanted you to meet my father and his friends.
I wanted to tell you a story.
I wanted to build a myth
as large as a hotel
strong as a power station.
Water to fall and tumble.
Coal to burn.
Steam to turn the wheel to make the journey
to pass through the line to finish the cycle . . .
But I was afraid to take

160

the glass of anemones out of the window
and they remained with you when
I was not there.
I wanted you to watch me shoot myself.

3

Here is a story.
The orange sun smiles up through
the coaldead river which has beached
a whale carcase on its bleached banks.
We are in danger of slagheaps
sweeping us to sea like tidal waves
in this place where I am condemned
to spend forever.
There is always something coming!
It is your love.
It will never reach me.

It is hell.
Why! Here I am!
Savage minds and fierce automobiles
shred the blubber from the carcase
and through its tiny dead throat
the whale makes low sounds of
water dripping through a roof of
a tree growing of
the fires of Sheffield raging of
the tick of my father's glasses
shining like sixpences in the night.
The robin is a sly bird
who turns away to talk to me
and pecks idly at the strings of meat
on the white branches.
The crow is a bird of love
who is always distant
who is always watching me
as though I am something
so small and indefinable
I do not exist.
The river flows through the sky.

MURRAY EDMOND

Here is the story.
Ants sort seeds
in an assembly line
several inches long
and the eagle does an heroic deed
in the teeth of the black waterfall.
Here she becomes a force in the telling
which until now has told only
of palaces and fragrant beds.
She is crossing a black river.
The fantail's laughter drowns her ears.
The earth is deep for her like the sea.
All tasks are impossible.
Divine help is hot oil, a puff of smoke.
No one sees as she falls through the horizon.

I wander in this cold northern land
and hear my feet crackle on last autumn's leaves
like your small midnight cough.
I follow the pitrail embankment
from sulphurstinking slagheaps
to abandoned farm and back.
Suddenly I abandon the idea of love
in a broken doorway.
It is just a whale carcase.
It is a line
which I draw round my mind
which infects the whole landscape.

4

No line left now to tighten round the world.
I look south to the light where you live
under the white slant of the sun
under the shadowy eaves of board
where time is sinking under the weight
of my constructions.

        Wonderful undersea life!

You are hunched in a green mossy chair
reading a letter which is an intrusion

162

a bathysphere a hungry scavenging eye.
I am as immortal as drowning!

You are the long swim down
the surge of leg on leg expanding
as thighs spread over sight
as your body becomes a colour and a thirst
which melts and floods.

The green ripples across the grey scoured face.
White stars sprinkle black branches.
Electric ends of charged twigs crackle.
Light splashes and soaks like
many small feet moving in and out of caves.

I stretch a leg, a finger, a voice.
The kernel of my eye undarkens.
Her hand is kneading my shoulder
like wind.

      Wandering down the road
this early morning through the green strokes
of hawthorn I am her full face
the size and shape of her new form.
I come to a place where the land
lowers and twists and I follow and
the road follows.   .

from *Poems of the End Wall*

House

Last night as I lay beside you all the desire had gone out of me
and I was cast up like a heap of sand, porous, shapeless, shifting,
a thing of shape, an entity, only by virtue of its million parts.

Here I live on a cliff in a tiny house at the end of the island
and in the face of the wind from the north and the wind from
    the south
I surround myself with this thin wall of wood, this shape in space

163

and you are there asleep in the bed, curled to the end wall
    of the house,
your breathing blowing shapes in the cold air, your dreams
    dreaming,
your dreaming holding up the whole fabric of paint and wood
    and tin.

If you stop wanting to dream it will collapse. Your desire to
    dream holds it up,
all the bare longing of the imagination holds it up, the desire
    of the nail
to enter the wood, the desire of the wood to embrace the nail,

the desire of the paint to hide the wood and reflect the light,
the desire of the roof to contain a secret shape of darkness,
the desire of the glass to shine like the sun in the face of the sun.

And the earth desires to lie asleep under the house and dream,
it dreams the very shape of the house as though it was something
    organic,
whole as a body, breathing and seeing and standing cold in the
    wind.

The house is the container and you are the thing contained.
Its membrane protects you and your life gives it energy
and stops the walls from collapse. And the moment of seeing this

and the moment of saying this are two separate moments:
the first, the moment of seeing is a moment without desire,
at night, by the bed watching you sleep, alone, still, chill,

but not cold, watching, as the silence of space watches the
    grinding earth,
when all the desire has gone out of me and I get up,
get up out of the bed, go out the door, out through the end wall,

and grasp hold of the string on the balloon and rise slowly,
    steadily
shimmering like a giant eye over the house, the whole town, the
    the capital city,
rising over the island and the ocean, the earth opening like a
    flower.

But the second, the moment of saying, involves me in the
    grammar of desire,
I have to touch you with my speech to be heard.
And grammar itself is a thing of desire, announcing its capacity

to evolve infinitely more complex systems out of bits of nothing,
to put together the grains of sand to make rock and the rock to
    build
a cliff and the cliff to hold a house, many houses, a city

to stand at the end wall of the island, the end wall of the land
turned like smooth wood in the yielding shape of the bay
to embrace the random desiring waves of the sea.

Somewhere a child is sacrificed and buried at the foot of the
    posthole
which comes to hold up the whole house. Building walls for the
    compost heap
I smash a post in half and in its rotted core a weta lies, soft and
    sleepy,

hiding until its new exoskeleton hardens enough to let it safely
    live,
to let it grow vulnerable, as earth to light, as sand to sea.
Tonight I embrace you and trust the roof will hold up till
    morning.

Two Paragraphs

1

The car moves through roots and crevices and passes,
dry nets of spiders dangle in caves of earth,
the car moves like a blind mouse in the tunnels
of a megalopolis of sand, reaching through marram
and spinifex to the unknown thing generalized
in a word as 'light' or 'death' or 'the unknown',
the car passes towns and trees and houses
inked into shapes of grass and concrete, the car

climbs like a tiny figure on stage climbs, dressed
in long white underwear, climbing through
the roads of Rochfort and Hochstetter and Te Kooti,
the car comes in three collapsible parts like a kitset
of ego and id and superego, the car carries all the goods
and worldly thoughts and conspiracies of dreams on its
royal road, all daft games of animal/vegetable/mineral —
a cloud, paint, a drumstick, a pinecone, a lightbulb, ice —
scissors/paper/rock — the car aches with photographs
and indigenous subtropical rain forests and pure bone grief
it has swallowed in its great hunger to get where it is
going and cannot now cough up.

2

Face east, face west, face north, face south — the four faces
of a geographic mandala which orient the moving object
        in space —
there is a classic gold out of 1972 on the radio,
there is a day ahead planned for you at the beach,
surf life-saving competitions — life, surf, saving, and competition —
words which willingly fall together like a recipe.
A sentence is a practical compromise to get
the thing done — light, flexible, full of feeling, muscular
yet elastic, with edge and a point where it tips
leading you into the next — the newspaper is yawning
at the precipice of a new economic era.
The car is driving past Hiruharama.
It is nineteen years since Baxter wrote
'Summer 1967' though in the antipodes it's always ambiguous
which summer you mean when you supply one year only.
In his poem there are no cars
and girls flower and die like girls on the beaches
of Algiers did so obligingly for Camus in his Journals.
Here are beaches with no flowering girls, but his poem
and this are full of the same sweet nostalgia of the surveyor
at work. Legend has it for 'car' you might read 'soul'
in the same way for 'girls' you might read 'literary influence'
or for 'the unknown' you read 'mouse'. And soul, spelt backwards,
is almost 'louse' and car backwards is almost 'rack'.
The car is also a mouse.

A Letter About Cars

to Russell Haley

It started with the implant of the poem about the hat
and came back suddenly to what we used to call,
'Mum's House' — standing, or swimming, feet deep

in the green Waikato flood, a dinghy roped to its steps,
just off the Rangiriri straight, the place which always prompted
Mother to say, 'That's where I wouldn't like to live' —

which gives you the historic logic behind the way we christened it,
'Mum's House', while you, with your dreams of owning
a pair of maroon slacks and a grey blazer were haunting Trafalgar

Square dressed in a death's head mask. A foreign woman came up
to you — 'Young man, you have made a lot of people very happy
tonight.' I connect us by this quality of being coeval —

like Malvern Hill and Rangiriri. Last year I stopped the Triumph
on the gravel-chip carpark ironed out for tourists like myself
below the battle hill — you can picture me, an apprehensive blur

half-turned towards the shot, receding against the 1960 National
Geographic green of the yet-to-be-turned-into-butter grass
and the white handrail climbing you up to the top where a
     noticeboard

orders you with military precision to gaze southeast and pick up
the low ambience of another fortified position while averting
     your gaze
from the southwest aspect across the river where the willows tangle

with the bank and begin the land Tawhiao sought back one
     hundred years ago
last year, coming up this road (or perhaps by train) to catch the
     London boat.
Or thirty years ago next year I took the road with my father driving

the Springboks out to welcome by Koroki. We came year after year,
first in a Plymouth with tartan seats and then in a '56 model with
small fins, then a '58 Dodge, slender-waisted, black and yellow

with huge fins and a sting in the tail, with flags and hats
(the hat in the poem) and red, yellow and black ribbons streaming,
always with a nod to Mum's House — you were emigrating
    to Australia —

the implant of the image flares up out of the water as words form
across a page of white sound — as though meaning meant
    accumulating loss —
the whiteness dropping piece by piece down spontaneous holes

forming the memory, always, in negative. He takes it this
    way when
writing about Mum's House which he carries as a residue of
    the incredible,
the impossible, a Ripley's sketch of local significance.

They both realize, in telling tales, they have been constructing
themselves backwards for the other in order to increase the level
of negative feedback, to push the print towards blackness without

complete loss of image. The history of seeing is contained in the
deceptively facile surface of this photo of his wife standing by
an unknown car in front of a house where both of them

used to live. At a certain point the history of a place
capitulates to its dreams — they are both far past that point —
he has inhabited two places already in this way — and so too

a narrative of beginning which goes on far enough begins to
contain another beginning. The text will alter subtly
    under weight —
as snow released from a branch for you — for me, the river
    over banks —

the house awash, isolated, dreaming of a car full of family
driving past. It is the way you inhabit character — coming out
of the airport and noticing the Triumph parked and the disbelief

on your face — allows the shared thought. We test drove it
down Taranaki St, into Abel Smith, up the top of Willis
        and across
Webb, and, back at the yard, the shared thought — 'It's too good

for us.' But already we had begun to inhabit a new origin.
Shifting the weight from foot to foot, reading the precise
        noticeboard,
becoming tourist, the hat becomes poem. I touch the back of

the earth with the nape of my sole. You lean forward to read
        the line.
Inside the letter is sealed another letter, and, on opening it,
another is found. Each allows you to understand more and more

of a rapidly moving, accumulative fiction. But memory strains and
multiplying versions of origin confound synopsis.
From time to time the river floods its banks and leaves the house

to stand like an island. The Triumph, grinning slightly, draws out
into the stream of cars on the Prussian blue seal. You can follow it
from your hill but it turns aside before becoming like a dot.

KIM EGGLESTON

(Born 1960)

Broad Bay

Sometimes when the light is slow down
the hill from the castle and the sea
is hammering at the heads

I walk across the hill
to where the albatross lives
and watch the sea bite the land

Sometimes when the light is slow
and the sea is flat
floundering in the mud

We wonder should we leave
or stay on the verandah and smoke
another cigarette

The fine net falls either way
as it does when you're arguing
about a jersey and you've

already got your coat on.

Gatherers

Macrocarpa, built to break
the wind is twisted
and further back the smell
is of rotting bush
calling the bluff
of these travellers tied
to their hearth

Their house is full of shells
and half grown children
Here the sailor is come
his back covered
with spider bites

His ship has disappeared
in the shallow river along the sand
where myriads sparkle
and the footprints are carved
huge and bright

Can this be love's spawn
that blackens his eyes
The river has flooded
and the wind thrashes the trees
like a wild priest

The spangle bright sand
now black and biting sucks
him into the bush where
his boat lies
rotting in a pool
a thousand years ago

Moaning and dank the wind
bends him in half
and he lays down
dead with kiss
to meet her.

High Dollar Wind

Ten o'clock when the phone rings
she's sitting up in bed
tousled and striped
like a French model from 1963
he thinks grabbing her bum
Someone outside is splitting

wood with a whistling axe
and the wind sweeps down
the hill rattling tree-ferns
breaking branches
burying them in feathers
It rings and rings rings
someone clumps in the back door
picks it up
says yes no alright
The house creaks and groans
in the high wooden wind
the kitchen fire sucked
roaring up the chimney
spills wild smoke
around the yard
where small people cry out
and dance their mad-flung arms
They are the children
and the parents
burrowing into the warmth
Splitting wood
with great chunking breaths
They are making home
in the warm mutton-fat house
of flat-eared cats
and crates of beer
The moon prowls across the morning
turning its silver dollar
high against the wind
and that is the money
they spend themselves on.

DAVID EGGLETON

(Born 1953)

Self-criticism of an Otago Poetry Worker

One whale doing a refugee roll in Foveaux Strait,
greyer than all that grey, holds out no promise now.
It's as if those birds and beasts, created for the salvation of zoos,
have withdrawn from the game —
(The Albatross Wars, Kakapo's Last Stand, Muttonbird Elegies) —
crowding a recess that hasn't been blundered on
and detonated into a spangled galaxy, a holiday car,
tripping up and down a blitzed stretch of the Dominion's
premier highway like a Tijuana taxi,
mariachi horn going hee-haw,
largesse of light spilling from festoons of chrome,
disgorging into foaming fields of daisies the Happy Family.
Furthermore, minds adrift, eyes agog,
their rugged bodies the only hard thing,
trampers, possessed by the land's self-possession,
plunge in deep rapture towards Memory.
Each reappears in it clutching a centrifugal shrub,
(those alloys of exploded light and leaf)
transparently healthy, stars of an ad for milk or Fresh-up,
beckoning, vanishing, grinning without effort in the fierce sunlight,
their faces to me as enigmatic as any African's
were I too, not part of the community,
able to read the fraternal signs of Invercargill and Rolleston.

I wish to say it's of Karangahape Road I sing
and to celebrate those haunting boyhood arcades,
but to describe them isn't enough and anyhow
this South Seas Hotel to which I return
looks out on swamps of islands and hanging tides of ice.
So I praise lighthouses, seaweed, pink roofs instead
and collect those myths of Maoridom,
about Chief Hongi Hika, for instance, because they grow on one,
like a fantastic work of tattooing spiralling
energetically all over.

DAVID EGGLETON

Also there's the poem on 'The Assassination
of Marion du Fresne' to be written,
a splendid antique theme on which it would be easy to be
    abundant.
But for now I'd like to escape this prosiness
and take you with me to the imperishable sheaf of gold,
sunbathing rocks,
diamond-hard lakes of light,
the turquoise ground at the core,
the moony inland wilderness.
There, ordinary dusty moths are winged celebrations,
night scares the daylights out of the stews
and the fly-blown mutton rots in its cloth.

Remember the delivery of your sofas,
O daughters of Aotearoa, twin garages chock-a-block
with the meaningful debris of a clocked-out civilization.
Some things we can share and will always have warm memories
    about.
More, I believe, than just say what belongs to us or how
you got saved by the Surf Patrol.
The Virtues should always be in our thoughts.
Why is there this wickedness in the world?
At times the promise of a Sanctuary is a gift.
I feel sure the rest of the world is counting on us.
Pre-historic ferns are struck like decimal coins beneath
the dead black beech pointed stiffly to the spreading light.

More afternoons of dry wit spent in the land of the golden
    skinned,
sudsy passions of the Sunday bar room,
jugs flung from the potter's wheel,
dim textures of wallpaper roses:
Kingdom Come shines with this very catalogue.
Firebirds and Stingrays have got nothing
on the belongings of the new poor,
nor have those electric hangi pits
or the edge on the Amcos spraypainted across the legs and hips.
Sunglasses at night!
Words made visible in the electric park.
Couldn't these parodies serve

as an introduction to the slow movement
of a sonata under all this blue fire,
which is where we left one another, the future rich with promise
    and distances?
Katherine Mansfield was a mere shadow on the horizon of
    Literature
within that bright ring of fire,
that particular, sapphire exclamation
which causes me to drift like roots in water,
collecting poems as casually as you brush your teeth.
And you, compost heap, humble sacrifice of rat and bird,
urgently reminding the home-maker harmony can develop into
    chaos . . .

Weary of revering cloud castles, I pass in under the porch
to rest on the hammock with clinking glass and a straw,
leaning to the steadily souring tones of a rock singer
broadcast *in memoriam.*
Hot night pushes forward its black, sticky champion.
The vanquished are bellying up to the victorious sportsmen
who, clinging to their toilet bags, are swept away from the vanity
    mirror
by the large crowd of well-wishers.
This mixed style is going flat out as fragrances ripple
from restaurants.
Those puzzled knots of Fijians fill the quota.
A net of lasers? Are you sure it isn't
a brick temple of medicine you mean?
I only say this because we are the people
our parents warned us about,
gone familiars getting lost.
Hey, what's this moving like a 'droid?
Something new from the mother country, I'll bet.
Well it's not to be contemplated.
She is without a stitch on her head in a room
of lost causes.
His moustache hangs before his face like guiding handlebars.
Fat raindrops fall like tiny frogs on eel-black streets
which flick their backs and drive closer together.
Swings and seesaws, slides and a jungle gym.
This provides everything you could wish for.

DAVID EGGLETON

The Alps of green glass tower sharp and clean.
The peaceful Sounds go down to gawping fish.
It's always the same,
monumental bottle of lemonade, wharf promenade,
tattooed palisade of flesh
just serve to reveal the pretty blue faces
of the Southern Lakes, which themselves have
no memorial, though now and then a picnic is held.
Tell me something I don't know about how
poetics collect behind the frail leaves
or drifting veil of rain,
spout issuing a silvery tongue —
the Annunciation is not very far away.
As for the Assumption, the young hitch along higher trails
to the pagan festival calling jubilantly —
'Free at last, fellow souls, free at last.'
I keep in mind
John Gully colouring a thunderstorm over Lake Wanaka,
whale-calf fishing in the white and blue,
varnished tatterdemalions in the Great Canoes,
the expressionism of the Saturday Night Headlock,
hot black rectangles in Gore on early summer afternoons,
winking bottles turfed into the drink,
the superb fizzy-soda light in Cook Strait,
Dunedin's sunrise, which, most often, is as gloomy as murder.

I say January and it is geraniums busting out,
red flowers with blue shadows carrying a full cargo.
The synthetic bossa-nova beat of the suburban
electric organ drifts prettily on a Sunday morning
over the pears, plums and gooseberries.
They are just little lonelinesses ripening.
Shades wander in their rooms and collect the spume
washing gently from the TV receiver.
A few Mongrels cross the square al fresco, they chew
peanuts and generally picnic.
The telephone booths have that surreal look of extreme emptiness.
The small panes cling to the few reflections offered
as a light breeze trembles the eyelash of Persuasion
launching on her frail barque where,
beyond a cakeshop window,

176

the inviting banks slope off into the river.

How odd we should be
so selective when, really, it's just you and I
and maybe a few coffee-skinned Papuans
sipping refreshments somewhere to the north of us
in what is obviously jungle.
I can see someone bending over to pick up
the jawbone of a cow.
Go easy, we are all fighting dawning realizations, gaiety,
discarded trumpets which won't stop playing.
Was it the muttonbird or merely some weird echo
of the fat wood pigeon?
Re-ordering the past
lets us lie in bed more lightly,
our dental-work wreathed with smiles
as we snooze in the vast protectorate of Sleep,
fantasizing for all the world
with the determination of young children
embarked on an epic voyage around the garden.
Ah! It's too hideous, the poet cries, his wet face
set before the waves
or lost within the penumbra of dimly lit
Chinese restaurants — walls emblazoned with golden
characters meaning 'Good Luck' and 'A Long Life to You'
when all the time
it's a question of your wallet and them trying to guess
a favourite dance tune.
Out back, great-grand-dad is an antiquity
who hunted fruitlessly for gold, they cherish him.
Yay! The Revolutionary Symphony groans on.
Brass shines amongst the kauri and olive green.

These rumours of hexagonal rooms in gone Bee City
over the Strait, just north of Leper's Footprint Island,
are like being in a hexagonal room, spectacular lattice,
stalking the sweet elixirs of rewarewa.
Homages, tears and smiles,
all alone with a spluttering kerosene lamp of shadows,
sodden, bruised blossoms,
fragile stems of herbs, embattled comfrey roots,

177

pale throats of mushroom,
and in the lounge the closed basilisk eye
of television, dense grey amid the shrieking orchard
swirling in the carpet.
It's Autumn, that gymnasium of harlequins;
snow's dirty coat's ready to appear in mid-year.
Velvet purple-cherry blood
on a saint's statue and the carved benches in a
cheapjack church early settlers slaved to establish,
bequeath the momentum of heritage.
They were so distracted by all this space on their hands.

Trifles of day-to-day lucidity are like liqueur chocolates
inside a shallow box decorated with blues and golds,
the bland haze of tapestry reflected in Lake Wanaka.
The boys disport in tee-shirts advertising soft drinks
in the exploding hollows of God's eyeball,
ducking and diving, scowling and quarrelling.
The radio emits wild, synthetic sounds,
jubilant fretwork buzzing and sawing,
heartbeat noises in gurgling glissando.
On delectable cabbage-tree-lined coasts
the sea swells pregnant with never-to-be-born light.
In a carton-shaped factory
the mirror-hard receptionist, cool as a pavilion,
remembers a shark-finned Cadillac
wobble between the dunes.
The small town glitters like a supermarket trolley.
The whole school is painting —
a fish hatchery, a deer fawn, stoned fruit, flossy wool.
Violet, violet, violet, violet
they pluck chords from the yielding tawny hills,
they are engulfed by the quivering froth of existence.

Abel Tasman, I salute you,
sailing these frigid cum tropic azure zones
from which would later spring such memorabilia
as whalers, nuclear testing, high-tech tourism —
the poisonous fruits of the Imagination.
The lost Elysium's England, they said, driving to Blenheim.
Newsreel spectres jog the elbow of Memory.

Boats pitch forward to Resolution Cove.
A small Honda winds past, tooting its sullen horn.
Inflation cycles from chainstore to chainstore.
In her make-up she shines like a mandarin slice
on a choice cheesecake, spreading illuminations.
Oh to live on beaches by the crash of waves,
solarizing with a brunette beside the polystyrene flotsam
of a picnic lunch, our wrinkly togs held up with elastic,
bladderwrack going pop.
The heroic ranges and the Empire of Sheep! We may never get
    another chance is a phrase never far from the lips.

O Christchurch, I can see how the flagrant heat sometimes wins
    you away
from that curious glacial pose in which so much absence
    is suggested.
Ah stung vanity, ah slippery efforts to have congratulations
    accepted.
The stone lids of Time will lift when everything has crumbled.
Those doomed splendours,
the dark hydrangea flowerheads, are radiant symbols of mortality.
This tattered foliage is otherwise harmless.
A reporter takes the fakes down.
Coal-black water springs back
its tense, soft skins,
curling under thin, slanting rays.
Light collects on the wing of the moth
and disappears into the brown monotony.

RIEMKE ENSING

(Born 1939)

Conversations for Miro

the drawing in the poem / the poem in the drawing

1

Signs and patterns are what is common.
That line might be a flock of birds
migrating, could be the first stroke
towards saying I've changed my mind
not liking trickery, the games we play
the line we draw elaborately across
time forgetting the magic of colour and the sun
going down red over the horizon
in one fell swoop being swept off
the edge of the world and you're left
completely in the dark as to where
you are going.

A painter might draw beside you
symbols of landscape recognizably centred
as cloud in the window of the neighbour's
house   not moving though the wind blows.
A tree perhaps to shape you by   its leaves
making any one of four seasons.
These signs we decipher.   They tell
stories ripe as aubergine or persimmon
tall as any dictionary where treasure is
kept.

> persimmon, n. diospyros kaki.
> American date plum
> yellow fruit becoming
> sweet when softened
> by frost / persimmon
> native of China bright
> fruits will hang on

the tree in winter /
persimmon deciduous
small native to Japan
can be in weeping
form attractive both
in leaf and fruit
after leaves have
fallen / persimmon
grows fifteen feet
persimmon dios divine.

So much for words lying
their way from one book to another
way of saying here are the words, they tell
me a thing or two mostly
they are not the sound I want
to hear the wind
in branches the sun orange lush
or persimmon / dios, divine
the word has its limits
go and see the tree
put the fruit in your hand, your mouth
mix shape and form with what
you feel and see and mostly touch
and smell or taste and hear.

Let the poet draw circles
round the moon   the painter till
his garden, plant trees for us
to sit under and smile
as the wind does when it's up
to mischief and blows human flowers
into the book we could be.

2

These words are about lines scored
with burin or pen   how charcoal spirits
away the harsh imprint of winter engraved
needlesharp on the mind like poems
the lithographs of sound shaped
by a point fine as glass drawing

181

blood and the full crescendo of cathedral
music singing from the stained window
of the heart shaped as magic flame dressed
gayer than harlequin riding on rooster
or peacocks reaching for rainbows.

3

The poem I started is already
lost.   One day I will find it
on a sheet of paper pulled out
from a pile of books or unanswered letters.
Perhaps it will be
a bookmark showing the way
to mushroom growing or porcelain
glazes delicate as the smudge of Puzzuoli
red in a sketch where nothing is
sentimental but all lives speak
clearly as words do when they cry
from the heart without design
or drama   plainly as a flight of birds caught
in the sharp magic of black surprising
with its coat of colours.

K.M. *at Garsington*

The flow of the pen scratching
bars on paper / small prisons
to hold herself and the shade
of vision / the bright beams
of sun taking off
as so many
freedom
doves
clapping
delighted above lavender
& rosemary (that's for remembrance)
the pot pourri
of garden all
around

the blue scent of life
fragile
on the open page.

Signal Blue

(the poem as tea ceremony)

for Helen Shaw

This is the blue I've been looking for.
The court sits in a Persian manuscript
on mosque blue in the British Museum.
1397 colours an ancient tale.

Majnun in the desert.
gouache on paper. Another blue. Later.
It is the blue of the night
sky you mistake for dawn / the blue
in the centre of the mihrab
or K'ang Hsi
sapphire in porcelain.

azure
lapis lazuli
byzantine
manganese
ultramarine

The stones in the garden are blue
where the shadow falls.
I make tea. Helen
you would have liked this ceremony,
the special room simple as bending
ink bamboo caught forever
in medieval gardens *where everything
moved at a slow pace.*

'Focus attention on a few objects / of beauty'
                                    (Sen'o Tanaka)

60: 'The ash in the brazier is moulded with a spoon.'
70: 'Wet ash is scattered on the pattern.'
76: 'The powdered tea is scooped up.'
77: 'Boiling water is ladled into the bowl.'
78: 'The tea and water is blended with a whisk.'

RIEMKE ENSING

Pick up the bowl in your right
hand and place it on the palm
of your left

make a small bow
of reverence.

Brushstrokes for eternity / each
                                    a single movement.

I watch the antics of clouds
building in the buildings
all done with mirrors.

white / blue blue / white
the sky a simple cobalt.

ANNE FRENCH

(Born 1956)

'it, then'

& from that time we pull
away up into the light   August and difficulty
lessens as we assume the old lives protectively
coloured and shapely enough & if it weren't for all
these journeys we insist on making
or get language to do for us the evasions
'it' 'then' as though something was and isn't   un-
stuck so uncouple & loosen this clenching

& when you are 'home' again Muntreal
staring back at here fisheyed by distance
where jasmine sprawls over tin fences
fingering in the dusk the airs of Parnell
Road scent solid as the Abels factory   recall
this one running and running on Museum Hill

Kite

On the beach the waves pour in furiously
the wind lashes the dunes
the bay fills with rain, smoky, and clears
and from the hill's bulk the flax bushes
shine out suddenly, like many waterfalls

So fly the yellow kite, a brave flutter
against grey and brown. It bucks and
dives, pulling down hope from the sky.
Behind, the thirty-foot scarlet tail snaps
in the wind, a red scissor of light.

It is a live thing, tugging
at the end of its lines. It is not docile

like the purple and green dragon kite
content to sit all day, bobbing as the breeze
drops and lifts, tethered to the fence.

It cruises, hungry
very small and spare, animate, fierce
its one black eye regarding us curiously
two greyish brown figures, heavy
terrestrial, shoes full of sand.

All You May Depend On

At heart it is not without
complications, which is why
there are several houses and children
and any number of marriages
and the red queen does not lie
neatly next to the black king but falls
crooked on a jack
of the wrong suit

as though they had been blown into dis-
arrangement by a strong wind
such as a sigh escaping
from the builder: edificer, that is to say, walls,
bones. At night you hear small
sounds there, as though they breathed; the bones
being a kind of tree, where the flesh perches, singing
and the heart a ticking egg in a nest of ribs.

That part at least you know to be illusory, and succumb
to an awareness of the fine distinctions. And you
are polite, restrained in this by a need to cry
out. It's an impulse which concerns old-fashioned things
such as possessions, intentions and the passing of time.
Take what you need. A white stone, the branches the moon
shines through, and a memory of how it would
have been, otherwise. They are talismans for a journey

against the cold winter nights, when a thin
man waits at the edge of the light. What
you have left is the conventional wisdom. Eat
well, beware small birds in the house and the song
of the riroriro which means loss. All this sun
which hangs down golden with dust
between the houses will go, and the rain,
a hypocrite imitation, will ease the heart nonetheless.

BERNADETTE HALL

(Born 1945)

Dionysus Sailing

(from a cup by Exekias)

wine slips
over the lip
of a red glazed cup

& there is
Dionysus sailing
nonchalantly

> the woven sail cracks
> a dolphin thwacks the water
> with his fish hook tail

> from the lashed mast
> fat grapes spring
> promising freedom

an awesome lover
great Dionysus
limbs loosed
in a slim grained ship

elegantly fit
to drain a woman
to dry black lees
& then sail on

Amica

for Joanna Paul

The house is a reliquary
of insects, flowers & fingernails
& this is rare, Amica, that you assume
with your Etruscan air its essence.
Lying on the hill arch of your arm.
On a sarcophagus. Someone is whistling
in the kitchen. Laying down new territory
with aluminium brightness. All the windows
are open. Ivory tides wash out, wash in
& you sing the mysteries: that love
is a gift; that nothing is ever lost;
that death is the centre of a long life.

Family Ties

Thin the slung chain,
silky slack, infrangible;
blood beads heavier than water.

Birthed we are like Russian dolls,
one from another from another,
mother, daughter, granddaughter,
red smudges on each cheek.

You stand at the open window
being never too happy in your own
time & place as she is always,
straddling blowsy branches, singing.

I bend between, frisking marjoram,
twisting in weedy aisles a breathing
space. The bright links burn on my neck.

BERNADETTE HALL

Lavandula Vera

shadow of a shadow
in paradiso
a small walled garden

the sun at right angles
touching with jointed fingers
bitter silk

grey on grey
a glaucous mirroring
of cygnets' wings

a lambent greening

Happy Families

for Kathryn

Warm I'll think you in the other island,
in Daffodil Street, though none grow;
leaning in a buttery halo from a shoebox
house. Your pretty brood and goodly man.

Remember the peg dolls we used to paint?
Soapy, rotten in one joint, between the legs.
And their archaic smiles. Years it's taken me
to learn to stop smiling. Anarchic in summer

you hijacked my garden, yanking bizarre tufts
of bergamot, blue hyssop, feverfew and thyme.
Held hostage, I'll always admit the obvious:
blood pricks, babies' shit, wet lips pursed

to kiss; true love's grubby baggage.
And never faltered have we, long? Nor shall.
But hug roughly and resume effective
breathing in a recovery position.

190

for Victoria Mxenge

Juliet has lost a hooked, milk tooth;
stashes it with petals in a jar.
So many losses. And not last, this least;
a syllable in our litany of grief.
The estuary flows black as the carved
lips of the women. And the sky too
round the white heel of the moon.
There should be music and I as beautiful
as the dancer. Holà, holà.
Elle sanglote, la mer.

(Victoria Mxenge: shot dead in South Africa, August 1985)

Iconoclast

Very tricksy are the Irish
aunts, adroit at half truths,

needing a tragedy for definition.
No one spins it quite as they,

gold from straw. Sometimes
they look at me, unsure, as if

I might say. And Eleanor jumped
from a bridge which alters most

things. Sharp as tin, the women
slipstitch outward signs to

fine linen; shuffle inner grace;
thumb rainbeads on fibreoptic

trees; rub crumbs for sparrows.
Uncomforted, in baleen clouds

I see the subtle shades of avalanches.

BERNADETTE HALL

I wave her name like a white flag.

Not knowing the god language,
I learn these things off

by my heart. Pulling down icons,
find I love them as they fall.

MICHAEL HARLOW

(Born 1937)

'Nothing but Switzerland and Lemonade'

Cézanne's mistress is in Switzerland drinking lemonade.

The mountains are white with snow.

A waiter appears bearing two glasses on a red tray.
Bending to the table he considers the remote possibility
of her breasts.

He is thinking: 'Green grape and you refused me, red
grape and you sent me packing. May I have a bite of your
raisin?'

She winks discreetly at her gentleman friend in his fawn
waistcoat and lemon gloves.

A glass falls shattering on the stone floor.

From across the terrace a pedlar smiles, flashing a fan
of postcard scenes from Provence . . .

The articulate suicide,
Socrates or Seneca, is rare

Magnetic north is deranged the south
cannot be found: you write of the dark

held in your hands, an old strategy
botched: 'nothing to praise, nothing

to desire', how rockfall scars the back
of a single blue cypress; on Hymettos

no song where once a mountain of bees-
essential radar is jammed to the asshole.

Here on the blue oval of the table a jar
sprigs of laurel brought back years ago

from Kos, inside it a 'bowshot of light'
some 'crazy' notion of cure that glints

there — shake it out, in the night, in
the night on the stones of your house.

Undiminished

— Nedime Hanim 3 years in detention on Büyükada

I cannot touch her; so taut with regard
the way she steps into first light, the
sea off Kadiköy; you can hear it seize her

'We throw water after those who leave us,
may it not dry before you return —
there are things that keep their identity:

kadin deniz gibi, a woman is like the sea;
scent of jasmine, the sweet waters of Asia'

Freud and a Lady in Vienna

I have titles she says and the sky
is true; she waves her fan and be-

hind it gossip hides — there is the
fine planetary blue of a policeman's

tunic — it is spring in the whorls of
her gown, in the brushwork of trees

She is strolling mid-morning along
the Prater, Vienna, with a bearded

man; behind two nurses airing their
prams, she touches him, just twice

there — and he says, Countess, we
are as strings attached to the end

of the century; may I, please, the
courtesy of . . . lend me, your fan . . . ?

Ein Programm sonnet for the 21st century:

If you wind them up they will shout
'hello' as high as a chimney, as low
as 'goodbye' they will jump through
windows, on the way down they will
waive their rights to wrongs undone
them & the time it takes to whistle
a zipper, they return from desire —
they are superb in latest colour &
they are happy, they love their son
there is no known crime, if you wind
them up on the way down they will tell
you of their new plastic lawn & yes
it smells of batshit in the rain, but
it shines and is, ah, forever green . . .

All the Gods Gone Over

Brooms have been ridden before:
a broken seal, witch with fox tail
moonrings built a myth — twigs, stake
burning fast as market closing
'all the gods gone over'

Cave walls have it: an arrow, sun
two footprints, paved way through

a hillside of quills, two forelegs
curved in flight, smoke curls

Tell me: when you sing it I will
sing it, too. As old as two charred
pots on an ashbed, white as
a stone whose bones you wear
some oaths cannot account for —
tell me, will you hear them?

Vlaminck's tie / the persistent imaginal

Vlaminck's tie survives.
It is made of wood & painted yellow;
it has purple polka-dot moons
that once were sighted floating around
the town, walking Vlaminck in every
direction.

      When I tell my son
it is resting now in a glass case,
it looks like, say, the beginning
of the world, he says, measuring
the space between his outstretched
hands, oh — like a crusader's sword
you mean.

      Yes, perhaps that's it
I reply, looking out over the yellow
fields, the tall sword-grass battling
the air. I see : now I see Vlaminck
in his wooden tie sailing right by
the day-moon, milky & far.

Before catching hold

for Brigitte Beierlein

In Ulm the talk
turned to those 'deep grammars of wish',
heavy words for that lightness of being
we desire when all the fancy footwork
fails to tell us where we're at
in a whirlwind of years flying by.

She said she would knit a poem
the length of a rainbow-coloured scarf.
I could wear it like a sentence chasing time,
what else. Was I planning to travel far,
and in what direction, returning?
Could I wait for spring to enter the city?

In the dark well of the doorway
she pressed into my hand a photograph —
'the light printing all my desires'

Below, under the street lamp
I could see only a shadow;
in the corner of the picture, like a fan
unfolding across the back of the century:
the imprint of her hand I failed to take
when you know the heart goes walkabout —
fearful of how far the falling is
before catching hold; before returning
in what direction, away.

DINAH HAWKEN

(Born 1943)

Writing Home

1

Bev, it's easy in this crudely driven
city to betray what is delicate

and what is deep. I'm writing 'delicate' and 'deep'
to you because they're exhausted

words and to avoid them now I know
would be a greater betrayal. Recently I've wanted to breach,

like the female whale I saw in 'Natural History',
right out of this pack (this pod!) of sparring males,

twist my massive body in the air
and land on the ocean with an almighty crash.

Behind me, behind her, at the precise moment
of suspension in the photograph

are the volcanoes of western Maui, halfway
between here and home, halfway between you and me.

2

It's October and the deciduous trees
and the homeless people I know are wrenching

me into their exposed tenacious lives.
Across the river, which still endlessly

saves my soul by running off with it
towards the harbour, a crane is dangling its steel claw.

Winter swings down so fast on Martha, Steve and George.
Already they're in their thick coats. Already

they need to dream of spring while I'm dreaming of them
trying to bring them directly and deeply inside.

The trees though go on as usual accepting everything
like the holy creatures we'd love but fear to be.

Let's excel ourselves, they say, let's set the world alight
before the long clenched collective withdrawal.

3

Judith is on the cold street talking to herself and I'm
in the park talking to trees. That's how lonely we are.

All along the New England coast oaks and maples
have been lashed and fractured by the hurricane and their leaves

have gone in shock from green to grey.
It's indifference in trees I've been resenting. And often

envying. But now I wonder why we think they have no senses:
how much rationality, on its own,

can possibly know. Coming off the phone to you
this morning I called out your name again and again.

Presence gathers weight by repetition. How we count on
repetition of our own first names. These oaks, on the verge

of celebration, are intensely seductive in a contained,
oh Bev, in a crucially responsive way.

4

I wonder if the journey from cob and thatch
in Devon, to rimu and totara in Taranaki — where

every tree was evergreen — is the longest my family ever made?
What we dread, at least as much as being snagged

away from home, is being confined inside it.
Madness easily happens either way. Igor has flickered off

like a tree with no roots into a world
where politics and espionage have a cogency

all their own. Martha has found some dough to knead and knead
in a trash can in mid-town, and now like a child

— or the best kind of clown — she is lifting out a carnation
bud with its stem broken at the neck.

If there's a knack to juggling attachment and
detachment, I'm writing to you trying to find it.

5

You have to laugh and you have to cry steeply
— without friction, fluently — in this climate to stay alive.

Coming here, into the firing line, into the shrieking
shifting centre of things, coming here nine thousand miles

from that slow green complacent place called home
where — at last — I'd gathered balance, I lost

my lightness, Bev: I fell down my own hollow
leafless trunk. Now you see me nosing my way out.

The trees across the river are still holding on to their gold
and today, as I began to drift down without a qualm

in the first snow, between the light flakes came Martha
with her precise, grimy, ungloved hands and Margaret

outside the liquor store door, stubborn — with a stick!
All I've wanted is to sing the seasons in — in peace.

6

Because you open yourself so widely into the world
but with care, not recklessness — which at first glance

is more remarkable — then turn without avoidance
into the haunted inner world — so that you become a channel

between one and the other — I keep steadying myself
by using your name. And because to most people

the two worlds are not equal, and you and I won't
sever ourselves from those outside, we'll each have to live

with a turbulence like the one just north of here where the Harlem
and East Rivers meet. When you come — and now I know you will —

I want to show you every simple significant thing.
Autumn is almost over. It's the sacred, sensual

time of year. In December the trees will be standing around
with great clarity — ignorantly arranging a better world.

7

Even though we are here together in the same room
my words to you are framed

the way the volcano Taranaki is framed
in the print beside the window, the way

Taranaki was tamed — to near extinction — in the arms
around my childhood and hastily re-named

in this tactful second language. Egmont. Taranaki

looming over us

the way the stark
delicate city
is looming over us

beginning to steam

the way
Fujiyama is beginning to steam

about to break

the way my sheer ancient restraint must break
if I rise

if here   waist deep   in mid-life
when I see that I can't survive, I rise

if I refuse this time to dive
and I rise

the way a tidal wave itself must accumulate and rise

massively, weightlessly   refined and ablaze

before it folds
thunders in
and eventually, subsides.

8

The week you left the Challenger exploded
over the earth and Stephen Hill finally died.

There's no way of holding politics out of this.
He was poor, black, gay and twenty-six.

Through a year of dying in doorways
and under tunnels, he kept on and on protecting

what was irreplaceable in himself — with anger
and a generous, stagy sense of humour. Bev, when

you see it, there's heroism every day in the feats
of the neglected. They are feats most women know

and if I ever make sense of his death
I'll have found the only place in this city

quiet enough to put rage and revolt to rest.
I can't stand the blunt, muffled violence of neglect.

9

If those who must control others would stop
for a moment and stand, face to face, for a long time

with their own hopelessness and the love
they can hardly bear, especially for their own sex,

then they'd see themselves exposed but essentially
irreproachable, full of poverty and endurance,

as we all are, even the greatest, even god, even the great
male God, and then they'd want to control themselves,
    then they'd fall

to a finer freedom. But, Bev, they won't stop. And there'll need to
    be centuries
left if we want to stop them. Occasionally I've seen a man's face

where strength and fallibility are so intricately
twisted in the living lines that you can't distinguish one

from the other. I could lie down with a man like that in
    a public place,
on the slow breathing earth, or in a bed, and join hands.

10

Since you left the trees have been standing against the snow
making those small inexplicable gestures

children make in their sleep. Today they were strictly
still. They gave nothing away, as if

they themselves were the dead
of winter. The sirens, the long echoing boom in the sky,

the angry traffic, made no impression on them, and I stood there,
as still as they were, acutely aware of my human breathing,

watching the birds move in them, moving them,
    making them move,

and I knew that too many people had given up, that

too little had been simply given and I decided, tossed back
on to my own faith with absolutely nothing

to go on, that their outstretched branches were not,
as they seemed, an empty gesture, but a sign of life.

11

Now I want to tell you my dreams: there were these
three in the same night. *I arrive in New York knowing*

I have been singled out, that I am being hunted down
by a group of armed, uniformed men. I am lying, to survive,

on the floor in the back of a moving car, covered
by a rug. I arrive in New York where I am met

by an old homeless woman who invites me down
into the tunnels under Grand Central Station for a cup of tea.

Then I am at home in exceedingly clear light.
In the dream I am telling you a dream. It is the dream

of a fifteen year old girl who has risen from the sea
and because you are listening to it so astutely, so

receptively, we can turn it with strength together
out of dream into the equally vital hard world.

12

While new leaves, like flowers,
are pressing out into the air

the paired outer husks are letting each other go,
settling back and disappearing into the branch's story.

What a colossal job they have done.
Lying down, on the steel tracks of politics and history,

part of the desperation is draining
out of my limbs into the past and into the future.

Sun is releasing the smell of things, blossom and dogshit,
and a mocking bird is singing for the first time — and warmth,

at last, is jostling in under our skins.
Homeless people are coming out — with unavoidably

mixed feelings — into the open.
How spring is here — with its double-edge!

13

Some women will tolerate anything to become
profoundly self-possessed. Yesterday, Anne, leaning with her bags

against a stone wall in Central Park said, 'I don't want to talk
      to you
because I have been waiting all my life for this time

to myself. I want to be alone.' The U.S. has gone obsessively
ahead with another nuclear test. Crudely, profanely

they gave it a name. 'Mighty Oak'. Do they truly believe
they are doing something beautiful? Are they longing

then to bring their brilliance up out of the ground?
Perhaps Igor — since he works for the K.G.B. *and* the F.B.I.

and since he was born 'as a matter of fact' in both
the Soviet Union and the United States — is far ahead of our time.

'This,' he says, pointing to his soft toy, Santa Claus, taped
to the back of the park bench, 'is Yuri Andropov in disguise.'

14

You have to enter an empty room to find
what you want is not there.

                              Mother has gone upstairs

to quieten the youngest child and when she returns
she must sleep because she is ill and may be dying.

Somewhere, far off,

shafting from round an old cellar door, is a deep,
almost tangible blue light, but when by chance

you discover it, journeys and years later, and see that even
a glimpse is more fulfilling than you ever imagined,

you don't open the door, not because you can't, but because
you don't want to, because what you have longed for

is too extraordinary, it would be too absorbing, and you're not
yet ready for it, and you may never be.

15

When the priest said in St John the Martyr on 72nd St,
'this Mass is being offered for the repose of the soul

of Stephen Hill', I was amazed — even though
I had arranged it — to hear his name

so respectfully, and solemnly, said. I noticed then
that prayer is full of poetry and that the sanctuary

is a beautiful shape. Of the Three — I thought —
I'd choose the Holy Spirit, as labour under the weight

of the Father, is finally, on its own, unproductive
while a spirit is reliably intangible: there is no one

it will not come to and nowhere it cannot go.
Lamb of God, you can never take away the sins of the world.

We need a harder, more delicate dream — opening slowly
out towards a place where each of us can breathe.

16

Bev, at last the park is a high green room.
All weekend I have been with friends who see,

and show that they know, how bleak things are.
It is a huge relief. This morning, the sun over Queens

has turned the river into a field of undeniably
light diamonds and the bright oaks,

which seem to have risen out of it,
look calm enough to waste the whole day

handling their excitable new leaves.
I wish you could have seen the speed

with which Martha, a mass of silver bangles
shining on her wrists, sneaked the last

chunk of chocolate ice cream out of the trash,
off the stick and into her old mouth.

The Romantic Entanglement

after John Ashbery

The adventure of the century is snaking about,
romantic as ashes, off-shore, forcing us home
in the lamplight for a final sermon.

Has something changed, I ask?
There's an unnatural beauty to this subject,
you answer, a kind of downhill aria

is being proposed and we are left, like pigs,
waist-deep in the night, in the brushwood.
Previously you'd noted how nature would compensate

for anything we shoplifted (not only mussels
from the steep sea-shelf!) and how the professors
coating our dreams and responses

with cold false notes, and no fun, were finally
just mistaken. New beginnings, you would reply
then, are not at all impossible. And the salespeople

arriving on the store floor seconds after us,
would see you and me marching in on their pianos!
What an itch, an urge we had for fun.

But I don't know if you too, having focused
on and gathered so little moss from the diminishing
story, can stay asleep, snoring along

close to the crackling grate? Time turns the eye
of the beholder — at the very moment of elision —
as when a river is met by rain — from romanticism

to a precise emerald stare. Now on the pinnacle,
five pipes stand — parallel — and ah, how we recommend them.
The vowels, the tunes — our very sustenance!

ARAPERA HINEIRA

(Born 1932; Ngāti Porou, Ngāti Kahungunu,
Rongowhakaata, Te Aitanga-ā-Mahaki)

Rangitukia Reminiscences: Soul Place

From Hikurangi the Waiapu
carves wide grey lines to turbulent seas
asserting mana vibrant sounds that
echo on the wind.

Eroding hills succumb to progress,
muted bush in hollows lie, with
bones of whanau undisturbed.
Manuka, puriri, giving way
to sunburnt grasses, creaking pine trees
now the home of shrieking magpies
swooping down on the unwary
echo on the wind.

Kumara gropes its way between
kiwi fruit and creeping grapevine,
Women weeding, rhythmic earth songs
echo on the wind.

Three miles south of Te Uranga
a battered one-way bridge still stands,
Monument to frequent bashings
by way-out drivers soaked in booze
at way-out cost in the Tiki pub
'Bloody hell I must be pissed'
splintering wood and scrunching metal
echo on the wind.

Down the road to Te Uranga
Paopaoku, Taumatapuihi
once the pa of shouting whānau
echo on the wind.

ARAPERA HINEIRA

Lima homestead round a corner
where our Aunt once ruled her family.
Uncle Tom her careful husband,
descendant of the Portuguese,
fed his sheep on worn-out grass
straight across the Waiapu
on the slopes of Pohautea
fattening on sheer wind.

Past Auntie Huinga's, Te Uranga
te marae o te whanau
Hinepare, tuwhera mai
ki to iwi marara nei!
Soul place of the gathering kin
for funerals, weddings, celebrations,
waiata, whaikorero,
echo on the wind.

Across the road from the marae
Tapere-nui-a-whatonga
where all of us kids went to school
echo on the wind.

Once upon a time my grandpa
dumped me wiggling over the fence
too whakama to go to school
with raggy pants and scabby bum
and all those kids yelling at me
Ya-ya-ya got a scabby bum
holes in your bloomers ya-ya-ya
Ka mau te wehi!

Teachers seeming all too clever
ruling with rod and ridicule
at my relations' morning talks
about shooting pigeons every Sunday
shamed into a mouth-dry silence
when a voice booms out don't you know
stupid child it's against the law?
Ka mau te wehi!

Untold dodging morning school
so that they would not have to read
coming too late for lessons
mumbling the worn-out dumb excuse
my father said go up the bush
Sir I was looking, looking for . . .
'A lost elephant I've no doubt!'
Ka mau te wehi!

You can't fool me I've heard them all
This village is a crying disgrace!
He filled his chest with heated air
'No wonder you're unteachable!
There's weeding kumara, shearing sheep
chasing pigs or bobby calves for
god knows what, since everyone's poor!'
Ka mau te wehi!

Water melons apples ripening
expert thieves in pine trees scheming.
Turanga and his famous notice
pasted on the shop-front window
'Persons caught in my pea orchard
will be persecuted by me'.
Children yelling 'Piss poor spelling'
farting on the wind.

No matter what one's sex or age
as long as one could walk upright
everyone learnt to milk a cow
before one learnt to read or write.
Warming feet on winter mornings,
on green hot shit from cows' backsides.
Knee-deep mud and raupa feet
Seldom bought gumboots.

Mostly in the cowsheds yelling
others in the pine trees singing
Miritene Miritene
he like a Heni Putia
his horsee, poro te waero

211

ARAPERA HINEIRA

pukutere skinny behind.
Fathers elsewhere occupied
Ka mau te wehi!

Home-made bread in the Gisborne Herald
pork-fat mixed with golden syrup
kanga waru pudding with clotted cream.
Grandma saying Ka mau te wehi
You don't appreciate how hard we work
I can't understand this moumou kai.
And my mother saying Don't waste a thing
Just eat and shut up, had enough!

What's important to me now
is changing seasons different songs.
Winter and my raupa feet
Autumn corn and puha rich
Spring and green and hope renewed.

From Hikurangi the Waiapu
binds many whanau to the sea,
on the other side her sister stream
the Waikaka renews my song.
Above her O-Hine-Waiapu
another soul place binding bones
Hawaiki-nui-ki Aotearoa
Rangitukia — Te Uranga.

Thus we are inheritors
of interwoven dreams,
whose paua-shimmering music ever
echoes on the wind.

TE OKANGA HUATA

(1922–88; Ngāti Kahungunu)

Tokomauritanga

Tokomauritanga maioha o te ngākau
Manawarū ana ko te kuku o te manawa
Ko te whai ao, ki te ao mārama, ki te hunga ora
Ngaropoko ki wīwī ngaropoko ki wāwā
Ko te aumārie te waikanaetanga kāpunipuni
o te wairua tangata, wairua Atua e

Haruru wawarotanga ngātorohanga
o te maungārongo o te Rongopai
Ko te pou huinga mataho o te whenua
rite ana ki te ngarungaru o rangawhenua
Pupuhi ana ki te hauāuru
Hau āwhiowhio, hauora matangirau.

Tūmanakonuitia rā ngā whakaaro ā iwi
Ko te whakapono ki te Matua i te Rangi
Te aroha aukume pupuritia rā
Ko te taura tangata tūhonohonotia ngā tīpuna
Whakapiringa whanaunga o te iwi o te mana
Heretia ki te pūtiki wharanui o Kahungunu, a Tamatea . . .

Affections

Heart's greetings, my love.
The assembly of survivors
disappears here and disappears there
from the light of day,
to the peace and tranquillity of the meeting place
of the human spirit, of the spirit of God.

The echo of the peace of Rongopai
murmurs and resounds

TE OKANGA HUATA

from that place of assembly so renowned in the land,
like seas tossed up by the gales of early summer,
blown by the west wind, the living wind, wind of spume.

The thoughts of people are filled with longing
and with trust in the heavenly father.
Love is remembered forever,
the cord joining people to their ancestors,
binding relatives to their tribe and their mana
tying them to the flaxen topknot of Kahungunu, of Tamatea . . .

Translation by Te Okanga Huata

Hinana

Hinana mātaratara ki tai
Pākato mai ki te tau aroha i
Mākinakina ki uta
Marara huaroa te hinengaro

Tīwhana kau ana Uenuku
Tuki nei ko te manawa toko i
Hoki anō rā ki haukāinga
Kua warewaretia nei e te ngākau.

Ka mihi mamao ki a koutou rā ia
Aroha tonu nō uki nō nehe
Kua hī ake nō rā te atakura
Tū ana te rangi ko te whenua.

Kai te rapa noa i aku mahara
Ōku nei tini tikanga kawa e i
Hua ana rā te wānanga
Taku ihi wehi mana mauri e i.

214

Search

Search when stormy seas subside —
thoughts of loved ones flow into my mind.
Let the murmuring breeze sigh over the land,
breaking with the swell of emotions,

curving away like the rainbow —
heart throbbing with excitement
should I return home
to that place my heart tends to forget?

Greetings my distant ancestors
still loved since ancient times,
appearing with the sunrise until
the heavens become light and land is born.

My mind searches
the many traditions and customs
until wisdom is born of me:
my charisma, prestige, power — my life principle!

Translation by Te Okanga Huata

Nei te Hunga

Nei te hunga kua memeha rā
Te whakangākautanga e
Wainehu te mātaki whakarehu ana
Kore te kite kua hinga kua wehe rā

Haukāinga te whanga nei
He kawenga hia tangi nōku
Ko te moe tū moe ara e
Takawai ana ki aku kamo e

Whana ko te ngākau pōuri
Aku moe tahurangi wawata noa

TE OKANGA HUATA

Whati kino mai ōku roimata
Koropupū ana i te ao i te pō

Tū mokemoke papaki kau ana
Ko te koinga o te ngākau
kakapa tonu te tau o te ate
Haruru ana ka kite wairua

Here are the People

Here, the people who passed on,
those whom we fretted for.
Vision is indistinct
as if in a dream.
We did not see the falling, the departing.

Waiting at home
induces me to tears.
I sleep fitfully,
moisture in my eyes.

My heavy heart frets
dreaming of a departed friend.
My tears flow sadly
brimming over day and night.

Standing alone
with the grief in my heart
beating still within,
drumming forth the spirit.

Translation by Te Okanga Huata

216

KERI HULME

(Born 1947; Kāi Tahu, Ngā Te Rangiamoa, Ngāti Ruahikihiki)

Tara Diptych

(the first wing)

You are just lying there on the dry hillside, near the top, in the afternoon sun. Your hands are under your head, fingers interlaced, your crooked arms making pointy wings either side of your head. Your body angles down towards the distant sea, and gulls are wheeling above you, silent and easy among the updraughts. There is not a thought in your head: you are gull-watching, hill-watching, sea-watching, nothing more.

You are just lying there on the hillside in the holy afternoon sun and the images are flowing through you, now a soap-opera — this character weeping tears of applied saline solution and this character stony-faced and stony-hearted and stony-voiced and *this* character, whilst tangling with spinal ganglion, still endeavouring to keep a brave fixed smile alight — and now a real-life blood drama [see the pistol jerk back and the head shove to an aside and the face just before dying grimace, similar grimaces from killer and killed], and right *now*, going through the atom-sieve of your left ankle, a barely boring barely interesting report on Ms Universal Torque Conservancy 1993.

This isn't any kind of fantasy: far from it. For instance, there is a skindiver off Cay Fear being penetrated by the gothic sonorific cathedral song of a solitary humpback cow a hundred leagues distant, and she is unaware of it, and her mother, nodding off in a fat armchair in Manchester, England, is being shot through and through with ten dozen heavy particles and straying microwaves and determined short waves not to mention nextdoor's telly dear, and *she* is unaware of it.

This isn't any kind of fantasy however: far from it. We are transit points and blubbery highways and temporarily fluid screens; indeed we are a finity of things to every light wave and every light particle and sonic particle and sonic wave, but

217

mainly somewhere to pass through in a hurry without so much as a by-yr-lve or a pardon.

These are not the kind of thoughts that steal through your brain while you are gull-watching, hill-watching, sea-watching — these are afterthoughts. While watching, and watching yourself watching, and watching yourself watching yourself etcetera and so on in an infinite regression/procession, it is much more apposite to pick that bit of spiky grass-stalk dried to dunness like everything else on this hillside (except the thistles) and chew it, wondering when the sheep were here last and whether they'd been regularly drenched, and where, and — idly of course but exceedingly quickly because this particular wonder takes about an nth of one second — just what was the cycle of lungworm? scrapies? again?

You chew absently — geez nice spiral, gull — teeth leaving silvery indentations at first and then fraying the stem, and bring your other hand down to fiddle — haven't noticed that hollow before I dont think — with that rattler, tohu, cloak pin, a long dagger of pounamu you wear by the silver cross round your neck, and all the while the sun cooks you with practised ease and the gulls soar and the waves roll in and the hill just stays there as it has done for a while.

And there is a clink.

The tara, you think lazily, squinting as its green length, and the undertow of your thought goes
green: pounamu/plasma/prase
plasma/prase: Moeraki
Moeraki=Puketapu
hey funny! think of all the taras in there! Tara tara tara!

An errant grass-stalk tickles and teases your nose and a fibre from the stalk you're fraying tickles and teases the back of your throat and, just as you're building up to a sneeze, the word tara tickling and teasing round the interstices and fenestrations of your brain (it all happens in the gaps and windows) there is another clink! and the sneeze erupts.

[A long time later, in the afterthought period, you are pretty sure that not only is the second clink louder than the first, but also that it doesn't come from the tara round your neck singing against anything else solid.]

The sun has drawn sweatbeads out of your shoulder-blades and they are rivering down the spinal channel, the buttock cleft, no longer beads but rivulets, and abruptly the rivulets turn torrent. Your body is running sweat.

Because you have become a shadow in someone else's head and body, not a shadow passing through —

silly to keep up this innocent pretence. I have become a shadow in someone else's body and head, while being a solid here on my holy hill. And it's not just a moment, there is a whole afternoon passing through me, a wine-tasting, a testing gossip-riddled party, a quarrel and a lover's meet, and such lovers . . . and I *am*, I am, I am still in my skull as well, chewing grass and sweating very heavily under the afternoon sun . . . but here the sun has gone and the thunderheads are swelling and here the sun is making me swelter and here the cold rain is sluicing down and it is growing black night. And I am telling things the tongueing things and gasping over my grass-stalk with amazement and you're not me and *you*'re not me and I am myself alone.

Again.

Now I know about all the waves that barge through us because we're not really there — or here — and now I know that there are at least 21 meanings for *tara* grouped under everything from gossip to rays. Maybe it was because it all took place on hills similarly holy, identically named, or maybe it was because a sneeze and a sound sent the soiling dance of my synenergy swirling through another place and other people and even another time. Don't bother my head: set up the frame — one marvellous 21-jointed word, full of diversities — and because I am merely weaver, making senses for the sounds — I shall weave anew.

KERI HULME

You'd be a brave human who would say where all the influences
come from, but I think the word sets the whole thing up . . .

(the other wing)

(For
all the lonely seas of people
who don't know living till they die)

Here in the afternoon sun, the lesser shafts
stealing through a barrier of window/outside
thistlehead demons with bright devil faces
blowing on the silent wind/and inside

still, the stridulation of cicadas gossiping
clicking scandal from powerpole to tree
to holy hilltop rings in my head.

I clasp a peach in my hands/while he talks
— It's been bitter he says . . . the musk of the peach
sweet on my hands . . . bitter for who?
and deep inside, the cyanide pit.

— You disturb me he says . . . the peach juice drips
he grips a finger pointed to groin
until blood swells it stiff — I have this this
unthinking ache

I smile at the cream of the joke
my own addition
— the laughter

the great clouds bloom on the horizon/blister pearls

other guests eye us eye each other eye coming
cold & storm/a whining king still plaintive
he joins the carrion eaters.

— A fire? A fire.
The flames swoop unguided
send a surge of chancy energy through me

a dance intricate as tattoo lines
and linked/to the vast spirals heat-engraven on Earth's hide
linked to the looping whorls on my fingertips' skin
linked —

it twirls winks by her breast a long stabber
of cloaksinew, an eyed jade we call other names
dark green rich with apple-colour inclusions aware
translucent lens . . . I've seen similar spikes show choler
in a stringray's tail, warning in the dorsal fin
of a fish, colour all the viewing
of the horn of the crescent moon.

Cicada song stammers   falls suddenly   silent

my skin rises/goosebumps/papillae/rough hide
against of course the coming cold — see there! Puketapu!
he nods coolly/goes/flinging a goodbye over his shoulder
(nobody caught it nobody
was waiting for it)

obligatory last gulps and obligatory last cracks and then
a flock of goodbyes going giggling into the rain
and   silence

What can I say to you?
That is clean, new, untrammelled,
free of smears and fresh from mothertongue?

                              and the rain is all around

a pin to skewer a cloak of flesh.

'Solitary tall hills
sometimes walk, sometimes meet,'

                    [sacred knob/holy top/Puketapu]

'and from ancient halls mounds vestibules
spinning out of the golden past

sometimes, the resonance of Words,
naming.'

> [O freebooter! A wing of seabirds aloft
> and hills shift and the clouds are in flight]

— the laughter of

this free gift
meant only entirely for pleasure for ever

— the laughter of

the quiet within:
hidden among the flowersoft pinksoft you think soft as skin
cleansed delicate newborn smiling thus soft/but it is
    excited lightning
toughened steel   a magnet ready gratuitous quick as sudden
sunlight/stronger than iron ever wrought/a brought gift
a nexus between spirit and turquoise brain/centering soul/
    an impossible mixture
the ribald and the decorous/the woman and the other/the child
and the mother of worlds

— the laughter of

wild sparks running through the chimney pile
a blaze of starmaps made wholly night
a second after

a ruby glance, that gauge and alignment for a second bearing
Puketapu

— the laughter of

Hei! he atua pi —
koikoi! Hu!

— the laughter of

the joy we bear alone/sharing a canoe of great journey —
a groove of mellow fire/a feud in understanding
subtle
pulse of breathing
exhale

and death against the wall of my house
would suit me fine . . .

[I mean I'm old already and ready for it
the still the sour the afterthought
mirrored in the deep of eyes

even if I can smile (Look!
stainstarred silverstudded caries-scarred grinning
no ivories but a mosaic of enamel and filling clouded with rot.)]

'But aren't we more
than twoten bones and a dozen holes?'

'Ten, my dear, all counted.'

— The laughter of

effigies of self
drawn by wishful thinking

— but, yeah
much more than skin and bone and cell
greymatter/eyejuice/energy curl
I am my by-the-wind sailor, the fisher of tomorrow
I have humours I think
what a nice skull I'd make
but a better head of hair

without
all that space

shifting now
replete with that free gift

KERI HULME

the laughter . . .
                                  let the wind of the void
                                  take it all away.

Here beside
a dying fire
midnight/cicadas fret fully click and pause/the dandelions
are folded shut

the wind sighing
the last of the wine/only an hour to go?
There is always tomorrow and in leaving

it is so still:
the moon's in the near north
[at two in the morning
you're late in leaning
round the world, lady . . .]

                                  and flitting over the hill
                                  in happy stealth
                                  an owl-child/songlight/raining
                                  childsong/lightwing/rainshine
                                  owl-light: rainchild: nothing else

SAM HUNT

(Born 1946)

Requiem

They say 'the lighthouse-keeper's world is round' —
The only lighthouse-keeper that I know
Inhabits space, his feet well clear of ground.
I say he is of light, of midnight snow.

That other lighthouse-keeper — he they say
Whose world is round — is held responsible
For manning his one light by night; by day,
For polishing his lenses, bulb and bell.

My man, my friend who lately leaves, is quite
Another type. He climbs no spiral stairs:
But go he does, for good, to man the night;
To reappear, among his polished stars.

New Words

New words, the words I have not
told, they gather for the night.

I send them out each day, each
tolling on its own. They reach

I know not where. They bounce back
reeling, some ready to break,

some merely echoing. They
bring back their news of the day

told in each one's way. They come
back tired, relieved to be home.

SAM HUNT

These words, the words I have not
told, they settle for the night.

Then, and only then, I light
the lamp, work on them, work late;

coax and grill. Interrogation
does not let up till the dawn.

Some nights, a few surrender,
tell me all I need know — her

dreams, the rhythms of her heart.
That's when there's a poem in it.

October in the Bay

1

Their mating is taking place
blatantly in front of us!
two tall blue white-faced herons —

they can teach us a thing or
two or three on four-day play!
For four days now around our

bay of bright painted shacks,
a Mr and a Ms Heron
have pecked and played and shied and

out of nowhere flown past in
unison, in pendulous flight —
four days we have borne the sight

of what — when it does happen,
when the event does take place —
will last hardly a moment.

And you can be damn sure
that we who have watched hardest
will miss it — like it flashed past us —

leaving us, the academic
bird-watchers we are at best,
to peck and play, shy and fight,

inhabiting a shoreline where we
can dream only, only dream
of such slow pendulous flight.

2

Old Mr Mitchell
whose wife Mrs Mitchell
died a month or so ago

is burning grass cuttings on the beach.
I watch him through
a pair of big binoculars.

Through one end
he looks close up, friendly
almost. Through

the other end not so
friendly. Indeed, ferociously
far-away.

Which is probably the way
God and Mrs Mitchell
are watching him today:

Games Time in Heaven:
Looking Back on Loss —
to move you must throw a seven.

The fire's billowing
blue smoke across the bay.
Mr Mitchell's fire's underway.

My eyes water.
God and Mrs Mitchell, too,
are maybe shedding just a tear or two.

Backyards

1

Drinking bitter instant coffee,
the day ahead an easy
breeze and only 10.00 a.m. and
high and flying higher:

the little girl across the
fence is running from her mother.
They're both laughing.
She's in the vegie patch,

she's pulling out a carrot —
and this, now, 10.01!
I want today to stay,
this minute, this instant,

crisp as any carrot;
celebrate
the high of the loving,
the sadness of leaving.

2

There's the little
girl and her mother.
They're playing still
and hanging out the nappies.

Across in the
neighbouring backyard
a woman in tartan I've
not ever seen before

and no doubt never
will again,
again. Again.
She's cutting silverbeet.

I,
I'm in love
in this backyard
rolling a smoke.

3

The mother and daughter —
they left soon after
but I can still
hear the laughter.

They drove off
up the main road,
off to
playcentre I guess.

The tartan woman cut
her bunch of silverbeet,
went inside her house
and closed the door.

And now very silent.
Evening, Sara, evening.
Tomorrow
I must be leaving.

Six Summer Sestets

At any moment — makes no difference if
you're there to witness it or not —
windsurfers will be out on the inlet;
and in the shallows, especially at sunset,
a group of Islanders will be dragging a net.
The feeling of being there; but not part of it.

SAM HUNT

A couple of kids, not long out of school,
have brought fish and chips down to the beach to eat.
I watch them through the big binoculars.
They are immersed, totally, in eating.
And now they're either playing or fighting
and their fish-and-chip paper is flying.

When I run out of things to write about,
I'm asked what I do . . . I pick up the big
binoculars I keep on hand —
either hanging from a six-inch nail or
somewhere on the jetty — I pick them up,
turn the music up; scour inlet, shoreline, sky.

I like people who travel on their own;
no threat about them.
One man, he drives his car along the beach
then reverses back up. I watch him
hours on end. He is a pest, for sure.
But there's something oddly likeable there.

Two girls, one plain. one pretty,
have wandered up the sand track.
The plain girl lives locally.
The other, fifteen, very
proud and pretty in purple bikini —
she won't be back.

The fairy tern outclasses the light —
but, I'm reminded now, depends on it;
reminded, once again: for shadow
an object needs light . . . I can put it
differently: for light *you* need shadow.
Like the fairy tern. You both know that.

KEVIN IRELAND

(Born 1933)

Expedition to a Mountain Lake

for Neil Perrett

standing almost to the waist at evening in a mountain lake
the rod unflexing the line curling away — the action
like knocking in a nail

thinking how we have come so far yet brought it all along
nothing forgotten nothing left behind
such odd remembrances as

picturing how I used to check my fire exits
when climbing stairs — and when I slept above ground level
I'd sometimes keep rope coiled by the bed

the line curves out again — I recollect some years ago
visiting a man who kept a silver ladder on an upstairs wall
my cure was this credential of dementia

the chill of the lake is like sleeping with legs dangling
from the blankets — ripples fan from the fly's jolt
the symmetry of dream

I can see him now telling me how he'd do survival drill
leaping from bed sometimes in the middle of the night
then — counting steps —

he'd unhitch the ladder swing it to the ceiling
mount it fling the skylight open scramble out
and escape over the roof

but the flame that gutted him was a slow carcinoma
no sprint from sleep and out — I remember the months
he lingered and smouldered

KEVIN IRELAND

an eye fixed on the one last impossible dash and vault
a cold combustion in the blood
a body burnt to clinker

the fly has the body of sunset — a twist of silver
a flare of orange and red — another cast unwinds
a shiver on the lake

and three times the tinfoil flash of the trout's rise
means eye betrayed and all that drilled response
becomes an error of dementia

then I know again the briefness of her lips — that searing
that splash of muscle leaping
silver orange red

her arm trembling her breath fanning ripples on my skin —
what makes me now remember exactly how she asked me
why I could not escape?

a setting sun — then at last the strike — a fish skittering
across the skin of the lake
a man now dead

the cold and darkness trembling out from the shore
the earth tilting away from daylight
lovers untangling and turning

memory is a rusty nail banged into an invisible wall —
the hammer-action of the rod the line uncoiling and dropping
the demented lunge

I rip the hook from the trout's eyeball — the whole weight
the madness the hurricane of its fight for life
snagged in a frozen look

a long wade through the shallows to the land
a night breeze braiding an outsize silver ladder
down the middle of the lake

the rungs of the moon hurtling by — darkness leaping
through the window of the sky — a day burnt out
memories escaping

Raffles Hotel

for Bill Manhire

you should have been there
swigging gin slings
watching Kipling and Conrad

swaying at the bar
doodling their slopped liquor
into lines immortal

it's not in the books
but the swimming pool
undresses everyone

I saw Coward and Maugham
exchanging strokes — and when
we dived in we cracked our knuckles

on champagne bubbles
and the froth
of all that smart chat

we thought we'd resist
but Style insisted we should try
to belong to the picnic

all those literary flowerings —
an obscure manifestation
for tropical palmists

we loved the iced water —
that was the best part
the sound of ice jigging

KEVIN IRELAND

The Scholar at the Funeral

his grief was inexpressible
he could not bring up the real
the terrible words which welled in him like bile

he was not short of handy declarations —
a smooth flat penny-round blabber
an out-of-date currency he felt he could not utter

the dealers in words had done him out
of his spoken rights — the articulations of the thoughts
that structured their world were cheap counterfeits

his schoolteachers had meant well
yet like dentists they too had drilled out
all the crazy usages and left the cavities unfilled

and tub-thumpers who rant constituencies
and spout whole countries had pilfered the common store
of sound-gift lip-secret heart-lore

a lover had once suggested
the sign-language of the deaf and dumb
her touch became the chiselled alphabet of a dead tongue

no one had set out to conspire against speech
he had simply been fiddled out of the best phrases
by those who put good words to better uses

and the sorrow which language could not release
suddenly resolved into a magic lunatic vision —
the earth heaved up and graves churned in convulsion

then detonated cracked apart and all the coffin lids
swelled and split — and he saw with a donnish eye distinctly
the wordless hilarious dead grin up at him and wink

from *The Year of the Comet*

3

Perhaps I never left.
A dream. Time passes. Eyes open. Still here?

How confusing was the voyage.
A comet clocks the seven-and-a-half decades

a lucky, Western health-freak might expect to last,
skipping wars, car-crashes or a late-night assignation

with a casual virus. Yet, clutching at a wisp
of heavenly fluff, we fizz past worlds colliding,

showers of meteorites like champagne diamonds,
the bursting puffballs of stellar clusters,

nebulae spilling hundreds and thousands,
a popping, swirling, dazzling, tinsel dust —

that's all. A planet implodes in a poem. A cosmic
exclamation mark. A huge hunk of black ice. Nothing.

24

'Now — imagine a voice from memory
across a half-forgotten bay

on a summer's moonlit night . . .'
It seems impossible to escape the inaccuracies

of the heart. I resurvey
the old, true outlines of the past and sight

nostalgia where the reefs of pain
jutted like needles from the surf.

All those years away, yet the habit remains —
I can actually hear the voice begin to laugh . . .

Between the curtains see the light like silica
track across the lawn to the beach . . .

A night distorted. Out of reach.
And the pathway of a falling star.

A Founder of the Nation

for Bridget Davern

The round, plain Limerick boldness in her glance
defies the eyeball of the lens:
Try your worst. You shall see me as I judge.

No lack of hostile courage in that look.
A childhood of famine, uprising, feud,
dispossession and her uncles hanged

and she had nerve to out-stare
the mechanical wink of the future.
Projecting herself in solemn, prosperous black,

she commands her descendants to respect the matriarch,
potent in piety, sovereign in success,
founder of nations. A fine performance

and a persuasive text: the advance party
of her kin had long struck it good on the Coast;
given their chance, position and substance

had come to them as naturally as their religion.
And why should they doubt it was sure to last forever,
their province astride the colony's pig's back?

When the girl had caught up with them it was to find
a Kumara that had everything: her townlanders,
her church, God's gift of gold, with more to come —

there were still the scatterings of the thousands
who had joined the first rush, ferried
by the skeleton ships whose sheets and chains

and shrouds had rattled the winds at Hokitika,
but whose doomed voyagings had already ended,
their remains sliding out of the old photographs

back into the white blizzards of the Tasman waves,
never to be seen again. Yet at the time it seems
Providence had found the way to right their grievances,

advancing family prestige towards a destiny pregnant
with municipal buildings, dignified houses, avenues,
spires of stone, industry and boundless commerce.

So, we intrude upon the truth to resurrect
the stifled conspiracy of loyalty, luck, rich promises
and dreams that opened doors to a country girl

leading to a forbidden vacancy in a widowed bed.
Arrogance, cash and obstinate love
held the whole impossible affair together

until it became accepted then almost respectable.
And, since — because of her child — it would mean
the rest of her life should have to be spent

outwitting injustice, it no longer mattered
that the town became deserted, the money was blown
and the men drank themselves to death.

There is no smugness in the way she has gazed on us
for a hundred years, just a matter-of-fact,
slightly belligerent assertion of herself:

if she had fallen, then by Grace and Will
she had arisen, and opinion and institution
could shift over and make room. And, though

KEVIN IRELAND

the Irish are a remembering tribe and skilled
at casting the first stone, who will now recollect
of that vast metropolis of gold-mad ghosts

the moonlight seduction of a teenage,
immigrant girl by a guardian old enough
to be her father? She was right,

there had been too much running away,
she had come far enough and now she would challenge
the times: *See me as I judge.* The portrait

that remains testifies to trials and strengths.
It takes nerve deriving from her own to detect
in her glance the shadow of a voluptuous cunning.

MICHAEL JACKSON

(Born 1940)

River Man

Should have a name
months drowned
should be known by now
this pilfered remnant of a man
they pulled from the river

Should have a wife a girl a
mother who has listed him missing
this sack in its cold cabinet
they joke about in the morgue,
that the eels enjoyed
that snags held up to ridicule
in the tow
that gravel by the bridge scoured
of fingerprint and finger,
whose mushroom skin
was the worms' home

Should have a name by now

But only this stretch of pebbled
water that yielded him,
all night and daylong
elbowing the shore
where tractors haul the eel traps out
in winter, and horses shy.

And his trade,
this lout of the weed and silt?
Scrubbing the stone
steps of the hill,
paving the sky
with the cement of his stare,

and with his pumice hands
rummaging through our lives
for a name.

The Moths

Our house had filled with moths,
a slow silting of lintel and architrave
a cupboard dust,
until I looked much closer
and found the wood-grain one,
the white quill paperbark, the blotched
shadow of a patch of bush,
an elbowing riverbank that had gone deep blue.

The soft perimeter of forests
had entered our house
fluttering around the moon.

Then for five days they drowned
in sinks and pools or seemed to wane
into sanded wood or ash on windowsills
until they became
what they were when I first noticed them:
fragments of a dull interior.

Socrates' Death

That he was ugly we have no doubt,
but little survives of what he said;
Remembered for his paunch, bare-
feet, indifference to death,
an ill-dressed master of argument.

I think of his accusers:
Anytus, a politician,
Lycon, a public orator,

Meletus, a tragic poet with lank hair,
scanty beard, whom Plato called
'a hook-nosed unknown man'.

Did death come any easier to them?

I see no change.
The thirty rule our city.
What we do not know we still condemn.
Sages wait without audience
and the trials go on.

The Primitive Form of a Word

All day I carry water,
gather bitter leaves, spread
grain to dry on a tar-sealed road;
at night I sit on the porch
remembering my brother killed
by a leopard,
a sorcerer's handprint on the face
of the moon.

Adrift in the penumbra
of my lamp
is a fallout of insects
that will not form a word.
At zero I no longer say
the etymon is filled with possibilities,
but here write: I 'fall prey'
to my fears,
I 'love' you,
we 'catch' disease.

MICHAEL JACKSON

Stone

Jedes Dasein scheint in sich rund
(Every Being seems in itself round)
    — Karl Jaspers

Life is probably round
        — Vincent van Gogh

Das Dasein ist rund
(Being is round)
        — Gaston Bachelard

Oglala Dakota

In the beginning everything was made round
except stone.

Sun, earth, moon are round
like shields; the sky
                a deep bowl.

Everything that breathes is round
like a plant's stem.

The circle stands for everything but stone:
the four winds travelling
at the world's edge,
for day and night when the moon
goes round the sky.

Therefore
we made our houses round,
our campsites circular,
and sat in circles when we ate.

I used to shut my ears when old men
            passed the sweetgrass round
                and spoke of stone;
it was the heart of those who ruined us.

We were deceived
            by their sky-blue skins
                        and uniforms of indigo;
watching them in their tents and yards
            all edged with stone
we wondered why they rode in lines
and laid down iron roads
                        on plains
            that flowed with game and wind.

Maori

Like wind far off
with great grave steps
came the rain.

Across the river
men with guns
slipped darkly on horseback
down the scree.

I called out to them
but the river drowned my voice.

I wanted you to tell me the darkness
was merely dark green,

our salvation the silver light
                        along the ridge,
that it was you we glimpsed
            at the edge of the clearing
                        through the rain,
that your love would come to us unbidden,
the circle be closed again.

I wanted to hear that the darkness
            was filled with snow-fed streams,
that our broken staves our fences
our plough lines our language
our songs our plantings
our selves
would soon be mended

MICHAEL JACKSON

by your words your promises
by a carved house
by the five voices
by the clover leaf, the diamonds, and the stars

Mihaia,

yes, and I hoped your voice
would recall for me,
my mother singing
                    in the rainbow room,
wild plums under windows,
                    where we threw the stones,
women with lacebark kits
                    bringing flowers and evergreens,
card players on a grey blanket
sheltering under a lean-to from the snow.

Achaea

The chorus began
in the noise of a threshing floor;
the navel of the earth
was a net of grain
flung round a stone.

A snake like a necklace
of onyx and emerald
drank at the air
then slipped through the ruins
at my feet.

By a cold spring
in a handhold in the hills
surrounded by cypresses,
the inarticulate syllables
of a wild girl.

At Epidauros
crushed laurel and sage
in a cupped hand

In the labyrinth
fat and limping citizens
dream their therapies

The scored bark of pines
bleeds resin
for wine

A mason's mallet echoing

Rain water collects
in a stone bowl.

LOUIS JOHNSON

(1924–88)

Because

Because I always like there to be
a little left for the morning don't
take it as frugality. It costs
to ensure there will be enough.

You could say it began with humble
origins and the hope of a better day
rotten with windfalls. My harvests
were not such fruit, my luck indifferent.

Or begin with the will to survive;
the reputed stubborn streak that couldn't
lie down to simply sleep because hours
apportioned came round like deathly clockwork.

Now, sensing it all draw in, I count
mornings singly and rejoice in dregs, even,
knowing the taste of night on the tongue,
and scents of love grown rank and tepid.

And realise the morning is not all glory
nor triumphs to be counted so much as kept
from turning to ash in the mouth. Tomorrow
will not be beautiful, nor enough. Some were.

In the Dordogne

In the land of many towers
the king's house has a flat top
but is set high on a hill.

The legless veteran suns in his doorway
practising smiles for passing traffic
or the fate he wishes upon it.

His ancestors lived here long
back into time so dense not even
the lifting veils of the mist can uncover.

On the walls of the next ruin
an anarchist has written
large, blaming and black:

Restoration is the Art of the Bourgeoisie:
down come stones of farmhouse walls
to raise the towers of holiday villas.

The essential blood of the tourist transfusion
frets in the veins of villages, unsettles
all with an itch that wills to win.

In Sarlat, the restaurants have two prices:
one for their kin and townsmen, another
for those oiled with the city's smell.

Man has lived longer here than he remembers time,
but the lodgers have been evicted
from the caves at Lascaux.

High in the blue air like premonition
a pilot has chalked his sign in a jet-trail
naming a culture plunging towards darkness.

And under the wings of the recycling mist
it will be colder tonight
in the towers of the Dordogne.

LOUIS JOHNSON

The Seventies

These days you keep on meeting,
stooped and desiccated, those
who laugh sadly, describe themselves
as 'the oldest living hippie', or
'the first bikie': looking back over a shoulder
uncertain how they got here so unprepared
for the ongoing, familiar, habitual world crisis.

They're a little out of tune
with the new music and cannot do
much about the falling birthrate.
Perhaps the world will not become
as young as it seemed to be getting
when they were. And if the roads are better
they are not leading anywhere now so soon.

A little less inclined to believe
what they read on placards, and more
amiable about opposing forces,
they see their strength had to be tested —
that even the new was not to be totally trusted —
and power still corrupts. In high places
they recognize no gods; sense father's many faces.

And pulse of the big machines
still revs between odd-jobs and going
to funerals. Change has indeed come,
they console themselves, between one suburb
of the global village and others. The road-houses
serve blander plastic steaks: their sons
commute to bread in the dying days of Ford.

Survivor

Don't close your eyes or turn your back
or bury your head in the sand. None
of these little tricks will obliterate
or cause me to go away any more
than wishing. Best to acknowledge
I've been around a long time and intend
to stay as long as I can. Not
that I like it here or want to settle.
It seems I developed the habit of survival,
of simply hanging around while shit and shell
shattered and splattered, and would not be told
to disappear. That's only one of the things
I would not be told. Unlike the official war artist,
released with a brush and colours, and orders
to paint no corpses and only bandaged wounds,
I've tended to yell when blood was drawn
and screech injustice when the prisoners
were lined up for target practice.
You know there was something in it, some light fell
from the ferment I made. It was the tone
you objected to, that caused discomfort.
Isn't it time we sought for something in common,
admitted each other's presence and rights
to see as we must? The tones can be adjusted:
a little blood allowed to leak through the bandages.

Winter Apples

In that worst of depression winters, the hawkers
and produce salesmen slid through our town
in their aged and sputtering trucks, greasing
their knuckles on knocked-up door-to-door sales,
rubbing their hands for warmth and the prize
of a few cold coins for persistence. Brushmen
and scissors-sharpeners: tramps with nothing to sell
but the fetor of fear and a shot of their hungry eyes

seeking more than the mere crusts their lips moved for:
mumbling and shuffling off into the bleak hereafter
of dazed afternoons that held no promise of harvest.

And the one we most awaited, from Pettigrew's Orchard,
in an old, cut-down Buick; his thick wicker
bakerman's basket ashicker with odorous apples —
a summer echo in a world of waste. We were wild
for them, the sharp sandpaper Sturmers, rough green skins
yielding a surge of joy to the tongue: the milder nectar
of Cox's Orange flooding all sense. We began to know
the truth of that story of Eden, the tempting white flesh
that could put purpose away for folly and pleasure.
We too could sell our souls for it and set to rest
the haunting in the tramp's eyes awaiting the exorcist.

Once there were Northern Spies the size of melons that milked
to a pint of juice apiece. And of course, the Red Delicious.
But most — how much most memorable — the firm Wine-Sap.
When bitten, a stain from the roseate skin flushed back,
marbling the creamy meat of this breast of pippins
with a picture of the sense that slashed the palate
with a naked blade of lust. You must embrace
the strength of your own clichés for such a fate.
I did not think I would live to see men shaped
again to such distortion as our times have made.
The good made useless while the useless rule.

Apple's my infant son's new word he proffers
to every query put. His gimmick. I cannot
easily eat them. I look out askance on a world
in which what we were taught to shape truly has lost
value and cannot be given away. There is not
consolation in crops, in buying or selling, or profit
while so many hunger. Yet I live greedy. The next plot
might be planted by anarchy out of a greater need.
It is the breaking of nations we might bleed for
endlessly, the stain running back from the broken skin
to the heart of our error. The air has a tang of cider.

Turtles

Because they live in a kind of underworld,
nosing green fronds of weed aside as they stretch
cadaverous necks above waterline for air,
we've named them Orpheus and Eurydice.

But expect no miracles or myth. To be exact,
they are red-eared turtles or terrapin, the size
of a rounded matchbox; though Orpheus,
in a few months, bulks larger. Is less timid

when humans of any size loom over the tank
with ministrations or interest. The smaller, scuttles
along the floor like a charlady, clawed feet
raising dust as she tidies eddies of sand

and gravel, preparing the house for visitors.
He seems inspired to climb always to light,
and crawls up on to the basking-log, the warmth
of the table-lamp, and does not stir when interviewed.

She remains subterranean. Someone has looked back
before her resolve was formed. She must be wooed
to further daring. Character settles upon them
as quickly as we invent or simply observe.

But it is not true we confer it — that animal life
is a totem for human being. They give to us
what it is we think we find there. Not our reading,
but their truth reflected on to us and expressed.

We are eager to keep them caged in their underworld
for safety's sake — that the world may get on
with its business. And look, she is crawling up after him.
'What shall we make them do now?' she is asking him.

LOUIS JOHNSON

The Critical Act

How do you learn to look? Already
at your watching-point you must know
where to go for the finer points you observe.

And a smidgeon of what to expect:
no sense in building the maimai
to shoot down ducks unless you know how

a duck is: its humping flight, the ways
its torso breaks the wind. The girl
on top of the sand-dune spying out the cruel

white coupling threshing among the tussock
might as well stay at home and watch goldfish
as think it merely a curious way to crush flowers

as an aspect and aid of memory. Best
to do that, perhaps, between the leaves
of heavy books. So much can happen in them.

You cannot afford less. Either you sense
a significance or take yourself to some place
where performance might count in an act you know well.

Coupling is a very special pleasure in which
only two are entitled to speak: the one atop
the dune or behind the peephole had best learn

to suppress comment till the scene is put behind
and the fire damped down. It's an artificial
heat for observers; something stirring at distance:

you have to invent another Muse. Govern
yourself to rules of a fair play nobody
possibly thought of. And it must all be surprise

as though you stumbled upon it and what occurred
seemed so natural there was nothing to do but stand
still till the threshing was complete. You cannot fake this.

The critic, first, must always know where he is
and be ready for transportation. It is not only
an act of anticipation, but a shocking to silence.

And then the interpretation. What was attempted?
What was achieved? Was it worth doing? These
you can only guess about: you can not begin willingly

naked and ask to be blessed with insight. Behind
the one-way mirror and the lawyer's guarantee
must lurk the suspicion that someone involved was right.

from *True Confessions of the Last Cannibal*

1   *The Last Cannibal*

You observe there are fewer characters
in what I write. A matter of taste.
Movement withers inwards. I'm seeing
fewer people. What can I draw on?
So many I've known are gone.

I have descended a long and knotted line
to the bottom of the cliff, and will never
try to scale back. Down here
the ovens are black and cold. Stones
you cannot count. No welcome

and no applause. I do not wish
to talk about it. One thing I confess.
What was once high and solitary becomes
simply lonely. I do not like the new
people. They are without qualities.

Perhaps, earlier, I was too eager
embracing precepts of the consumer age.
There is no one left I can talk to:
none with qualities: well, it was for these
that I ate them. Memory is rich as gravy.

MIKE JOHNSON

(Born 1947)

from *The Palanquin Ropes*

salmon leap, buck
float past my window

shingle moans, inhospitable beaches
around the Rakaia river mouth

at early dawn the gumbooted fishermen
hauling them in over iron light

pound their heads
with a flat stone

chucked into an old potato sack
in the boot

memory!
not so easily put to rest

glimpse a window
spilling open to the street
passing cars, voices
red roofs
the dusk of lawns
the chastity of sparrows
odours of seas, dark pines
women

life! life!
the sky slaps down light in chunks
across the East Cape

eyelids chained, dolphin hands
turned to trout flapping
on white sheets

I hear rumours of the moon
pushing aside a net of stars
over Whale Island

from murky caves stencilled ghosts
appear and reappear
fronds of shadow

what's all this about confusing
the real and the true?
my veins have grown numb

I've gone about as far as I can go
with these analgesics
and fear, fear
fear

lightning probes
enamel surfaces

winds uproot yellow skies
where butterflies drag

from birth to birth
sad ruined mountains

the terror of raw clay
or the sick man's bed

from cemeteries wounded birds
flicker to the open air

a wind bends to carve its storm
upon a single leaf

MIKE JOHNSON

serpent cold coiled
through the groin

mind cold bone cold
tight four a.m. cold

dripping lizard tongue
quicksilver moon

the claw of the rose
scratched on crystalline eyes

and veins, the staggering heart
cruel linoleum on the feet

here one thought
may take a million years

branch, bare dawn
holocaust of blue

touch of warm wind
sudden tranquillity

at its roots the tree
recalls early spring

Chung Tzu once dreamed
he was a butterfly
dream a man
dreaming

such men they call sages

others serve phantoms
but draw real blood

such men they call realists

what hope for the rest of us
ordinary men
with dust in our eyes

I could never emulate the Buddha
or Christ, turn into a bird
at the hinge of morning

I've been like a cow, thrashing
in the reeds of Rotoiti

quiet now, hear
the wind playing the river harp
at the Whakatane mouth

no regrets

why pay heed
to the myths that crawl
through the subculture of the mind?

the mouth of the wise is stuffed
with dead leaves, kisses taste
of lilies from mass graves, straw bodies
on the battlefield a mock funeral
bleeding from rock
& tree, eyes
stolen from tribal gods

as a youth I too talked
over the backbone of the sky
with a lizard and the bird
and the voices of elders

aue aue, Kua Mate Te Atua
why invent more

MIKE JOHNSON

dawn light traces
wingtips of the gull

wind through my hands
seeds of stone
musk of valleys

whisper of dust

few things
flung clear

SHANE JONES

(Born 1959; Te Aupōuri)

He Whakakaro

Ngōkingōki iho
Kōpiko mai
Whakaraka kau
Kōpiko atu
Totoro mai
He ahakoa
Matikara noa
Kapohia atu
Hiki mai taku reke
Hīkoi ana ahau

A Thought

Growth for me was small
and the pace all so slow.
Floundering I tried to crawl,
stumbling I hesitatingly
made a step.
Fingers beckoned
clasping one, two, three.
I stood and now
I walk.

Translation by Shane Jones

TE AOMUHURANGI TEMAMAKA JONES

(Born 1927; Te Whānau-ā-Apanui, Kāi Tahu,
Te Aitanga-ā-Mahaki, Ngāti Porou)

Ngā Uri a Peti

I noho au i ngā tai moana
I te riu o te ākau o Whitianga
Ngā hautonga mai te moana
Pūpuhi nei
Te waka rā nō ngā tīpuna
I heke mai i te Ao Pākehā
Ngā uri a rāua ko Peti
e pupuri nei — ngā taonga
ka puta ko — Te Kohi Erueti e
Ka noho i a Metamu Ngarori e

Oe, Oe, te karanga a te mātere
Ko wai? Ko wai e haere ana i te moana? Te pakake!
Ka eke, ka eke te tohunga ki runga rawa
Tainapu! hāpuna! Ka mate, mate rawa
Te pakake! Hei Auē!

Ka ū, ka ū ki uta rā te pakake!
Ka ora! ka ora! te iwi nui tonu e
Hei! ha!

The Descendants of Peti

Here ashore was I born on the sea coast
in the valley near the shores of Whitianga Bay
where the southerly winds
blow from the sea.
There sailed the ship of our forefathers —
a migration from the Pakeha world.
Now the descendants of that man
and Peti hold on to these treasures.

Kohi Erueti was born of them, e,
he married Metamu Ngarori e.

Ahoy there, ahoy there is the call from the lookout.
Who is it? Who goes out there on the ocean? The whale!
The skilful captain brings us right over the top.
Stand up! Harpoon! Death comes swiftly
to the whale! Hei aue!

Beached, beached is the whale!
Life returns for all our people,
Hei! Ha!

Translation by Te Aomuhurangi Temamaka Jones

Te Pakake

Oe oe ko wai te pakake
E paute haere rā i waho o Pokohinu
He kira pea he rāti rānei
Whītiki takahia te iwi ki te wai
Āhā hā!
Whakaeke whakaeke
Ki runga ki te waka
Āhā! hā! kia mau
Puraheti Hī hā!
Puraheti Hī hā!
Ākina mai ripia!
Hī Hā!
Hī Hā!
Kōpare kōpare ō whatu
Kei hea te pakake
Kei tērā tō pea
Kei te kai o papaka
Āhā ha hā!
Tainapu! Hāpunu!
Āhā! Hā!
Mate mate rawa!

261

The Whale

There she blows! What is the whale
that's spouting out off Pokohinu?
Is it a killer whale, it might be a right whale?
Up and away, the people race down
to the water's edge,
Aha ha!
Places aboard! Man the boats,
in to the long boats,
Aha ha! Take your oars!
Full ahead! Hi! Ha!
Full ahead! Hi! Ha!
On together! On together!
Hi! Ha!
Hi! Ha!
Keep your eyes peeled.
Where's that whale gone?
Is it following the ocean current,
or following the shoreward current?
Aha ha ha!
Stand up! Harpoon!
Aha! Ha!
Death comes quick and clean.

Translation by Te Aomuhurangi Temamaka Jones

Waiata Tangi mō Paora Delamere

Me he rau noa pea e Koro
I kapea e au
o roto i ngā nohoanga poto
Tāua e te tau
Tētahi rau o ngā karaipiture
O ngā tikanga pea
O wawata mō te Hāhi Ringatū
Arā, mō te hunga whakapono!

Moe mai! te okiokitanga
Ko Tokata rā, e koa nei
Kua eke katoa koutou mā
I a koe, te whakamutunga rā
Ngā taura roto o mātou mā
Wehe atu i te wā poto noa e

Huri kau noa ake a Te Whānau-ā-Apanui
E kore e whiwhi he tangata
hei hiki i ngā tikanga!
Kei te moe! Kei te moe!
E moe ana!

Lament for Paora Delamere

Was there a leaf?
If only I had plucked it Father
during our short visits together
when I stayed a while —
one leaf perhaps of scriptures
or the traditions,
your dreams for the Ringatu Church
and those who believed!

Sleep sleep at your resting place.
Tokata gladdens,
while those who have preceded you
rejoice in your homecoming.
You are the last of your generation,
of the inner threads in
the lives of all of us —
all taken in a brief moment of time.

Te Whanau-a-Apanui is lost without you,
the church will not find people able to uphold its learning.
They sleep! They sleep!
For evermore they sleep!

Translation by Te Aomuhurangi Temamaka Jones

TE AOMUHURANGI TEMAMAKA JONES

Poi Pounamu

Taku poi pounamu
mai Whangamataa ki te rohe o Te Waipounamu
Ka rere taku teka rāua ko taku poi
ki Taupo rā e — e — e i aha! Tērā!
Hurihuri noa taku teka
kore rawa e tau ki te whenua — e —
Ka rere anō taku teka ki Kotorepi
Hūtia ake ana rā, ko ngā maramara pounamu
o te Waka-a-Maui e, ka peka taku teka
ki Waikawa rā he pounamu he pounamu
Ka kake whakarunga taku teka hangai tonu atu
ki Hokitika rā ka huri pōhēhē noa taku
teka rāua ko taku poi e
Tane: Kei whea rā kei whea rā e Poutini e
        Tikina atu te kei o te waka o Poutini e
        Ka tahuri! Ka tahuri! I tēnei te waka
        Poutini e o Poutini e
Ko Mata Tahua ko Mata Tahua te wahine
e tangi e taku Tangiwai taku Tangiwai
ka rewa anō taku teka, ka rere ki ngā pūtake rā
o te Pounamu a Te Inanga
Inanga Inanga Auē Taukuri e!
Ka hoki whakarunga te rere a taku teka
rāua ko taku poi ki te rohe o Ārahura
te takenga o Poutini e — he māwhera,
he māwhera — he whatu pounamu — he tipua
he taonga, he kārohirohi pounamu
Tīhei Mauri Pounamu
        Poneke ka huri

Pounamu poi

My pounamu poi!
From Whangamataa to the boundary of Te Waipounamu
my magic dart takes flight with my poi
to Taupo e — e — e i aha! Tera!
My magic dart spins around.

264

It does not settle
but takes flight again to Kotorepi, Farewell Spit.
It fishes up the scattered pieces of pounamu of the Waka-a-Maui.
Then my magic dart diverts to Waikawa; pounamu! Pounamu!
On upwards it flies, directly to Hokitika.
Confused, it spins around with my poi.
Tane: Where, oh where is Poutini?
      Fetch the kei of the canoe of Poutini
      It capsizes! Capsizes! This is the canoe
      of Poutini. O Poutini!
It is Mata Tahua. Mata Tahua the wife
mourns and weeps. Alas my Tangiwai! Alas, my Tangiwai!
My magic dart takes flight again.
It flies to the roots of the greenstone known as
Inanga. Aue taukuri e!
Then my dart moves upwards with my poi
to the zone of Arahura, the source of Poutini mawhera.
Mawhera! The eyes of the greenstone — a supernatural being,
a treasure, a plane of pounamu.
And so I state, the life force of pounamu
    bids you well!

Translation by Te Aomuhurangi Temamaka Jones

265

TIMOTI KARETU

(Born 1939; Tūhoe)

Te Tumu o Tainui

Papaki kau ana, āki kau ana
Ngā Tai o Kāwhia moana,
O Kāwhia kai Kāwhia tangata
Ki uta rā, ki Te Ahurei,
Takotoranga waka tapu,
Ki Auau-ki-te-rangi,
Te whakairinga o te kupu, te whakapiringa o te tangata,
Ki te Tumu o Tainui ka haruru nei,
Ka ngātoro nei tōna reo whakamene, tōna reo whakaōpeti
Ki te ākau, ki te pātaka a Tangaroa
Ki te tuawhenua, ki te pātaka a Tāne-Mahuta
Ki ngā whakamarumaru, ki ngā whakamataku
Kia tau mai, kia pae mai
Ki te whakamānawa i te kawanga o Tahua-roa,
E pārekareka ai te korokoro,
E pangoro ai te whata roa a Manaia
E tau pai ai te mauri, e rere ai te wai o te puna kupu.
Kāti, inā ake nei tā tātou taonga,
Hei penapena, hei rauhī, hei tauwhiro i te marea.
Kua rite tā te hunga whai whakaaro i whakarehu ai!
Kia whakatau noa ake te ngākau,
Auē! haere mai rā taku nui, taku wehi
Taku whakatiketike i ahau ki runga rā e
Haere mai! Haere mai!

The Mooring Post of Tainui

The tides of Kawhia,
of abundant and populous Kawhia
crash and surge ashore
at Te Ahurei,
resting place of the sacred canoe,

to Auau-ki-te-Rangi,
where words are timeless, the refuge of people,
to the Tumu of Tainui, the cradle of Tainui,
whose welcome and invitation resounds
as far as the coast, the food-store of Tangaroa,
inland to the food-store of Tane Mahuta,
to the protectors, to those inspiring fear,
that they may come together
to bless the opening of Tahua-roa, that hall
which delights the throat
and fills the stomach,
which brings peace to the spirit and causes the well-spring of
     language to flow.
Enough — here now is our treasure,
may it nuture and protect and tend the multitude.
Here now, what those gifted with vision saw in their dreams!
Aue! My sincerest greetings to you, the great and the powerful,
you who have honoured me.
Welcome! Welcome!

Translation by Timoti Karetu

HERA KATENE-HORVARTH

(1912–87; Ngāti Toa, Ngāti Tama, Te Āti Awa, Te Rarawa)

I Ngā Rā

I ngā rā o mua noa atu
Waiatatia te waiata o mua
Auē! e hine mā, auē! e tama mā
Kia mau ki to reo Māori e
Auē! Auē! Auē!

I ngā rā o mua noa atu
I mahi i ngā mahi Māori
E te iwi, e te iwi, hāpai ake ki runga
Tēnei whakatupuranga e
Auē! Auē! Auē!

Akona ai te haka taparahi e
Akona ai te poi pōwhiri
Poi poropiti, tāpara patua!

Kia mau ki tō Māoritanga
Ki ngā taonga a ōu tūpuna
Tēnei hei kahu kiwi mō tōu pakihiwi
Mō ake, mō ake tonu e
Mō ake, mō ake tonu e.

In Days Gone By

In days gone by
the ancient songs were sung.
Young women, young men,
keep your Maori tongue!
Aue! Aue! Aue!

In days gone by
whatever happened was Maori.

O people, bring up, raise up
this generation.
Aue! Aue! Aue!

Learn the war dance,
learn the welcoming poi,
beat the whirling double poi!

Hold on to your Maoritanga
and the treasures of your ancestors
as a kiwi-feather cloak for your shoulders.
Forever,
Forever, and ever.

Translation by Hera Katene-Horvarth

PIKI KEREAMA

(Born 1961; Ngāti Raukawa, Ngāti Whakatere, Ngāti Manomano)

Tūrongo

Tūrongo, Mahinarangi
Ko ngā mātua o tō mātou tūpuna
Na tō rāua moetanga
Ka puta mai rā a Raukawa

I whānau ai ia
Ki ngā waiwera ki Okoroire
Nā te kakara tōna ingoa
Ko Raukawa auē, auē, auē

He maha ngā mokopuna
Arā te iwi nei a Ngāti Raukawa

Turongo

Turongo and Mahinarangi
Are the parents of our ancestor.
From their union
Raukawa was born.

He was born
by the hot springs at Okoroire
And was named after the scent
of the Raukawa tree.

There are now many descendants,
hence the tribe of Ngati Raukawa.

Translation by Piki Kereama

HUGH LAUDER

(Born 1948)

A Visitor in Rome

In the bar 'Caligula'
above the coffee machine
she catches the face
of a waiter
and a young man
in the newspaper
slumped behind
a shattered windscreen
eyeing her.

As the waiter folds
the man under his arm
a moment's
recognition

touches her
like a blind map-maker
drawing the contours
of the young country
she has disowned:

the frosty mornings
loading the slinkies

the geography lesson
when they were told
the Queen lived far away

and the first
strangely familiar
smell of womanhood
drowning
in the aftershave

the preening glance
in the rear-view mirror.

HUGH LAUDER

Cave Painting, North Otago

1

What is on the outside
we can only guess.

The birdman
rises on thin wings
through the uncertain green
light.

2

With a greasy crayon
the archaeologist colours in
the chiselled bones.
As she works
she begins to reconstruct
how the world must have been outside —

the sun is increasing in power,
soon everything will become so clear
the furthest mountains and people
so familiar
the horizons will walk empty-handed

and the biographies

of flowers, stones and people
will sparkle equally brilliant
in the singular light.

It is a vision she understands
is impossible
she modulates the light
a shade darker
for the colour of blood
a shade lighter
for the flesh of stones
and in between
in a moment of carelessness

the jagged shapes
of the two shades
are fatally confused

at that moment
the birdman enters.

At Kaikoura

All day we watch them,
these experts at the margin
inch-perfect in their judgement
as they patrol no-man's land
between earth and water.

Their flight is beyond desperation,
they are the shock-troops,
memories extinguished,
imaginations framed by unknown
shadows. Already, the wind

has stirred the oceans and clouds
are massing to drive them
from their ruthless parish.
Calculating to the last
they cruise the fabulous spray.

The storm breaks, the quick
retreat, silently, inland.
Those about to die
confront their purpose.

Later, the priests militant
will return to feed off their dead.
What the storm leaves undone
they complete.

HUGH LAUDER

The Descent

cosi bello viver di cittadini . . .
   cosi dolce ostello
     Paradiso, XV: 130, 132

It is a spring dawn,
it is the wrong century.

                    Here
on the edge of Florence
we shall sleep
through the summer
dream of what
we have forgotten.
Guns cradled
in our locked arms.

The stones of history
are not so strong
we have pounded them
into rubble;
here a fresco's fragment
shows the carnal love
between wolf and man,
and there, the inscriptions
of a dead tongue.

We have come far
from the memory
of flight.
Soon we shall
sleep,
feathers falling
like ash.

Then She Read

for Susan Johanknecht

Then she read at that moment the walls
turned to ice and she could feel her surfaces
glaze and crack as she tried to keep warm.
It was the moment she felt where she began
and where she ended like a man falling
between apartments his outstretched arms
and head first seeing the firemen
unravelling the safety-net or the half-dressed
woman against the green upstairs
watching the man below with the ten dollar
note tucked into his hat. Something

like this driving westward into the mountains
the cars hunched on the road and the drivers shiny
as the cars and the moment passing
in the oncoming faces with the snow capped
mountains always rising and never quite
there so that if you stretched out to touch them
you'd have to say something
to make them present and just by saying it
or drawing it on a glass there's something else
added like the fireplace and the chimney

standing alone on the plains not exactly
human but perhaps getting closer
to them you can sense what it is about yourself
not needing anyone but to make a mark
in the way of a fish rising preserved
in the alpine lake or a figure in a room
at the end of the day finding the familiar
edges prey to a new curiosity you have stumbled
upon that moment you want to ride
the carousel horse into the sunset.

MICHELE LEGGOTT

(Born 1956)

think this
into abalone
nacre no body
embraces
acheless or
necklace
wrack free
breaks

reckless
that kissed
detritus whist
forsake and

dance
unsounded

fortune on
wild waves

forsake and
leviathan

never
look back
at the smash
nacreous

deeps
unless
eyes crescent
swimming

ascent

MICHELE LEGGOTT

from *The Rose Poems*

4

there's
dwarf bramble
all over
       Alouette
mountain
      in August
            ah
            gentle
                gongle
            air
            for
              jangles
            raven
            jokers
                gentils
                jongleurs
paired airs'
zenith

6

saw oregon
          grape bloom blueberry
          maillot
   my eye
bayou
    saw fat bunches
    wrap
        so
           delightedly
blue blue blue
no rose but the apple
              my eye
        ripple
watched that tree
spring wind

                    counting time to
                    time from
                                Tydeman wind
                                falls early
                          now

7

and then
more comes
                    prune plums bloom
                    blue in the leaves
plum under the blue
bloom
          prunus
                    spaces
the sky came through
saying
          the dark leaves
          open
                    summer's
                    catalogue
we began
keeping
          and can't
          finish

An Island

An island for Easter   an Easter island
in the pacific Pacific

    of the Inside Passage

    grounding the dream and dreaming the ground
    with the Sunshine Crew

           that's daffodils

and a shack on the water   whatever the dream hands out
whatever we can bring
what

   ever

   these spring nights no-one can sleep   days set to roll over
   showing long flanks and a bright mammalian eye

Other imaginations fired easily and here we are
headed straight into history

        other stories breathing   spaces
          between the quotidian hauls and the junk we saved
   a walk out to the plane at infinity
   or a face turned south smiling meridian co-ordinates

               at the sun   *oh merry days*

great circles roll over our heads and we're breathing even so
the fish can't tell if it's
    air like water

  or *water like air*

      nosing in among the sailing islands
      whose hills roll in the gentle swell of the Gulf of

Georgia   you sent us a west wind and Florence saying
welcome to Roseland here comes the water
          back up the bay through the fruit trees
     coming into leaf
     walnuts apples veranda pear around the corner
              mad with blossom and
the high diver who danced courtship on dynamo wings
                  all weekend
              long
                  in the orchard
     which blew its own scents and those
of the rock breaker
          elusive unlikely unreal
                       to us
            in the green cinnamon evening

Canoe   sun   showers   arbutus   dropping those honey flowers
into the sea
   bird of the other laugh circling above them
          and out on the point
          cabins breathe in the trees
     with the help of that redesigning wind

the pictures we wanted to paint badly
will be tacked up
    robin's egg tender with the yellow blown out
    hearts and stars and squalls
        rattling through a silver-pen narrative
        the strait can do to a count of minutes   (fast passages

or ricepaper wash
white sheets and open doors
        on closed eyelids (the dream)   (the curve
                  of a dyed egg
             a hemisphere
        or a line of longitude
        my ache for yours
                trading in the dim cabins of possibility
                for the wingspread facts
                   of the dream

                                    and so
                                                they travelled west with the sailing islands

              the whales came in like the naturals they were
              throwing off rowboats of improbability

                        the world turned some more

                                                                                  flowers on the water

                                                                            or

                                                                        signs of the pace we set

and both archipelagos
came up for air

            gulf and pool

                        and eye of the wind *palagi* blue

                                                grey

                                                    green

                                            gulps
                                            of Pacific lilac and the wild red currant
                                                around the headlands

The dark pointer has an Easter face and northwest light
is flooding that outflung arm
                            of the sea   sun gone over the edge
                                or beyond the hills of the bay

            she called him the Sentinel

and he stands between us and the wet light of the Pacific
        islands like the moon passing through a phase

    he guards this passage

perhaps us

nights in the cabin with the kids asleep underfoot
or listening in the dark

        days running for the tops of hills
                        the ends of points

            any place a line might sail in
            (that curve

                breathing tenderness saying   we are so close
                need so much

                        so many times over

                                unless the wind on your face
                                is also my breath

                                        in the hollow of your throat

                                    and we go on like that

we keep moving tangling the lines
and the great distances grow dangerous

            forever

for good

        times   feet on the porch rail in the late sun

roasting paschal lamb stuck with rosemary
waiting for the others
the canoe the car
the crab-catchers line-casters lake-finders
letter-writers lily-sniffers
the shore-walkers bird-watchers book-readers
snake-chasers shell-hunters egg-painters
the eaters of spice buns and bacon
(the Sunshine Breakfast warm at the oven door
phenomenal scrambled eggs
the whole crew
coming in now
dice-rollers gin-drinkers hangovers
crowded round the table again
light on their faces reflected Pacific
morning's say-so
or the sweet chiaroscuro of candles
orange skins thrown on the fire
wood brought in for the night
under the skewed eyes of the woodgrain beast
whose portrait hangs over the hearth
bear   dog   coyote
or ocean chart for those who flunked the tacky gestalt
who saw only stars

who took islands as they came
        here

   here
      here
       and here
         and had to be shown   eyes   nose   mouth   (Pacific spaces
         or head
           fins
             tail
               Te ika a Maui   (a blue eye for the fish

or the navel of the world away off to the south there
Te pito no henua
    attached by the cords of memory and desire
    to the improbable the very delicate the invincible
                   beginning
           'my' Easter island

Show me the star charts and I will show you
plans for a future hung between Georgia and Hauraki

                Auckland and Valparaiso

        Easter and Pender
        place where the whales came in
        and
          space where they used to sing
             a future the shape of a bellied sail

          twenty-eight names for the winds of Rapa Nui

and what matters is the distance they're blowing into the sail
that it be navigable
        to the mind wanting voices   (the mid-ocean gam
        gathering word
            from wherever   whatever
               walking out on mnemonic extremities
                   eyes   nose   mouth   navel
          to the plane at infinity
          takeoff!

The bird-men of Easter Island were egg thieves
and so are we
            out in the orchard where the kids hunt what's left
            of the chocolate cache
                        among dripping trees

                in cold spring

I lie awake before sunrise
    even breathing and eyelid curves all around
        the crew is dreaming of crabmeat salads and exorbitant lamb
and somehow

a fantasm of island raspberries and double cream gets into the picture
with a flourish of past summerings
            and the whiff of a biddable future   (is it greed
    or appetite
        has us out wading the terraces again for the big red crabs
                    basking on beds of gently waving sea-lettuce
which turns a wistful eye on the great shells
left by the ebb on the bottom of Ella Bay?
                        a bed of grandaddy clams out there

        feasts and delicacies
        we come back for
                    singling out

                        making sense (and love

of the things
we find
getting hungrier by the moment
or maybe just sure of the victualling stops

the depopulators of small paradises

I'm happy I'm afraid

Emily's Sentinel looks out on the sea
and that (improbable) arm has kept the blackbirders out

the grid-men with their hands-on madness
who have also covered the Pacific spaces (hold it right there
and might oneday come in close (don't
move a mussel

to make us an offer we can't refuse

then say

goodbye to the beloved junk the holidays out of cardboard boxes
off weekend crockery
in good company

goodbye to the voyages the small paradises the bellying sail
goodbye   and would you let it happen

just catch an early boat and never   look   back?

Within the month we passed close to the island again
put a glass on the bay and saw

a flag snapping on the whitewood pole of the point
                                                    hola!

and the panorama moved right along until next it was
Roseland's cabins vanishing

                    into the leafed-over orchard

        so green   so sunlit
        minimal kinetic glitter in the dancing glass

and the same wind rolling the clouds back off heaven that night
would have shown us the first of ten moons

                        sliding up over the islands   phasing in

                                            was making another start

the time of our lives
could have told us that love's growing season

                                            close to the first

                a second heart begins to beat

GRAHAM LINDSAY

(Born 1952)

Lesson in Place (over Hills

Where's Baye where's Jill where's Damien
  & Marcus & Sandy?
                  They're over there, by the sun.
Where's Peter where's Kevin where's Lisa
  & Rupert, & Lones?
                  They're over there, by the sun.

  I've taken some photographs
  with my eye
with hills like noses to the left & right
of the view, depending on the eye.

They have my two-year boy standing on this hill
in Havelock North, looking down the hill
grass & sun around his knees.
  Also my favourite rims, which
  I'd like to teach him —

                  A zone of space in line
with Amners' great lime block in the orange altocumulus.
  Thence to the ranges, & a place south
  where the homestead is.
Where the people are who we left today.

Maiorum Institutis Utendo

1

Gulls flying
motes of ash in the updraught, up in the sunlight
the sun declining on the western faces
of hills, houses

290

people readying themselves to go home from work
to the pub from work:

see them in the Oriental
faces afloat in a dark tank
the old gropers grinning boyishly
holding freshlit filtertips aloft in their fingers
spilling first glassfuls from full jugs on pedestals
easing their arses on the awkward hotel furniture
settling in for the night;
others walking
head down along the golden streets.

Two wood pigeons on the powerlines
great fluffy feathered white breasts, forest green necks
red eyes red collars red crowns transcolouring
three purple claws visible on each leg
symbol of transcendence of the carved ancestors.

Signal Hill in the binoculars, that place that presence
the War Memorial statue on the peninsula, away over there
the stone hillsides.

Bracken View by the Northern Cemetery
where the lovers in cars cradle each other blind
behind the windscreens to the view
which nevertheless settles down through their hoods and
      all around
where the hoons heave their empties vaingloriously
in beautiful glinting parabolas of bad taste
leave their piss in half filled bottles on the parapets
beam headlamps like searchlights in a swathe across the city
      as they
drop clutch and depart
in slithering mud-spinning vollies.

In the Northern Cemetery east of the main gates Bracken lies
under a view he would not have cared too much for:
wharves, cranes, gasworks, bits of railway track
silos, oil depots, chimneys, sweepage of houses and industry
probably the earth has caved in his bones —

he was dug in there in 1898
and fastened with a monumental plug.

On the Lookout pedestal we're accorded
this civic charm of his:
Go, trav'ler, unto others boast
    of Venice and of Rome
Of Saintly Mark's majestic pile,
    And Peter's lofty dome;
Of Naples and her trellised bowers;
    Of Rhineland far away:—
These may be grand, but give to me
    Dunedin from the Bay.
He didn't get it, we don't either
more than a glimmering.

A bronze compass disk points out the places of 'interest':
Cargill's castle, First Church
Otago Boys', the Technical College
and other architectural and engineering amazements
of the city fathers, the councillors those mothers
monuments in masonry to their everlasting memory
their forsightedness;

Queens Gardens, the Early Settlers' museum
a bust of James Macandrew beside plaster colonnades and
        acanthus leaves
D. M. Stuart D.D. daydreaming through a hole in the past,
        out on the reclaimed beach front
Queen Victoria with down-turned orifices
the mournful cheeks of the chaste maids Justice and Wisdom
tears of rain rolling down their heads
Wisdom suffering impressment, her eyes direct
merely watch what you say they ask —
hard pips of the nineteenth century
in the brown core of the present:

the Cenotaph like a Mandarin arms folded
until you see the crosses on its breast
to THE GLORIOUS DEAD 1914–18
an emaciated marble lion guarding the plinth
griefleaves of shadow cascading up the spotlit spine

(the Sixty-Fifth moves out on to Anzac Avenue
elderly men running shickered to catch up with
the Holsum Bakery Kaikorai Band
it's too much)

Norwich Union breaking wind with MFL
monstrous mausoleums transfixing the night-time gaze
of out-of-city children
AIRPORT HOUSE about to take off
the Gresham Home Supply not going anywhere
men spitting vomit alongside the Café de Curb.

The directions — get it right — that way north, trans-border
stand with your arms flung like a weathercock
planes coming in from the upland
crossing the Sorbonne of the low night sky
over Swampy and Flagstaff (Johnny Jones's highway)
the geophysical barriers reducing to silhouettes
way over them the world flies out

that way the aurora
over the cold flat plexus of the southern ocean
all the way to Antarctica our kindred land-form from
        Gondwanaland days
an odd angle it seems, with us on Te Waka a Maui aslant like this.

2

Bell Hill in the harbour
grief envy, what keeps us back
'The estimated cost, £355,000, would be covered, it was believed,
by the return from the sale or leasing of the land created' —
between thirteen and fifteen metres were cut off
and First Church erected in its stead;

the pommel on Saddle Hill sheared for basalt
the great girth of the hill underneath sliding toward Mosgiel;

the reserve on Signal Hill, contrary to statute, leased to a farmer
who bulldozed the bush regenerating on its summit, presumably
because it was eating up space and nutrients

his dozen or so sheep could increase on
because that's the model for the New Zealand male,
      if you mean business;

two quarries on its spurs
the lower a great amphitheatre for the prevailing winds
and detonations jumping in the bowels of Black Jack's Point
the upper a silent auditorium for the post-mortemed rock.

The peninsula heavily forested from 'shoreline to skyline'
once-upon-a-time
when Tuckett came through looking for the New Edinburgh
where Kahukura stood, one foot on Hautai the other in Tainui,
watching over the ambergris of the cells of man
as it floated landward.

George O'Brien painting the lines of his times:
sunset over the harbour from Waverley
the 'kidney' clearly visible at the Heads, where they plan,
the councillors those motherfuckers, to raise an aluminium
      golgotha
so they and their cohorts can continue buying in
their bright new Japanese cars, and dispense with the bumper
      stickers saying 'We Love Otago' and
'Otago Needs Jobs'

they're going under
the Skeggs' eggs Bolgers Birchs Coopers Couchs, minions of late
      Western capitalism, are going under
and they're taking with them their
charismatic catastrophe;

painting also Kaituna, from Te Pahure o Te Rangipohika,
      or Signal Hill
where he was, 1860s, deforestation already commenced
the passive imperturbable upper harbour ringed now
by the orange lights of Portsmouth Drive on the Southern
Endowment (sic).
Reclamation

protestation . . .
Pelichet Bay, Mud Terrace:
the former taken 'chiefly for the convenience of land-owners
      in the vicinity'
the latter through the surveyors drawing Princess Street through
      blue water;

Andersons Bay, the Southern 'Endowment':
the decreased volume of water in the harbour reducing 'tidal scour
      necessary to prevent shoaling';

proposed widening of road facilities beyond Careys Bay
proposed reclamation of twenty-nine hectares at Te Ngaru
pretty soon plans will be revived
for an international tarmac on the upper harbour.

A dead octopus suspended in the tide
where the water empties through the causeway laid by
      Taranaki prisoners
many of them dying of bronchial and tubercular diseases
the nineteenth-century equivalent of germ warfare

stretch-marks on the water's surface
black spools of current unravelling
into seemingly insoluble bird-nests
riding over rapids and dissolving
in the coves the water like moiré
reflecting hanks of copper light from the lamp-posts
on Burns Point shimmering wind-rippled.

Across the Bay those spaceships the highrise are readying for lift off
from the cavernous dark roar of the water-front
the gloom of night pours heavily into the hill above Ravensbourne
cars battle round the bays and headlands
an ambulance flashes deathly scarlet beside a prone cyclist
the industrial isthmus looking like a ghoulish school playground
the curvature of the world evident
in the meniscus of the Bay.

3

Fancy finding New Zealand on an AA Otago roadsign
the 'New Zealand Centennial Memorial' beside the simple seal
    of a country road
simple grass verge-hedge-paddock, and
ten-acre farmlets on a hilltop!
Eucalyptus trees full-grown, kennels, nurseries, stone out-houses
a hamlet 'over the rainbow'
a stone's throw behind the city shoulder.

Alone at the wheels of their big cars
the poets who lost their lives, maybe lost their wives and children,
have been up here
gazing into the crystal ball of Separation
they descend now through black gates, back to the shadowed
    trenches
of Caversham, Maclaggan, Leith and North East Valley
the cattle-stops rattle behind.

We must grow into the immensity, the phantasmagoria of
Dunedin, New Zealand, the World: that large!
That way north, over there, over those hills
stand with your arms flung like a weathercock
over Maniototo, that plain of the fruition of vision
where the world flies out, outwards and upwards
that way the aurora
east-west the transmeridional
demarcation of our spirit.

'At the beginning of the Dominion's second century this monument
    is dedicated to the memory of the pioneers who braved the
    first'
History and The Thread Of Life commanding the vistas
the patriarch heavy-browed, in boots
with a hollow book and a solid pencil, gazing west — padme gate
    padme gate
the hooded woman in sandals with a bale of twine or
fishing line, gazing into the birth. And

Edinburgh, here!
'This rock hewn from the rock on which Edinburgh Castle stands

was given as a centennial
memorial token by the people of Edinburgh to signify the
bond which forever binds the cities of Edinburgh and
Dunedin'
cloaked in indigenous lichens
and here too is Robbie Burns inscribed: Auld Lang Syne.

From the Seal of the Province of Otago — Maiorum Institutis
    Utendo*
looking down on our home town
a freighter casting chevrons and demi-spheres in the harbour's
    mercury bulb
the bridge of the Memorial soaring out over the city
old brain of the chieftains Pukemamaku, Whanaupaki,
    Kapukataumahaka, Te Pahure o Te Rangipohika
demurely regarding the slip of gold at their feet.

---

*'By following in the steps of our forefathers' (translation from K. C. McDonald,
  City of Dunedin).

Black frost

Leaf-fall across sash windows
orange glow lighting the cornices
    thrush flight transecting telegraph wires
traversing the cove

the hills arranging the harbour
blue whales abreast in pointillist mist
    on the verandah a chipped rockinghorse, a
church pew — veneer peeling,

a grey oregon ladder like a slide-rule
the nextdoor neighbour shouting
    'Get out! Get out!'
a rooster crowing

a man walking over the convex road
to the cemetery, bluegums rattling

GRAHAM LINDSAY

a man going down to the sea
through the lurid debris

of autumn in Careys Bay
catkins, basket-willow, leaf-strewn clay
    Alice rising
shrugs into her blue boilersuit

tilting headlong at the mirror —
stars, the grinding keel, Herta
    wheel in the updraught
of her dream's aftermath

the sea washes round stones
reefs rip shreds off the ocean
    gulls dupe the cliff face
stunning the silences

between waves sucking back
vesicles of blood . . .
    Morning putting us on
our best behaviour

'taking extra care in the shower'
the hospitality of the guest stirring
    black tea on the balcony
at ease inside a popped bubble.

RACHEL McALPINE

(Born 1940)

Zig-Zag up a Thistle

1

A lot has changed here since the day
he left.
Fig trees have thrust up
their chubby fists,
tiny thumbs are dangling
from the sycamores,
cabbage tree's rococo
in her blonde embroidered plaits,
fuschia bleeding pointedly
from every joint.

Some things remain the same:
the cat is happy.

And my fridge is over-full
of half-forgotten love,
marbled with islands of mould.

2

It's hard to fix your pronouns.
I was happy with 'me'.
Then we made an effort to be 'us'.
He retreated. I had to learn
'you' and 'him'.

I still say 'There are fig trees
in our street.'
I belong to many an us:
the family long and wide,
the human race.
Nobody lives alone.

RACHEL McALPINE

Romans began their verbs incognito.
I (a part of us) got
two Christmas presents.
A Latin grammar once belonging
to my mother's grandmother.
A four-leafed clover
which I keep between
'idem, alius, alter, ceteri'
and 'hic, iste, ille, is'.

3

I used to have a friend and people said
how strong she was. I sanded
the banisters yesterday.
If only she were here! Her eyes
are nimble and her fingers slick
with putty, brush, plaster.

Today you touched my breast and so
I must be near. Thank you, thank you.
If I could find my friend
I might supervise your loving.

A final decision every day.
I check the calendar —
so far, thirty-two: nil.
Poetry's algebra,
love is arithmetic.
Some people say we are living
lives with a shape.

4

Sometimes you forget your lines
and have to act them out
again. This time,
should I flatter him, or cringe?

I have had such an urge to tidy up.
But I can work in a mess
and I usually do.

There is no
single perfect gesture,
and there is no amen.
The world will ad lib without end.

5

On a dry hill I look
at small brave lives.

A lark aspires to the orgasm
of a Pegasus. A ladybird
uses cocksfoot
for tightrope and trapeze.
Spiders zig-zag up a thistle.
Butterflies rely entirely
on their buoyant colours.
No one but the skylark travels
in a straight line.
The rest of us polka and pussyfoot.

6

The dandelion opens twice,
first to a dominant gold.
Then discarding petals
it clamps up tight,
and leggy seeds develop
in its grip.
And later — froth.

Love must change or die.
The future needs no feeding,
no permission.
It is white.
It happens somewhere else.

Love, work, children.
Angels fly on
two wings.

7

A good decision, that,
deciding to live, and properly.
Down on the beach it's hard to play
the tragedy queen for long.
Fathers watch their toddlers waddle,
lollipops laze in candy togs,
the sea explodes with kids
and yellow canoes.

You popping seed-pod of a world,
I love you, I love you,
let me come in!

Before the Fall

After the bath with ragged towels
my Dad
would dry us very carefully:
six little wriggly girls,
each with foamy pigtails,
two rainy legs,
the invisible back we couldn't reach,
a small wet heart,
and toes, ten each.

He dried us all
the way he gave the parish
Morning Prayer:
as if it was important,
as if God was fair,
as if it was really simple
if you would just be still
and bare.

Energy Crisis

1

Now I've settled down again.
Reward me: send me away.

Some days Wellington behaves —
the air is sedimentary,
and workmen smoke on girders
and forget to demolish Lambton Quay.
One for the sauna,
one for the Scripture Union.

I know we're all God's children.
I reserve the right to say
I don't care how left wing you are,
if you're going to be a paranoid cynic
I'd rather have a motorbike
or a polyanthus, thank you.

2

But the wind is our prophylaxis here —
we need the wind to suck the shit away,
or we'd never do a thing beyond
renovate, regurgitate,
lock the turbulence indoors,
because we're all so terribly mature.

I'm always going on about clouds,
but look, on Tinakori Hill
we've got very fast weather.
We do have sun, but it flirts,
and nobody dwells on that,
and our hair is rightly pulled
by flying water.

The point is moving fast and often,
diving up the air, inventing blue,
all of which alters the prospect.

RACHEL McALPINE

I am opposed to closeness, which
implies being met at the airport.
Will I lose my multiple vision?
I will not, or I'll leave.

3

The world is improving.
Look at apples, and underwear.
My grandmother called me a peasant
and that's OK: planting
no theory but many anecdotes
with my potato hands. It's much
like being no lady, but a woman.

4

The aim is to stop them falling in love
but juggling does not function. I suppose
that proves something, but
should I stay home from the circus?
and what if I break the eggs? and then again,
who needs three men just to keep her cold?

At least this is not the end. Love might hatch,
I could love some friendly lover,
one and not a clutch,
one who keeps his distance, one
who will go away for sure.

5

The children do their duty all the time.
The big ones make a noise, that's their job.
They talk by colliding and they don't break much.
The tiny children visit on their microdots
and write important letters to the Queen.
And the very large ones do assignments
and withhold significant truths
about boyfriends and girlfriends
and their baths are very long but they all
have the right sized laugh.

None of them knows about benzene or bowzers.
They do not repeat themselves.
May the children grow up? No they may not.
They must do assignments forever.

6

And one says 'Lo, I am fluorescent.'
I'm more keen on the rough ones,
not for themselves but because their job
is liberating rivers and they walk on eggs.
They wear their clothes like a boat.
They're the only buoyant saviours
in flip flops and punctures,
defending the ends of the earth,
pathologically heterodox and fizzy.

In a single day they'll tell you
one hundred remarkable facts,
like the use of an old school atlas
to steer the 'Pacific Charger',
or the specific gravity of music.
I'm watching them, since I'm afloat
and I'm a remarkable fact.

7

There's nothing to hide:
that's how I know it's spring.
I've never seen that before.
Every hour the ponga pops a G-spot,
rapidly getting unknotted.

8

Leave me alone. I can swim.
I harbour a lake of Bach,
the Tinakori jig revs up inside me
— nothing fancy, mind you,
just a tree of roaring feathers
in revolt.
It's all physique,
it's all impeccably proletarian,

305

RACHEL McALPINE

I'm up and coming all the time
while the phrases queue like breakers
and their shapely echoes.
Remember a woman's multiple stem.
Don't you see?
Even for me who likes a hornpipe
waxed in flame
it's no contest.
I'm overboard, I'm going,
I'll be back before tomorrow,
I'll give you the news of the world
when I get back.

A Trip to the Recent Future

(to Sweden, where I have not been)

It's true, isn't it?
I'm really looking for a great truth
about a yellow light,
a trip to the recent future.

It's dark in Sweden, I believe;
an occasional lack of trees
is much admired, and language tickles.

Imagine yellow lupins on your legs,
see, they light up hills and bays,
clarify a visible horizon.
Pohutukawa trees
spit out their crimson hyphens,
bloom pools at the roots of middle age.

Hey Sweden! Talk to me!
I'm brand new, I can prevent the past.
You live here, and here, and here,
you're my favourite part of the planet.
What can I say that you
will understand?
Put your ear to this volcano.

We are so intimate,
we're poles apart,
this is the very limit.

I am the talking stock of the institution.
There are only so many words,
and so many marching girls.

Poor Swedish poets, straining their eyes
by the lights of a Christmas tree.
We type in our polaroids here.
Here we often say 'here' and 'we'.
You are my father who sent me abroad.
Left auricle, left ventricle —
it's a fire drill, right?

You're not collecting strawberries like me,
not today, it's dark all day,
it's Christmas.
The woods are not red with cloudberries,
the bush is not blue with blueberries,
this we have in common in December.

Now don't get sentimental:
faith is no excuse for
eighty thousand workless,
our laws are jelly,
we talk the syntax of despair.

Keep your eyes on the hop
from yin to yang.
You can see that any time;
simply buy a ticket.
Only the lucky tourists get to see
the marching girls.
They travel in tens around a car park,
they are terrifically brave,
they arch and march and it's Christmas.
They are the blompol of your tomtar,

---

blompol: puddle of petals at the base of a flowering tree
tomtar: little people with red hats and white beards

and a single marching girl is like
a single Father Christmas.

Back in your roomy vicarage,
bear in mind the marching girls,
the paddocks blind with opposites,
the yellow light in which
it's possible to preach,
it's hard to tell a lie.

Life is dangerous, thank God,
and we are natives nowhere.
You are lucky to be sad,
here
in the light of the recent future.

HEATHER McPHERSON

(Born 1942)

Theology and a Patchwork Absolute

                              Time and again,
time and again I tried to write a goddess song.
Now that I have fleshed the lyric tongue a poem
stirs. It breaks from its inhabitants. Red shapes
blaze in the patchwork quilt. Here are two women
naked on a bed.

    Such proximity is heretical and a sin
to theologians and borough councillors. Their voices
shake the boardrooms. Bearded ones look stonily
from blazoned coats of arms. Thick carpet corridors
choke between the walls.

    And we strip absolution. We have become
our own theologians and counsellors. Our skins are
moon washed. Our laughter escalates. If sometimes
we hear Unclean Unclean we ascribe it to the
mythical leper, mournful behind his bell. From
driftwood fire to loft we heal the biblical
landscape.

    We have unpicked the spiral staircase.
We have pieced out a goddess ancestry from digs
and neglected pottery to risk her gifts.

    One is the faculty of clearing a Selective
Hard of Hearing. Libraries and presses yield
their fast. Shelves inch out to accommodate new
limbs. A poem holds the shell of an inner
chamber.

    Voices between the breasts. Satin
and seersucker edged with feather stitch. Arms
that slide down forearms. Yellow plums.
Serenities.

    Proximity of old lyric tongues and this.

HEATHER McPHERSON

I Sit Here Dreaming Woman and Woman

I sit here dreaming woman and woman —

    This one preserved among antiques in a darkly
    drawbridged face
        (she lives like a nun, smacks her pomaded
        poodle with a hairbrush when he squirms)
this worn one still uncornered but for a
    sickle mouth pegged tight across the outbreaks
        (she bore eight children, lies in a darkened
        room among headache spaces)
this one low-slung, the barmaid wary behind her
    eyelines and warpaint lips, a swashbuckling
    high-heeled ship loose-moored among
    half-full glasses
        (she lies under changing faces, since the
        admiral's so long landing she'll taste the fleet)
this one afloat in a lakeland aura, pale-haired
    wraith with expensive suits and a waste of
    untouchable views behind pink-rinsed eyes
        (she was groomed to be mute in a
        sound-proof room)
this one heavy of hand, block-boots and shoulders,
    precise at the rifle-range, stern at the steering
    wheel, stacked in a watchful somnolence at parties
        (but clenches, momentarily, in the record-
        player's blast)
this one absorbent, seismograph and moon in a puffy
    body — cue to cue the antennae feed
    her thirsts
        (she turns a dispositor's eye on grabber and
        presumptive)
this powdery one, inflammable, in butterfly lens
    and a habit of prescriptions — feeling capsuled to
    function, function to patrol the healthy womb
        (since women breed she'll see they do it
        properly, for the man)
this one owl-deep in policies, speeches, tactics,
    user of resources till her own burst flawed with
    angry love and insupportable expectancies

(since women bleed she'll see they do it
     properly, as they need)

I sit here dreaming woman and woman
   women who walk grandly, quickly, a concentrate
   or lost —
   who crush themselves in their bodies
   who outreach their bodies
   who move as ceremonies in their bodies,
      or as packhorse —
   whose presence electrifies the air
   whose presence magnetizes stares
   women as sunflowers, eagles, goddesses, gulls
   whose eyes retain late remnants of joy, pain, rage,
      audacity
   whose eyes are questioning

I sit reflecting woman and woman
   as if I could recreate them
   as if I held a licence to call up spirits —
   clairvoyant, to forsee births, paths and sequences
   to cast the witch spell hastening loves and cures
   or high priestess lead the chant on sea-swept beaches
   or fossick yellowing journals for the genius
      we lost — planners whose cities wore too visionary
      a façade, idealists whose relief schemes lasted
      with their lives and slid away, queens whose
      people washed back into slavery in one generation —

I sit here dreaming woman and woman
   as if I could be the voice of woman-hungers —
      of pioneer and tribal rite and strangled wife
   as if I could commune in firelit circles with
      the elders — learn the mysteries, the rituals,
      signs and powers
   as if I, poet, had learnt some true words of our
      lives

HEATHER McPHERSON

Miss Eyrie Testifies

Seeing the world through spectacles
alters it. Tonight I rub bared eyes
while two clock faces slide to a blurry
one. Doubly received, a supposed still bottle
floats above the table, a jar of cut bell
hyacinths becomes the horizon's island —
and you, through imperfect peer, my peer,
disperse among hunched shadow —
are blotted eyelid, half a cheekbone,
a moving twist of knuckle as you lift your cup.

An ordinary distortion this —
hereditary, adjustable with ground lens.
My glasses like some portable locutory
refine the mass to substance within outline —
and are less inconvenient — mostly —
than the defect.

It's said El Greco's vision was distorted —
that astigmatic eyes diffract solidity,
prefer lean limbs alive with fitful shadow.
So, in the Visitation, two figures mutely face —
pale wasted flesh consumed in massive cloaks
they and the streaked sky rise and whitely blaze —
and fade as lightning swallowed into dark.

Isn't all vision so? Half-seen, backdrop
and figures merge; not line, nor colour
differentiates made, maker, or the grown.
A stone portico will writhe in intricate light.
Shapes become human seem in a bulb's arc solid
till they speak — broken with words, the beams
reform eyes, lips, in alien planes and ambush angles.

So then I make my sight the world's?
True, I see roundly and undazzled,
dark-glassed to face the caller — but glassed
or not, as you, see bottle and bell hyacinth
with mood, watch a visitant stranger move
as vision moves, trying for balance.

. . . *and underground*

in Kelly Tarlton's Aquarium
a stringray sweeps slowly, Nemesis
overhead . . . whisper, sister
no figurehead, this.
A huge white sculptural belly
hairless as ad-men's nudes — but
smooth libidinal thrift — no breasts,
a gill-grid of little louvres — six
vestigial ribcage wounds above
one puckering slit . . .
a prima diva's ease,
a ventriloquist's lipless
craft contrive no discharge.
Sightseers trundle past on noisy
discs. We're visitors and transfixed.
Till the current shifts and a giant
hybrid — moth? or bat?
swans by . . . in
skin-tight evening jacket
and sinuous cuffs . . . undrownable
forebears buoy her night-club lap.
Her praying mantis eyes stalk through
the smaller fishes' stream, behind
speedy half-grown sharks
she's a circling
fish-prison matron of bad dreams —
and Queen of the Wine-Green Deeps
she stares into. Wing by wing
her lazy skin-flaps peel, a ripple
pulse slides down each soft-disc
edge. Effortlessly.
She coasts into a rock
bay and back-turned, hovers . . .
monumental aplomb in a box-office
dead-end. Mock sea-bed music
pipes through engine grinds,
speakers jar in the roof jib,
the surface froths . . .

    a tank thrust up
there twists her blind side
out. A grotesque tragedian's mouth,
black in a bloodless front,
gapes up the transparent moulding
between us and density.
It chills our chat . . .
    till deadpan
fixity diverts to droopy eyes —
droll in a white-face mask — and a
grinning spectre floats up the arch . . .
hang-bag of old deterrents!
mummy chucked off the wharfside,
nightmare trailing a lash!
    or first-born crone
dropped out of the half moon
light years back, into the filmiest
green dimension, marrying —
barb-tailed flatfish —
gender and dissolution after
the waters broke . . .
    Piebald, unembraceable,
she tows a provocative virginalia
through floodlit Tarlton windings . . .
sunk Anat, her bargeload and no
Nile — no airy exit into the street
and off to a corn sowing,
the god-twin dying . . .
    The fruitless rounds,
the woman-ghost crevices looking up —
we find them hard to abandon.

Our Wall Has Fallen

Our wall has fallen down. It lies
face down on the footpath, two blocks
split. The garden is exposed — a piece
of rope hanging off the porch roof
swings in the wind. The grapevine dips

on the fence, the figtree in the barrel
shakes, a sparrow in the plumtree
flies away. This grey trickling day
I am haunted by the sense that nothing
stays the same — like the blown-up
restless weeks after a broken love
no buffer, no fences stand — the road's
too close and my hand picks over
the sewing basket for wool and holey
jerseys. I must mend, must mend . . . this
autumn's draughty, and winter's brewing
up, and the stonemason to come.

After a Formula

Simply let go a while a while . . .
Let words flow though they don't though they cross
cut and scatter and skirt into underneath hide . . .
Ride, ride . . . Into the word tops that sit in the centre
of half what they mean Into the broil the boil the bloat
of a bunch crop with rents and alone
A stilt craft a fly path the animate by-blast
of oughts and split eye. Not picking about itself
sliding half true till a final say flitted away Not
scuttle out ebbing dry webbing and tinny When thin
finger rings rattle plaques on deft rubbings When
pedestals tilt with a breathless and sense drops in
preen. Marble and please argue lean.
Set other distinct after mean. Double is audience,
luggage. Form forced to barge, formed to breaker
still single absorb . . . Relating distorts. Halfso
and bitmade and hard and a mess of explain. Gaps
under tension attention will petrify.
Alone see alone into swathe.
Ride, ride . . . till the moment the mountain, mountain
rise isolate, word owned entire at arrive.
Only unaudienced choose The exact the exacting word
fit for its being fits a being fits being.
Being freed.

CILLA McQUEEN

(Born 1949)

Matinal

Alice on the croquet lawn
is nibbling   at the morning
high   as a tree   she is
appropriately placed for
contemplation.
                    In the garden
held down by webs
                              anchored on
leaves,
            quiet as trickling
the wind unknots its branches.
Alice goes in   to the garden
leaf by   leaf:
                        such small things
as transparency in the sun's light
move her.
                The blackbird directs an eye
at veins   under the
skin: she watches a moment, and
laughs her
                    disappearing laugh, unpicking
nets of shadows.
                        Alice's balance
is delicate;
                  yet see
the quiet spider journeying
from point to point,
repairing her small wounds.

Hokianga Poem

The sea
sprang.
The shy
lady in
the yellow
uncrushable
sun
dress
folded her
dark
glasses.
The hills
were
blue.

The sun
sprang
yellow.
The blue
hills
folded the
uncrushable
sun
dress. The
shy sea
darkened
the
pale
lady.

The crushed
yellow
paled
the dark.
The lady
sprang
in the
blue
sun.
The sea
folded.
The shy
hills
folded.

To Ben, at the Lake

See, Ben, the water
has a strong soft skin,
and all the insects dance
and jump about on it —
for them it's safe as
springy turf. You see,
it is a matter of ensuring
that you are lighter
than the medium you
walk on: in other words,
first check your meniscus
And also, to hell with the
trout — you can't afford
to look down, anyway.
You and I have lots of
golden sticky clay on our
gumboots — the world
is holding us up
very well, today.

CILLA McQUEEN

Vegetable Garden Poem II

Silver beet stalks glow white
neon tubes. The sun goes in to them
and shines back off the dark leaves.
Clouds come over the Potters'
roof travelling fast scored by the
cabbage trees. The telegraph poles
have remained alive. They have
branches and shiny brown knobs that
hold wires and pass them across.
The power lines are straight and
curved, parallel crisscrossing and
converging. The poles are anchors
to the ground and vectors out of
the earth.

Looking down, the vegetable garden's
chocolate brown and green. I'm
down here beside the silver beet between
two thistles. There is a very old and
rusty iron drum we brought back from
Aramoana lying to my left. The skin
of it is stippled orange indigo and violet.
A starry daisy's shadow polishes it in
coming and going breeze. I turn to face
the plum tree. Red eyes wink in there.

The ash whispers.

Suddenly in a gust we are all swept
sideways hair in a glitter. Now here in
front of me is a corrugated copper red and
green and black hot water tank, elegantly
eroded. A pile of soft orange old bricks,
corrugated iron, docks and blackberry.
Up the hill the big gum tree is the shape
of the clouds travelling east. I strip
a seedhead and let the seeds go flying.
The thistles move slowly their purple
crowns. A slow silent willow dances behind.

The grasses each have their exclusive
seed head design. Whatever it is, the idea
is to get up very tall and slim into the
maximum possible windspace, and start broadcasting.

Parallax

for Joanna & Jeffrey

Out or in or simply looking quite through
as if cut glass or tears more likely (but

not sad) oh heavens no a great delight this
seeing it differently, knowing the boundary

between one vision & the next. Beta Street
black rubber gumboots off into the middle

distance while the houses jostle in the view
finder & a window in the heart suddenly opens.

The window opens in splinters & droplets, the
window opens in a shower of little flying worlds,

the window opens & opens out in yellow & white
edges in fractured vistas, & the light is seen to be

coming from inside a sure calm wholeness: one
might suppose a vantage point within the egg.

Outside (22.1.85)

love
kin
place
springs & anchors

CILLA McQUEEN

present stability
surfing on illusion

a light
wave

Aramoana
the black rock
the tall sand
the gulls

skylarks
ancient loves

air electricity
earth spring

place
kin
love

the past,
dangling in the now

& the truth is so little & sharp

HARVEY McQUEEN

(Born 1934)

Anything New

The face must languish behind the dungeon grill:
    Mussolini's upside down on a butcher's hook.

The fortress must possess one gate to breach:
    a bomb bursts open the Czar's rib cage.

The younger bull must fight to take the herd:
    Savonarola flares like the Maid of Orleans

The polar bear must stalk its frozen 'berg:
    Viking blood stains rock in Labrador.

The axe must hack the rimu and the oak:
    the tides crash back on Pharaoh's frenzied men.

Delacroix as Centre

the appetising thighs of a lady

or death

or heaven

cool Nature moved centrestage
when sceptic Hume broke that circle

then as Wordsworth prattled on
the French rediscovered the sphinx

vultures plunged from the ancient sun
the lack of rain fell on barren terrain

infinities of space
                & temperament

in vain
violets, mistletoe, anemones
attempted rescue from the massacre of the senses.

'Nomanschatter'

Childhood's horses stumble in the shingle,
scoop a channel through the tight, stone spit,
Lake Forsyth, Birdling's Flat.
               When my parents sold
memory's farm, did new owners call the paddock,
the third one past the dip, Foxglove Knoll, my first
day christening?

               Norwest tennis as I struggle for my
school, Okuti, introduction to the times when I would
rise shouting to my feet as Buddy Henderson banged
home another goal or Sylvia Potts fell inches from
the tape at Edinburgh, three times the set is deuce,
before the gale lobs my final shot into the perspiring
pines. Country kids mustn't cry, talk instead to
sheepdogs, Rag, Sharp, & Meg.

               After he was shot I dug
Rag's grave. Once started the lake devours its own
channel, spreads like the retreating German lines,
Stalingrad, Smolensk, Kiev.

               The entire British fleet
could anchor safely in Akaroa Harbour.

               Unbelief begins
when the 1943 birthday globe doesn't square with the
treasure trove atlas, St Petersburg, Matabeleland,
Bosnia. Green smoke obscures the sun as the comforting
dogs watch me clear manuka, or loll beside me under

the walnut tree as William, Douglas, Ginger & Henry
romp across intoxicated space or the villainous white
rose close in with swords at Barnet on the last baron.

Theology promises theories to explain experience.
Sin, salvation, penance. 'I will lay open the flanks
of Moab from the cities on its frontiers, the glory
of the country, Beth-jest-imoth, Bael-meon, Kiriathaim.'
The symbols fail to engage. Indiscriminate, I read Brontë,
Bonhoeffer, Bulldog Drummond. The only style in existence
is me and that is pretty vulnerable.

                              Hannibal can lose.

'I will execute judgements upon Moab and they shall know
that I am the Lord.' A broken clavicle doesn't mend by
name. Spinoza, Hegel, James, infatuated fools candle me
along my way, prayer and grammar learnt by text.
                                        Although
I've never sailed to South Georgia I have swum at
Acapulco & Peraki Bay.

                  My present salary claims I can
'maintain, improve & where appropriate enlarge arrangements
for consultation with statutory and other interested bodies'.

Thoughts on the floppy discs of time to mythologize
the present, as much truth as any author's fiction.
Agapanthus bloom randy out the back midst convolvulus,
nasturtium, ivy & wandering jew. Each wind, Easterly,
Norwest, Souwest bends the newly planted cherry tree.
I smear rosemary, garlic on a leg of lamb & place it
in the oven. Scents linger like doubt upon the mind. I
have spent blood navigating with words from strangers;
time to start hacking my own path through the prickly pear.

Without nomenclature we live in noman's land. I am Harvey.

HARVEY McQUEEN

Oasis Motel

After long days of green manuals
the odd decision or two, it felt
great to swing the car along route

one, head north away from defeated
men, curious neighbours, relentless
kids, arrive here, where the plural

waters of the lake, driven by winds
straight from the mountains, hammer
into what was once called hot water

beach. Maui's brothers, we section,
cut and claim, like most of us
moteliers must make a living, decor

of the unit neutral rather than
vogue. We sit, warm, relaxed from
a thermal swim, while floating

buoyant on my back I could hardly
see the stars for steam, and watch in
colour, nothing comparative about this

performance, Fonteyn, Nureyev dance
la Dame aux Camelias. Outside refuelled
trucks head for the desert road. Inside

we live every step, every movement
into the final drowsy grief. Somewhere,
someone else is making the mistakes.

Ballyhoo

That childhood hero, Shackleton
flickers in my consciousness,
crushed ship, ice, an impossible
voyage, incredulous welcome at
the whaling station,

                     penguins
nest now in the rusting iron,
albatross tumble still over
cliffs to soar the southern
latitudes.

         Tonight, *Swan Lake*,
swirling buttocks of the ballerinas,
snares, relics, violins, the ultimate
romantic.

       Bones lie through the thorn
bushes of Chunuk Bair, stone plinths
on the outskirts of forgotten townships.

the lonely cross

           the lovely arms . . .

Turning points for every myth
          the stars are delayed light.

AUNTY JANE MANAHI

(KĀI TAHU)

Te Kōtuku — Te Manu Wairua o Te Toka

Takoto mai rā kā wai e piata ana
O Okarito i raro i te maru o Aoraki
Te mauka teitei o Te Toka.
E karo atu ana te tihi o Aoraki
I kā kapua o Te Raki.

Whānau mai kā Pipi Kōtuku
I roto i te kāhere o Okarito
Te kōhaka wairua o te kōtuku.
Kia tae ki te wā e rere ana
Ka rere te kōtuku ki tua o kā mauka.

Ka huri te kanohi ki te Hau Māru
Rere atu kōtuku i ruka i kā pakiki
Whakatekateka o Waitaha.
Ka pā atu tō reo
Ko Piki Kōtuku tēnei e rere atu nei.

Hoki atu Kōtuku ki tōu kāika tūturu
I te tihi o Aoraki, haere ki ōu mātua
Ki te mauka teitei i Te Raki.

White Heron — The Spirit Bird of the South

The glistening waters
of Okarito lie there
in the shadows of Aoraki,
the majestic mountain of the South
with its peak obscured by heavenly clouds.

Nurtured deep within the forest
of Okarito, the baby kotuku will

emerge as the beautiful
white heron
Spirit Bird of the South

Flying above the Canterbury Plains
kotuku changes course flying into
the nor'-west wind. Then you call,
this is Piki Kotuku in flight
to my permanent dwelling place.

Return, Kotuku, to your spiritual ancestors,
to Aoraki where the summit reaches
the sky and is lost in heavenly clouds.

Translation by Aunty Jane Manahi

BILL MANHIRE

(Born 1946)

Declining the Naked Horse

The naked horse came into the room.
The naked horse comes into the room.
The naked horse has come into the room.
The naked horse will be coming into the room.
The naked horse is coming into the room.
The naked horse does come into the room.
The naked horse had come into the room.
The naked horse would of come into the room
again if we hadn't of stopped it.

The Voyeur: An Imitation

How long a minute seems out in the falling snow
and how pale the late Victorian girl is, sleeping
in her bed. How small she is, the same shade
as the curtains, sahib, sleeping even as she chooses.
We look at her but don't 'relate', living too late
in another century. The lighting is soft and clear
but not intense, like a royal court or the modest glow
of a radio at night and really, she is
somehow medieval, quite flat upon the paper.
And we should put the book down now and just return it
to the shelf and then that way at least
be done with it. But that would be too much like
putting down the ancient family pet, not possible,
even if the mind is gone, the form of what was loved
remains, a passive thing demanding to be cherished.
Also, we have not finished reading. We learned our early
slow advances out of books, getting the answers
off by heart before we knew the questions.
The books showed how the bodies grew

though the books themselves weren't bodies.
We put down other questions and passed them
to the front, and that was reproduction.
The trees we saw were diagrams of trees
with bodies underneath. How far away
those bodies seemed, how cold
they must be now beneath the skies, making
their way through snow by word of mouth
and multiplying as they move towards us. It is
probably their life of whiteness we desire
and probably desire is why you stand
behind the curtains, sahib, and I am here
beside you, persuaded I am also in the picture.
How easily we might partake of what is pallid!
Now you are awake and I am not awake
or I am awake and you are not, and anyway the picture
is a theory: the room itself is luminous.
And we can put this pleasant evening down
entirely to experience, whether or not we find
the girl agreeable, whether we choose to make
advances now or climb back through the window,
postponing the moment once again,
whatever it is we go on imitating.

A Song about the Moon

The moon lives by damaging the ocean
The moon lives in its nest of feathers
The moon lives in its nest of clamps
The moon lives by aching for marriage
The moon is dead, it has nothing to live for

The bodies are dangerous, you should not touch them
The bodies resemble our own, they belong together
The bodies are weapons, someone will die of them
The bodies will not lack for wings, someone will find them
The bodies are maimed but you will not remember

Do you still suffer terribly?
Do you always speak French?
Do you stare at the moon for you cannot forget it?
Do you long to be emptied of nothing but feathers?
Do you want to go on like this almost forever?

You must abandon everything after all
You must abandon nothing at least not yet
You must abandon hilarity
You must abandon your flags
You must abandon your pain, it is someone else's

You must abandon poetry for you cannot forget it
You must abandon poetry, it never existed
You must abandon poetry, it has always been fatal
It is like the moon, it is like your body
It is like the ocean, it is like your face

Water, a Stopping Place

There are places named for
other places, ones where
a word survives whatever happened

which it once referred to. And there are
names for the places water comes and touches,
but nothing for the whole. A world

released from reference
is travelling away. Its monotones of swell
surround the modest island nation

where a man and woman
lie together by a stream
on a blanket anchored to the grass

by stones. She has turned a radio on
and as their passion comes to rest
she hears the first commercial break

which advertises cereals, then tractors.
Later she walks down
to fill a bottle from the stream

and stands, bare feet on gravel,
meaning to scoop water out of water,
her dress tucked up. It is late

to be changing the topic of conversation
but she is searching for a word,
something to tell him why he something huge

about devotion, some other sound beyond
this small dark gargle from the past,
not vowel, not consonant, not either.

The Selenologist

Is gazing at the moon again.
He stares as usual through his optic lens,
The length of tube with glass at either end.
There, as it happens, is the outside cat;
And there are the fox & the flower & the star.
Among all these his life takes place.

There also is the river of light
Which moves past stars with golden rays
Too bright to contemplate or gaze upon.
The river itself begins in snow,
Far out in space. It travels under cloud,
And those who travel in the boat upon the river

Are pleased to hold beneath the cloud
Because there they are always safe.
(Of course, they will never again traverse
The space they have just left
And which they have just deserted forever,
They will never again embrace brothers or sisters:

331

BILL MANHIRE

They are looking for life on another planet.)
Imagine, before the selenologist was born
They were on their way. They dipped their oars
In cloud and thought of water. Even now
They hardly know if they are touching water
Through the cloud — for they are going with

The current anyway. They are unknown life
But not to each other. They know each other
By their voices and the songs they sing; yet
They can only assume the content of these songs,
The golden stars past which they journey,
They can only assume the water.

This is not strictly true
For they can almost guess at death.
They can imagine the faces, growing older;
Also, they know that if one should fall
From the boat, then it is one voice less;
And yet that such a splashing will confirm the water.

It is then they sing with purest pleasure.
The selenologist can hear across all space
The sound that water makes when violently displaced
And fancies he can hear them singing.
He knows that before he was conceived
This noise was on its way; and smiles

And sighs and gives the cat its supper.
He tells the story of the fox & the flower
& the star, he writes how happy all these are.
He sighs and writes: 'Life is motionless
In consequence of all the time it takes.'
He sighs and writes: 'Distance sets limits

Where our vision fails in space.'
He tries to imagine the boat upon the water
But can see only grass in a small field
By the river at the edge of cloud.
It is immense vegetation, fixed in place:
Green as emerald, soft like a lake.

An Outline

First we disowned parents
because they always said *after*;
and friends promised to be around
but were not. Our teachers gave
encouragement and then prescribed
the lonely flower inside the brain.
One showed a picture
but soon would kick the bucket.

At home, away from home, but mostly
nowhere special, we took our own advice.
We got in the car and then just drove
along the road past cliffs and river,
and when we stopped
we slept on the parchment floor,
taking it for the real thing.
We wrote out the poem and slept on it.

Still, there was nothing good for us in words,
or nothing couched in formal English,
while being good itself was good for nothing,
and then again there was always something
coming next, though no particular direction.
The baby lay in its cot and cooed
or it lay afloat in water inside mother.
When once that baby grows, we said,

and put away the car. We built the house then
by the side of the road
at the end of the road beside the river.
Friends came and were welcome
though many failed to make sense
except in pieces, and others
had only rested quietly by mistake.
All day they took their boats

upon the water. We felt alone.
perhaps, but full of promise.
We still possessed the poem in outline,

we had kept some image of the flower in mind.
Now, too, there were provisions, jars of preserves
against the future, photographs to remind
that nothing entered the picture
save cats and children; and the telephone rang

to tell of father's death or just
in other words to ask who's speaking.
We sat by the road and watched
the water tremble as it still stayed perfect.
We woke and slept and that is how
we kept in touch. The children woke in the night
and cried and we sang words to cure.
One crashed the car

and the others soon shot through.
We were young too: we thought
that every goodbye was the last goodbye
and that every last word was made to be careful.
We waved and we waved of course, and now
we find we don't stop waving: believing we see
our life at last, and thinking it over,
knowing how far the road goes home.

Zoetropes

A starting. Words which begin
with Z alarm the heart:
the eye cuts down at once

then drifts across the page
to other disappointments.

★

Zenana: the women's apartments
in Indian or Persian houses.
Zero is nought, nothing,

nil — the quiet starting point
of any scale of measurement.

★

The land itself is only
smoke at anchor, drifting above
Antarctica's white flower,

tied by a thin red line
(5000 miles) to Valparaiso.

London 29.4.81

Beach Life

Early morning, there's

a slice of light
(electric) beneath the door,
someone going along

the corridor. The baby's
asleep between sheets
of pale blue water

while outside a tractor
tows the first boat
down to the beach.

In the next-door
room and nearly
dressed, you're reciting

an early twentieth-
century poem — benign
neglectful cadences, still

pining to go home.

BILL MANHIRE

Our Father

On one trip he brought home
a piece of stone from the river,
shaped like a child's foot

and filled with the weight
of the missing body. Another time
he just walked in

with our lost brother
high on his shoulders
after a two-day absence;

and it seems like only yesterday
he was showing us
the long pole, the one out

there in the yard now,
taller than twice himself,
that still hoists

our mother's washing out of reach.

Synopsis (Handel's Imeneo)

for Peter Walls

*Since a Handel opera consists of a succession of short scenes, any detailed
synopsis tends to be confusing to read. As the action unfolds on stage,
however, it is perfectly easy to follow, provided that one identifies the
characters and bears in mind their basic aims and attitudes to each other.*

Disguised as women we at last drop anchor;
then we herd the ladies back to Athens
where all the senators are stunned and hurt . . .

But this is not Toronto, why have the pirates
entered our conversation? Are they trying
to restore romance or do they want

to leave us in confusion? Any one of us
might be the father of Stephanie's baby.
You know how it goes: you fall in love,

you fall to the floor (oh cruel misfortune),
and by the time you are lifted to your feet
you have become the understudy,

you are just another little ship
drifting towards the Saturday matinée
and in the end you retain your misguided

sense of duty but that will never
see you through. Turn up the stereo,
it speaks not for itself

but for a friend; it sings
through speakers while we can only speak
through song. Meanwhile

things go from bad to worse for Tania
and Ken finds that the horrors of jury duty
are not yet over. Then during the interval

Kate decides to tell the truth — or does she

know about her uncle's ultimatum? Why
is the chorus offstage playing cards?

Why do we rise so often
to applaud the absence of a plot? Spurned
and unrequited! poor Clomiri, rebuked

and beckoned by the music,
and tuned to the contrasting angels
(the one called Sorrow, the one

called Amorous Intention) who hover now
above the darkening orchestra. Perhaps
they are friends of the conductor.

Theirs is the language
of the wild and stormy heart. (We hear
and misinterpret, then depart.)

PĀ MAX TAKUIRA MARIU, s.m.

(Born 1952; Ngāti Tūwharetoa)

Ko Taku Titiro

Ko taku titiro te riu o te waka ki Maketū,
Me mihi atu Whakaari ngā Kete-e-Rua,
Te hono ki Pūtauaki.
    Whakahoki mai ai ki roto Te Arawa,
    Tarawera moe mai rā!
    Hiki nei te kanohi, Tauhara te
    Pikinga tuatahi;
    Pere te rākau Taupo papatu-manawa,
    Kia rere Waikato. Hai!
Ohorere te ngākau, Motutaiko ki Horomatangi;
Me uta Waitahanui te waha o te awa
Arā ko Pīhanga te wahine, Auē! Te aroha!
Whiti mai ana te mahana o te rā,
Te Ngaurutanga-o-te-hoe!
Te riu o te tiro Pare-te-taitonga,
Ruapehu, Whanganui e tere, Taranaki.
Nei te kiri whakaora o roto o Ketetahi,
Taku tūnga ake ko Tongariro te Puhi o Te Arawa,
Te karanga o te rā nei eeee!

I Gaze Out

I gaze out to the boundary of the canoe to Maketu,
I greet Whakaari, nga Kete-e-rua,
And I pay homage to Putauaki.
    I return to the midst of Te Arawa,
    Tarawera at peace!
    I lift up my eyes, Tauhara my first ascent,
    I hurl my dart, Taupo pulsates
    And so flows Waikato! Hai!
My heart races, Motutaiki at Horomatangi;
I rest my gaze on Waitahanui, the mouth of the river,

339

PĀ MAX TAKUIRA MARIU

See here, Pihanga the maiden, how deep is my love!
   The warmth of the sun bursts forth,
   My paddle quivers!
   The boundary of my gaze is Pare-te-taitonga,
   Ruapehu, Wanganui flowing, there Taranaki.
   Here I am being revived in the springs of Ketetahi;
   My standing place is Tongariro the plume of Te Arawa,
   The reason for our gathering this day.

Translation by Pā Max Takuira Mariu

HIRINI MELBOURNE

(Born 1949; Tūhoe)

Te Pūtōrino a Raukatauri

Te pūtōrino a Raukatauri,
iri, piri runga peka e.
Kei roto ko te puhi o te tangi,
porowhitawhita e.
He tangi hotuhotu mokemoke e,
mo te tau kua rere e.

The Flute of Raukatauri — the Bag Moth

The flute of Raukatauri
hanging on a tree:
inside is the goddess of music.
The lonely notes of the flute
crying out for her loved one
who's flown away.

Translation by Hirini Melbourne

Pūtake

Mai te kakano,
ka tipu te purapura;
i ruia mai i Rangiātea.
Mai ngā pūtake
ka pū mai te waipuna;
i ū mai i a Papatuanuku.

Mai ngā rau reka
ka pū mai te hau ora;
i ū mai i a Ranginui.

HIRINI MELBOURNE

Ka puāwai, ka pū ngā hae
ka pū ngā hua, ka kakano anō.
Ko tātou rā i tēnei rā.
Tīhei mauri ora! Tīhei mauri ora!

Foundations

From the seed
the seedling sprouts
sown from Rangiatea.
From the roots
absorbing clear waters
that spring from Papatuanuku:

from the sweet leaves
absorbing the living breath
that springs from Ranginui:

from flowers to pollen,
to fruit and seed again —
hence us today,
to breathe the living breath!

Translation by Hirini Melbourne

TRIXIE TE ARAMA MENZIES

(Born 1936; Tainui)

Ki aku Tipuna Maori

Where are my people of the tonuitanga
I have shared the love-hate politicking of the family —
Once there was a whanau but we are separated —
Ka raungaiti au.

Once there was a black-eyed woman who was my ancestress,
She lurked behind the innocent eyes of my babies,
In the sweaty beds of love she was the one I sought but did not
        know it.
I never heard her name, this forgotten woman
She was my blood my bone my pulse my smell my breath
When I first danced with death she was my chaperone
Later to be unmasked as procuress.

Sometimes I sense her in a patch of garden,
A place where crops grow by themselves unplanted
Or a certain stretch of coast touched by a warm late season.

Worms gnaw her bones as one day they will gnaw at mine
When I find where she lies, there would I lie contented.

Watercress

We sensed the place from fifty yards
As we passed the white upstanding trees,
Then walked along the railway, on the sleepers,
Or holding hands to balance on the lines
Charcoal rock intruded under our feet
Gorse interfered on the side
We knew the storm was coming, by the wind and the oddly
        yellow light

343

But we thrust through the gorse to the fence
Tearing up young puha shoots as we went
To go with the watercress we hoped to find.
You said, dreamily, this doesn't look like watercress country
But we spotted the barrow, a small swelling
As if the earth was trying to hide something under her coat
I was embarrassed at intruding on something private
I felt I should walk away
Burnt gorse and manuka, and a cabbage tree
With the first peal of thunder we were knee-deep in mud and
    watercress
We filled our kit, letting the rain soak us
Searching the mound for bogs, penetrating the earth's
    secret places
Feeling in each patch of mud for food.

Harakeke

Roots clustered, entwined in the body of Papatuanuku
In slow searching plant time, patiently growing
Seedheads leaning, reaching upward to Rangi
Gathering light and air, sunshine and strength
Into fibres for the scraping, the soaking, the rolling,
Delicate golds and half tones of different green
Humble colours, not dazzling like scarlet kaka feathers
Not striking like the bright plumes of kotuku or hawk
But homely, strong as a woman built for childbearing
Provider of warp and weft, the fabric of being.

Wharikitia te whare mo te manuhiri
Kia pai te whare mo te manuhiri

The house must be prepared to welcome the manuhiri
The whariki woven and spread, life is the guest —
On the whariki we were conceived and born, and there we slept
Feeling it firm beneath us, sheltering and warm.
The whariki supported our coupling and when life was spent
There we were laid to be mourned, our spirit farewelled
At the last we were wrapped in a whariki, returned to Earth.

Season succeeded on season, dark followed light
Unblinking eyes of our foremothers gazed to the future
To us their descendants, knowing their strength was sufficient
Despite betrayal for guns, death in the swamps
Bequeathing a cloak to cover us, a kete for treasures.
We are part of the pattern that must never be broken.
We must continue the weaving, even the bruised ones
Our work will fashion the nets to catch the stars.

Flight North

In my father's house are many lounges
Many balconies and many gardens
And also many points where three tracks meet.
Father not of sons but of three daughters
Our separate begetter, Laius, Lear,
Which is Cordelia, which the ugly sisters?
The birth of children is the death of parents —
I am the long awaited executioner
First in the line, the missing generation.
In many transit lounges I have waited
Flying the blue Pacific with my message,
A season-changing migrant, titi wainui
Seeds of the fall are my guest's gift to you.
Now as I eat your green and rosy apples —
Salute the sun! Soon he comes south with me.

MICHAEL MORRISSEY

(Born 1942)

Poem About Left-handed Alternatives

one of your cauldron castoffs
I dry like scum on the lawn

sweet glitter of sex
luring me on like fake rubies

Pluck one! Pluck one!
I am your priceless future

your eyes kidnap my body
holding it up to ransom

love brings one of us to the boil
the other yearns for gas

come brother Onan let us spill
our seed on womanless ground

Assassin! Assassin!
sperm have such dirty mouths

Movie Madonnas

Wounds of Christ
Are not more saintly than the delicate
Tracery of crimson from your lips

I salute you Heroines of B grade grief!
Your handkerchiefs are wet with intelligence
You know far more than we

When the blood and rosed affair of Romanticism
Ceases to 'drive light up your spines'
You will come to our 'emotional rescue'

Your wash of tears permit our guilt

2 Borges/Some Oranges/A Tambourine

Along the Avenue of the Americas
Señor Borges is smoking a cigar
That is if Señor Borges indulges —
I am not certain (the Señor has not
Recently written) whether that learned
Gaucho can be the one who blindly
Turning his Easter Island visage towards
The secret miracle of his twin
Shakes the tambourine from a skateboard . . .

As the first Borges reflects
That no shade exists save the roaring
Yellows of the taxi cabs Borges (numero
El Segundo) hurls his instrument high
Above the Chase Manhattan, the Waldorf
Astoria and the World Trade twins where
It descends with . . . genius. Doubles have
This knack; anything you *can't* do they
Can do better. You can live with that.

Have to. It's a fine day for walking.
Luis bring your pogo stick and let's
Hit the well-cornered streets. Cross
Over Brooklyn Bridge (so full of sweet
Suspension) where on a clear day you can see
Your self swinging, witness with indignation
Your double selling oranges and tossing
In the Bridge for good measure. There are
More messages below street level than you

Thought possible. Upper East Siders
Flushed little white fluffy pussy cats
Down the toilet last spring and how
Quickly they turned into sabre-toothed tigers.
Meanwhile your foolish twin is ransacking
The subway walls for lyrical graffiti.
What's he trying to prove? That two heads
Are better than one? Old dinosaur

It's best to straighten your tie — especially
When your better half is pulling mirror
Faces overly confident that he exists.
Don't smoke too much Señor Borges, cancer
In the labyrinth of your lungs remains
— cancer. If your double (who reads you
Like a book) jumps up and runs his fingers
Through his hair, it's a tribute.
Don't knock it, amigo. Write it down.

Taking in the View

The far reaches. The far reaches of Whatipu
seem to be stretching down to the ship

on which I am sailing. It is not a ship, it is
a species of emptiness. But who can be lonely

in this vacancy when the lack of artifice
is ready to confess a truth or two, when

you are walking the earth 'sublimely' sure
that it is walking you. You can be reaching

up to touch the orange sky and think:
it is kissing my eyes. Such a soft full kiss

like the lips you dreamt as sexually sweet
and no mere milk takers. At any second some

special effect leapfrogs the black surfaces
where you stroll like man Friday looking for a

second set of footprints and knowing the longed
for miracle is just as possible as Our Lady's

apparition gurgling in a stream near Te Kuiti.
Amnesty International reports 98 countries are

using torture but New Zealand isn't one of them.
Neither is Whatipu. Nature is the serious thing.

You start thinking silly things. Like why is the
sea beating up the rocks and why does it whiten

the sand every time it lashes out for more.
And why does it stir the genitals by lifting the mind

up to view the far Waiuku side like a nineteenth
century painting in which you are the only form

for miles that can sit alone and not be lonely.
Pretend to your big heart's content but don't

be fooled. You're *in* the frame, the one nobody's
buying so why not step back into focus way

beyond the far green wash where light is dreaming
up some new form of courage and where you

remember something you can't imagine
forgetting like being on acid and seeing

bright red bulls leap up from the sea. And why
shouldn't they? Especially near dawn when sandwraiths

begin to caress the mind. And I nearly said soul. Is that
why I'm climbing the lighthouse: to take in the view?

MICHAEL MORRISSEY

Beautiful Theories in the Capital

philosophy & ice creams & the choppy sea & old men
smiling in yellow raincoats   construction workers
from Babel's tower proud of their differing languages

one being self pity & a pigeon-necked walk   I've
seen it all before   because in a lifetime's walking
you glimpse the cripples   & their sun shielding

gestures so off-shore waders get wet under Oriental
Bay's very Occidental fountain   & nature before artifice
seems to win arguments in winter   well   this is April

& a high-heeled girl is reading her Lawrence beside
the untidy sea   what her white wrists mean is anybody's
guess   how about the Chinese woman pulling weeds

in a purple hat   or a child hopscotching his mantra
in chalk   it's got to add up   & those   dark stones
visible beneath the sea   so much existence eggtimed

by a nod   the French say I bore myself   there could
be difficulties here   but over there a man has found
something alive and well in his shoes   it could be

serious having a toe out of place   did you know
angels are drawing the unemployment benefit   that their
long silver wings caused a beautiful crash   yet no one

has death prepared right down to the last detail   the coffin
may be crammed with wonderful surprises low rent & such
a marvellous view   ah when it strikes we've had good chances

to catch the lion I mean scrub the lino   oceans may
look bald without fountains   I'm buying an ice-cream
renting out the sea   that should cure philosophy

Venice

Remember a man with brilliantined hair and hypnotic gestures
that changed reality? Well the flicker of your waves
resembled Mandrake's fingers solidifying a few

reflective shimmers   just as the waves make impermanent
the Istrian stone   and after the thousand year old speeches
you lay garrulously silent   like a martyr with a tongue

ripped out for praising the one true God   So I embraced
you in the moonlight   I mean the floodlight
canals extending like the arms of a great courtesan

who needed no amours   as they stroked themselves
to fretful ecstasy   and all I did was sit and watch
with feet   reluctantly shuffling the litany for

a perfect marriage   not to be sneezed at while catching
cold beneath Maria's salute   Oh Venice we ought to love
your corny barber poles   wittily refuting notions of short

back & sides   better than the slap slap of the Adriatic
and we do even though your solid tinsel is full of wicked torture
if nothing else gold weighs heavy in my cat-reeking room

an eight foot stud is no practice for Tintoretto
for heavenly cities you can't shake off even at night
all that splendour weeping in the shadows

isn't just love sick horses   history is stolen beauty
and I'm ravishing yours   dear shimmering Venice
because gently reclining   you're everything Disneyland

is not   meanwhile sweet sinking Venice I eat your chocolates
and listen to the lap lap of your smelly centuries
as you grandly gesture yourself out of gilded existence

ELIZABETH NANNESTAD

(Born 1956)

The Witch Speaks Gently

Night of my imagining —

Where fish are running in the sea
and soft-bodied stars move
in all heaven's inhospitable grace
and winds feed on beaten grass
as wildfire in the hills
before the hills go down. Oh, my Dear
take me dancing.

I love to dance
as cold queens
long to die
laughing,
I like to dance
and this
is life
in life to me.

You, my silent and lonely hero of the hour,
you are my flower. My snapdragon.

He hardly replies. I
will not ask again.

Night of wild and easing sorrow. Night of reason.
Where now does your disappointment lie?

Somewhere in the night
a lover with dead white skin
lies breathing, thinking
I do not want to breathe again.

Your hip's hollow where you lie
is warm, and holds the smell
of salt and vinegar
like your skin, like mine.

You don't open those eyes.
Why not? You might as well.
There is no end to the number of times
the little death will come again.

Queen of the River

Here the boat set me down, and I wait. The oarsman swung on
    the pole
and we came to the bank, lifted my belongings, and I got out.
Four days and five nights, the canoe does not return.
I waited at the river bank. Oh, the river. How I wept, and now
how dry I am.
            This is only a tributary, and a thousand miles to the sea,
a lifetime to the other side. The river bends, or is it that my eye
bends what I see with distance and time.
                            The military walk in the town.
The old giantess behind her stand in the market refuses to bargain
selling fallen fruit smelling of diarrhoea, golden and black.
She looks down. The tiny captured monkeys
tethered to her, they also look down.

In the evening I walk to the river, at the end of town
and I watch the sun set in equatorial calm.
I see the circles on the slow-swift stream
and I hear the monkeys scream. It is all one.
I walk back to my hammock and lie down.

Opposite in the street is the tailor's shop, a carbox with an
    open side
where the tailor works through the night. In the evening
his family comes and sits with him, a laugh breaks, and one
    sings out.

Outside my room the night has turned to flowers. The tailor's
    daughter
lines up her back with the side of the shop, looks down the street.
The military drift, looking in at bars.

                        I am the Queen of the River
and I go as I please. The river is as wide as this arm of mine,
I reach out and measure the river with my arm and touch on the
    far side.
I will leave now. Why should I not go down?
A mosquito steps on my arm and clings.
My arms are bitten by the dark bougainvillea
and ignored by the spines.
                        I am the Queen of the River,
and I know by now the one song they play, over and again,
down in my throat I know them, all the songs to this hour in time
and I will drive the oarsman mad.

The tailor's little daughter kicks a foot at midnight.
It is cool now, and I who have flown in my dreams and died
stop sweating, pull the sheet up on to a shoulder, and sleep.

The Altiplano

Who knows the altiplano? Who's been there?
No-one breathes the air of pure silver
and stays steady. Living on spit-beer and corn
no-one there lives long.

There are the thin dogs running and the thieves
by walls eroded by rains, and the sun
and the writings on the wall say:
Sing me a song of New Freedom.

Mother of mothers, whose eyes shine
what is she saying, on her knees in prayer
to her nailed saints in their niches?
Three hundred candles are weeping. Offer one.

Whoever flies over the altiplano and looks down
sees red backs scored, and the white road
drawn out around and over them, a signature
by an inventive hand.

Portrait across a Room

When I see you moving in a room with other people
your lips outlined
shining and going from one to another

I think the first of your line was a marketeer
and poor, who fought in crowds
for part of a carcass
and won the tail, or the eyes.

Mountain

Down comes a silence from the sides of the mountain
to feed out of my open hand.
Mountain with a lap like heaven
Mountain with a voice like an empty sky
and no other mountain to talk to:
How do we get down from here?

Last night, in the pillow
I heard avalanches,
heard the small cracks of doom
in an ear to the ground.

Perfectly clear across the swinging miles, the spume
stands in blue air, before the back-breaking sound.
If I with my flying heels still don't know how
one of these will hunt me down.

ELIZABETH NANNESTAD

Portrait of a Fisherman

The fisherman changes none of his ideas
through weathers and seasons.
He's the beetle man, carrying
the dinghy down the beach
on two bent legs.
Underneath,
his face is lined
away from the mouth and eyes,
the smiling frown means
salt weather stings.
The fisherman's
hands are hard,
his shoulders
shift like ferry piles
and his feet are far apart
for pulling in the long-lines,
bringing up over the stern
fish with pouring sides and weary mouths
that bang out daylight on the floor of the boat.
The fisherman rests
in stronger arms.
He ships the oars
across the harbour
to the mooring.
There are plenty more fish in the sea
and again and again, the loved sound
of the current on either side
slips behind.

JOHN NEWTON

(Born 1959)

National grid

1

I was five or six when the cable came through,
too young to remember the road being built
or, before that, going in and out by boat,
but I knew the bulldozers, ploughing through the waterfront,
had unearthed adzes
and a flax-pounder
which was now a doorstop.

Putting down the pylon feet
they dug and blasted, yards deep,
while I scoured the turned-over rock and soil
for artefacts —

which I never found
though I hung round to watch the towers go up
and stare at the huge bulldozers
hauling cable drums.

2

The line of towers ran
on and out of Robin Hood,
through Ocean Bay and Kakapo,
over the back of Port Underwood
to Fighting Bay
where the cable finally runs into the sea
and under the Strait
to the North Island.

I was shown an off-cut
from the underwater cable,
six inches thick,
ringed like a tree trunk.

3

For all that, it was five more years
before we had power ourselves, at the house.
The whole Waitaki was pouring through the cable
while burning off scrub
meant permission from the N.Z.E.D.

But in the quiet
after the men and machinery
I spent hours picking up odd bolts and rivets,
split pins, bits of copper wire,
scouting round under the shining towers.
Days when the wind blew spray off the sea
you could hear the insulators

buzzing in the salt and wet.
Thistles grew back in the bulldozer tracks
while under the wires
the static
stood your hair on end.

Night fishing

1

The red sun slips
below the rim of the valley, the breeze
stills, poplars prick the felt air.
A whisper of wheatstraw
brushing my ankles
follows me in the direction of the river.

Chaff sacks piled
along the stopbank to try to hold the flood
spill sand beneath the weight of my foot;
milk-fat, waxing on a tide of silt,
a wedge of corn between the road and the water.

Three ducks angle across the last light,

disappear in blue hills
behind Tuamarina. The Withers still
give back the bone and gold
colour of the wheatstraw.

A dead branch
hung across the current
houses a lone shag, skinny as leather,
throat bobbing, watching
me splash through the shallows,

then spreading black wings and the night comes,
flooding the valley. Current
closes around me, feeling my way into quickening water,
bare toes gripping in the polished gravel, stripping
fly-line, feeding the river.

2

The water this winter took
paddocks and left behind
stones; it turned the small streams on Northbank
into deserts, glittering bleach-white creekbeds
scoured of slime and feed, shelterless,
barren.

This year there are no fish up there:
instead I come looking for them
down here, in reach of the sea.

The sea's mouth opens and closes
on the mouth of the river, and the lower river falls
and rises. Here, on the back
of each full tide, the kahawai
come riding, and old bony jacks,
and then, as the March nights grow deeper, the sea-heavy

spawning hens, weaving their way back
upriver, headed for Cat Creek
headed for the Goulter
headed all the way to the head of the
valley, to the Rainbow

359

and further, to Tarndale,
where the first of the river
slips between mountains, and where
when the gentians and daisies and mosses have been buried
    under snow
and when they've brought down the cattle

in a river so small you can jump across it
the spawning fish build
their shallow nests in the gravel.

3

Tail lights
bloom on the bridge

as the tide drops, as the night
becomes thicker. Swinging

through the current my weighted line explores
the fluency of the river. The taut line

gives back the beat of the current, which is the beat
of an artery, the pulse of the valley,

and the line which runs back from the river runs
into my own blood. I balance its weight

on my finger and concentrate,
waiting for the suck and the boil

and the rod bent double by a pull
like the pull of water.

4

The valley is subject to the river:
the bucking rod
divines a whole walled world.
The Wairau is a long sum of rivers,
the river in flood this winter
a total of floods.

In the high country
snow fell with rain on it,
slush, a torrent of it, gushing out of Hell's Gate
and all down that side of the watershed,
the Branch, the Waihopai.
                    On Northbank —
the opposite catchment — more rain, feet of it,
feeder streams roaring,
a whole grid of floodwater, millions of
tons of it, pouring down the throat of the valley

to the sea. And sometimes
it came through glass doors and the insides
of houses were washed out and spat around
paddocks. Pictures and pieces of furniture
swam with the overturned tractors
and caravans   fuel drums   wattle stumps
mattresses   mailboxes   rocks. The live

stock took shelter on porches
and haystacks. The drowned sheep collected
in fences, netted like bait, while the great swollen river

pushed its thick clay-yellow
tongue out into the mouth of the ocean
and over the Strait
you could look down from aircraft and pick out,
still swimming, the red shapes of
cattle
on a bright yellow   ground

5

When the moon comes
it brings the tide back with it,

and stray late whitebait and silveries
climbing on the tide-swell, and sea-trout

which scatter the bait.
Fattened all summer on sea-life and heavy

with spawn, the trout
now stream back from the ocean,

and their scales, like a herring's, are soft
from their sea-spell, and slip

off in handfuls, and are coloured
like the moon. They glide by me

wading in the deepening current, and push
for their breeding grounds, steering by mountains.

The lapping tide
rides up the willow trunks, drowning

the bait-stand decks, bellying
around me in flood, and the rhythm

of season and sea-wash absorbs me.
The big river, salty and swollen with tidewater,

brimming with moonlight, climbs against
my body, and I lean with it, buoyant

in the bloodstream of the valley, in the lit water
sliding over gravel, over skin.

Inland

Get out this early, while the mist still
leaks through the floor of the valley, and the road's
your own. The roller doors of the cherry stalls
are closed, broadbeans sag in the dew,
the morning has yet to take on its colours
except where the AA roadsigns glow
like corn, their long fingers drawing you

inland, upriver. The sealed road
unwinds through the barn-studded reaches of river-flat
pasture, nosing out contours
itself like a river, fitting

its form to the shapes of this landscape you're

driving into: a mob clicks gate to gate
on the move now before the heat and the traffic,
a hawk lumbers
grudgingly up off the fur-strewn tar.

Brighter:
a first glimpse of sky
through the top leaves of poplars that
begin to lean over. The road
gets tighter,
the valley walls steepen,
the big river pushes
you hard against the hill,
climbing, in second,
boxed in by boulders till you're
through the top and as the valley re-opens you can let

go, planing away up the river
through willows and wattles, and a cattlestop
rattles as the seal gives out and you
plough into metal. A pair of fat
quail beat for the scrub.
The road in front of each farmhouse is oiled
for the dust that comes pouring through the floor of the cab.

And the lifting mist upwraps
acres of purple
borage carpeting the stony flats, and wheel tracks
rifling down the tops of the stopbanks,
horizons that carry you into the riverbed,
shouldering back the lupins
and the golden ragwort running thigh-high to the water:

Here comes the warmth now,
here come the honking

paradise ducks in their paired skidding flight,
pippits and yellowhammers dive round the windscreen
the sun arrives
the valley fills up with light

RANUI NGARIMU

(Born 1946; Kāi Tahu, Ngāti Mutunga)

Okarito

Okarito te wāhi tapu o te kōtuku,
Okarito te papa rā o te hauāuru
Taumarumaru i raro i te maunga Aoraki
Te awa māreparepa o ngā īnanga
Okarito — Ngāti Mamoe te hapu e
Okarito — te Tai o Poutini e
Kia ora rā, tēna rā koutou katoa.

Okarito

Okarito is the sacred place of the heron,
Okarito is the place of the westerlies.
Shady beneath Mount Aoraki
The river splashing with whitebait.
Okarito — the people are Ngati Mamoe —
Okarito — the Tide of Poutini.
Greetings, greetings to you all.

Translation by Ranui Ngarimu

Te Waipounamu

Ko Tuhua te maunga
Ko Arahura te awa
Ngāti Waewae e te iwi
Ko Tuhuru te tipuna

Ko te wāhi tapu o ngā taonga nei
Kaikanohi, Kahurangi e
Hineraukawakawa, Ahuka,
Kokopu, Inanga, Totoweka e

364

Ko Aorangi te maunga
Ko Arahura te awa
Ngāti Waewae e te iwi
o Poutini Ngāi Tahu
ki Te Waipounamu e

Te Waipounamu — The Land of Greenstone

Tuhua is the mountain,
Arahura is the river,
Ngati Waewae, the people,
The ancestor is Tuhuru.

It is the sacred place of these taonga:
Kaikanohi, Kahurangi,
Hineraukawakawa, Ahuka,
Kokopu, Inanga, Totoweka.

Aorangi is the mountain,
Arahura is the river,
Ngati Waewae the people
of Poutini-Ngai Tahu
to the land of greenstone.

Translation by Te Aomuhurangi Temamaka Jones

GREGORY O'BRIEN

(Born 1961)

from *Old Man South Road*

1

Past tired lawns and
rock-formations, the falling
powerpoles held

only by wires
driving south with a Number
Eight discussing the Holy Shroud

of Turin and the wiring of
broken bones — he says he
has heard of a poet

called Longfella
had his cheekbones cracked last
season — while I tear pages out

of old books and listen to rain
on limestone and quilts, rewriting
the family history

between sand castles
and drug overdoses in the seaward
suburbs. I offer him money

for petrol but he refuses, says
he would only spend it on beer
leaves me staring

back at all those
miles of lines and twisted poles
wondering how word ever gets through.

4

The world arrived
after closing time
in the small town's

misshapen lap, a second
son of a lawyer with busy
hands and an overshot jaw

a mere sketch of a son
born in April under a
half-Maori moon while

my father in a public
bar drank the shadows
of half-empty glasses

and discussed the immaculate
conception with a traveller
in suits. I was born into

the bandaged hands of
morning, hardly touching the
stables and railway lines

leading into the town
I have never left — the boy
who two years later fell

down a fight of stairs
but still refuses to die
or pay for a drink.

5

Rosalie tried the convent
   but went into real estate
instead — selling swimming
pools and verandahs in the
streets she drove in
   contact lenses and a

company car — subdividing
Polynesia to build Spanish
   villas with electric garage
doors and watchdogs.

Rosalie left the church
when the pope and his
   bishops became dupes of
the Kremlin — left the broken
voices of her sons
   one who spray-paints on walls
another who breaks bottles and
writes speeches, waits for
   cheques in the mail —
the lives she cannot accept
that will one day sell her short
   to the collarless barefoot angels
heralding in eternity
      with a garage sale
in a state house on Taniwha Street.

7

Hear aeroplanes rustling the undergrowth
waves ransacking the seaside baches
   now deserted, penguins huddled
beneath the sky-abandoned ferris-wheel
and further inland
      kumara pits at the old pa
sheep occasionally stumble into
next summer only their skeletons remaining
   and a painting of 'one's good angel'
which fell from the end bedroom wall
the day the tractor rolled into the river
'now and at the hour'
      the eels hardly moved.

While we were miles off
   our eyes on 'one's good angel'
scapulars swinging about our necks
pausing long enough to take aim

(Mount Egmont ducked behind a tree)
   and shoot the ear off a rabbit

then taking it home
   to show your aunt
who was still preparing
the strong man's dinner.

It will be better then

It will be better then —
those rose clouds gone boldly off
over blue plains . . .
        I will leave an unpaid bill
for you in a small wine-stained café
in a city you will one day reach.
        I will order a bottle of wine
for you and leave before the waiter returns.
He will still be waiting when you arrive
        perhaps years later
other customers will have been and gone
his arms will have grown stronger
        the wine matured.

We will sleep on our stony ledge
the rustling of a gown
        will mention your name
and I will have it

and I will not have it
        any other way. It will be
a harsh time of year — you will have broken
three umbrellas, torn a fingernail on a
doorhandle. You will discover a statue
I once sat under in a foreign city.
        You will brush against it
and it will feel like a familiar arm.
A day later the statue will be gone and
the city will have moved half way around the world.

It will be better then —
and I will mark time in its appointed place —
       a lop-sided dinghy by the breakwater
flipping shells over the wakes of eels.
You could set your exact course
according to the stars —
              there are a million of them
it doesn't matter where you go.

Comfort for the sick child

If there was a sequel to the life
you are living as, say, the island
    becomes a fist releasing birds

which fly through the broad grin
of the harbour bridge, cars like
    teeth travelling north, Summer

would be a bicycle with two wheels
and nothing between and that's about
    where you happened along

I wanted to name you Little Hat or
Speckled Red but, by way of Bo Weevil
    and Sleepy John, we arrived

at Jack then drank your health
another feather plucked from the
    Great Bird. The whole time

you never lost your step, feet never
touched the ground. Now you are realizing
    the movement of a tiny fish through

the many fissures of a rock, narrow
body tucked inside a towel. We understand
    each other. It takes time.

370

The hilltop, the green tablecloth

This is where, in leaving, she enters
plotting a course around the edge
        of a familiar room
a kettle full of tea so weak
all she can taste is milk

        and a trace
of a shag that flew under the reservoir
water three days ago. She holds it
in her mouth, tastes the angle of
        the bird's descent
the surfacing, fish in mouth (yes
there are fishes in the water she drinks).

This is where, sleeping, she travels
to a hill where a man is pulling a cart
        stacked high with all the objects
his lifetime can muster.
There is the weight of a woman
and the hungry body of child
        to hold him back
but inch by inch
he continues. When he reaches the hilltop
suddenly the cart is speeding down

the other side and the man is swept
into the cart with all the other objects
        and is carried off.
This is where, in being here
she becomes this place, her face
pressed against the window, the spacing
of articles along the mantelpiece regulating
        the flow of her blood
from here to there (with her body
somewhere between). Outside, the harbour

is a green tablecloth, yachts move
like moths, linger in corners
        from the balcony you can see
as far as the Mediterranean
        just by looking.

GREGORY O'BRIEN

Her voice is the tidying of a house

A woman is kneeling in a stream —
   the mist is a sponge drawing the town
up into itself. Dogs lie around the park
like battered violins
   their music scattered
among the long grass. Trees grow straight

only the leaves curl like dollar notes
on the arms of a skeleton. A man is standing
   beside the stream
cold as charity, beautifully shaven
a dove is whispering into his ear
   a drizzle of light descending . . .

Now it is night, the woman is climbing out
of a car. The string of pearls around her neck
   breaks and the man crawls down the road
trying to scoop the beads up
out of the darkness. Later, on a couch
the woman realises he has handed
   her a palmful of tiny wet stones

by now the pearls have rolled
miles away
   into the hands of a child
on the pavement who is waiting for her mother
(she will recognise a woman with nail polish
   on only one finger) — her voice
is the tidying of a house, her handclaps like rain
the patter of her feet like the first
   fall of snow as she recovers
pearls from the streets of the moon —
and two shadows move
   further up the road
leaving the child who wishes
   their hands held more
      than hands could ever hold.

BOB ORR

(Born 1949)

Cargo

Sitting on a stack
of mahogany
planks
I have seen
a ship
in thick blue sunlight
whose bows eclipse
the city.
A black barge
weighted with a universe of sand
the illusionary white mantle
of the ocean's
snow.
Japanese squid boats
sailing out
beneath a southern sun
into the dark slits of the waves.
A red container ship
that turns upon the tide
until embers
burn the green keel
where it rides.
I have watched this now
until all cargoes
have become like dust.
As seagulls swerve
above the tracks
of tough old railway steel
it seems that I
have cut
from the sky
a piece of glass
to make some kind of window.

BOB ORR

The ship
beside the wharf
begins to listen to the callings
of a city
its white sails
               its windows
                              its cargoes
& I am one.

Sugar Boat

The black sugar boat
across the bay
beneath the chains of Chelsea —
we saw it from the other side of town
moored up by the refinery. We were sitting
on the hard steps of a jetty in Herne Bay. The waves
kept coming in — a yellow crust
of cool volcanic moon
flew up above the
city.
       We were close
to breaking up. We could only see ourselves
through images. The jetty was adrift
in jagged light. A dark wind was blowing in on us.
I saw you as I never had before . . . as you
swam slowly towards your freedom
as the phosphorescent sea
became the tail of a mermaid
between your feet
as I kept turning
& as a black sugar boat
                        across the bay was burning.

Thelonious Monk Piano

Thelonious Monk
has just walked in the room
he's playing some sly tune
here it comes again you can tell it by its funny hat
Thelonious Monk plays a piano
as big as a matchbox,
he's walking it & talking it
just like he always does
that's Thelonious Monk for you
shit there's more than one piano
in the room
Thelonious Monk makes music
out of aircraft carriers big floating pianos
out of refrigerators real cool pianos
out of a bus on the last trip out of town a late night piano
out of a bus on the first trip of the day a real late night piano
out of a hotel bar call it a drunk piano
out of a long distance truck call it a piano with a load
Thelonious Monk can play any kind of piano
but listening to this record you can tell
there's only one Thelonious Monk though
Thelonious Monk does the talking
the piano does the playing
Thelonious Monk does the listening
his life begins to play
the memories are in his hat
the music is in his head
the ivory is in his heart
the elephant is in his fingers
walking out of Africa into the New York snow.

BOB ORR

Return

Rain
dripping
slowly from
deserted cattle

yards

space travellers
ancient voyagers

or simply people
who have gone
astray

sequential thought
is sad

water
from dark railings
ducks nothing

*

a kitchen
floor

the linoleum
the colour of dried blood

the yellow heat
of January

swimming through
the sharp exotic leaves

of a date palm

is memory

*

a cattle
truck

streams
shit and piss

toward
a feudal

freezing works

through
the karmic dawn

of the Waikato.

VINCENT O'SULLIVAN

(Born 1937)

from *Brother Jonathan, Brother Kafka*

6

It is because we are other people she had said,
because you and I are now really others.
I am then supposed, she implies, to replace the phone calmly,
to reflect on it before going back

to the kitchen, to the book I have not been reading
but simply let rest on my knee like an idle cat,
think 'Once I knew a woman not unlike her' —
and philosophy eases the stone through the gullet

because the mind is turning like a vane
in the fresh gust of honest vision —
new worlds laid out, chrism on daily things,
now that east swaps west, now truth roosts!

Yet aches the perverse skeleton living in me,
the man I am not, who took five years to get here,
to stand at the window and watch the dried grass
cross and blur its fragments with the eyes, presumably,
        of the dead.

13

To be in a place for spring and not have lived its winter
is to get things on the cheap — it is asking from sky
as much as taking from earth, what has not been earned,
it is food without its growing, pay without labour,

love and not its unpredictable effort
at kindness, tact — in fact, it is how we live.
I sit in a room where each day the heaters
burn for an hour less; I see trees

which I saw neither in leaf nor when their leaves
were called for, prepare for spring,
                                I am like a man
arriving too late for Friday's riddled flesh
or Saturday's dreadful inertia, and then on Sunday hearing

a corpse walks on the hillside, shining and placid,
asks 'What's so special?'
                        A man in spring
without winter or the fear which is properly winter's
is Thomas's gullible brother,

                                so much sillier than doubt.

27

A figure who stands on the beach and beckons,
invites to the green room behind the fangs of surf,
walks again in my dreams — a little too far off
to catch is features.

                        He is patient, sure.
He looks back, pauses, moves further on.
He could be a parent walking with a child,
waiting while shells are pocketed, while driftwood
the shape of a bird or of a figure is brushed and carried
to prove how the child had come to the sea's edge.

He walks on a bit, once more he is waiting.
His shirt is open at the throat, the sun
razors his stubble,
                        his step is pretty much my own —
then that slow encouraging sweep of his signalling arm.
Through his hands the sea glitters, the hands which are glass.

40

Last things:
                the turning leaves slip in the wind
as turning fish; the wind stills and the long branch
outside the window rubs at the late sky,
behind it the library tower, the power poles,

the dead paraphernalia of an ordered world.
The leaves if you like are now spread hands
or clipped identical banners or metaphor
fading against the stalled comparative sky.

The slight ephemeral leaf is the size of night.
The single word swamped in the gob of silence.
There is sky at the window, dark where even dark was.

    The veering fish slip on, there is breeze again
outside . . .
             an undersea of leaves is schooling,
a branch berths at the wall.
                One remembers light
as a quaint hook let down
through day's wrack,
                home.

Look Sheila Seeing You've Asked Me

Life is *not* a horse with a winner's garland
on its sweaty neck, across its chugging veins;
not a rosette hung to a pair of agreeable norks
the world pants at like a scrum:
nor *quite* a flushy sunset and its pouring ribbons
from God's theoretic bosom either, lady —
Yet *I don't know what it is* says Butcher
            hardly know what it is
if it isn't this as well —
          which is light walking
the dreamy edge of steel
which is pulse where his wrist lies on complacent death
which is water pure as silence before speech is thought of
from the tap in the back room
             splashed on face, on boots,
so he stands with chin tingling,
            with feet like jewels.

Elegy

Today, because I am not dead,
I notice the red handbasin,
the green curtains,
the knot in the veins behind the leg
of the woman who pours our tea.
I see the world because my eyes are open, thus,
as nothing could stir me, being dead, thus.

Today, as you've guessed, a funeral.
The corpse was my first cousin.
I leaned forward in the cold, kissed my other cousins,
the corpse's daughters.
I said to one, who had lovers,
'There is no answer, no consolation.'
I said to the other, the virginal,
'Perhaps, somewhere, an answer.
We must let time drench us, its river.'

A day of a red bathroom,
of two women I have lied to,
of green curtains in the morning,
of bad weather, hills whose cows
mumble in a paddock next door
while the last prayer promises
the last dream:
the new, the eternal, the shining Jerusalem,
eternity brilliant as cow-spit
in the dripping wind.
The usual slipping of the coffin
into usual earth.

The angels whose wings are paper
we can see the ink through.

VINCENT O'SULLIVAN

So We Say at Sunset

'When I put down the visionary's book
after an afternoon spent reading of rather
a plethora of angels' wings and the wisdom of lions,

I am glad of the kitchen tap, dripping
since lunchtime behind its door; of the telephone
like an ordinary plastic idol which may bring

disaster next time it rings, or great joy,
or an apologetic grocer out of anchovies —
whatever, I shall not know till I answer.

I am glad of the jade-leaved plant
that makes children think of groping green hands,
of nectarines in a wooden bowl,

of the sunset lighting little dashes of reflection
on a framed photograph of a wedding or a team;
of walking, simply, from one room to the next.

I'm grateful of course there are lions with strength and knowledge
and angels, and conflagrations of great splendour,
but my mind already is somewhere else:

I rejoin the armies and armies and further armies
who stretch ever beyond the wings of illumination,
who fight, I suppose, if compelled to,

who find filling buckets, paying for food,
singing the odd song, seem to occupy a lifetime.
And for the old miracle of I, *as distinct from you.*'

Don't Knock the Rawleigh's Man

Don't knock the Rawleigh's Man
when he opens his case and offers you
mixed spices, curry powder, chilblain
ointment, Ready Relief, brilliantine,
don't say *Not now*, don't think
Piss off, but remember:
think of a hill called Tibi Dabo
behind Barcelona and the legend
that up there Satan
showed J.C. just what he was missing.
What he offered was not simply
the vulgar things — the girls
with buttocks like mounded cream
or enough money in brewery shares
to take a Rotarian's mind off mowing lawns
for octogenarian widows,
or the sort of drink we all know
Vice-Chancellors drink when they drink
with other Vice-Chancellors —
not that but more deftly
the luciferic fingers fondled
buttons nostalgic with little anchors
as in the Mansfield story
and bits of coloured glass from old houses
and variously, these: good punctuation,
unattainable notes, throaty grunts
at bedtime, the nap of the neck
of lovely ladies caught in lamplight
like the perfect compliance of the pitch
in the last over when the last ball
takes the intransigent wicket —
yes, he did. Satan offered those things,
those were the things turned down,
that's how serious it was.
And what was round the corner as we know
was a tree already chopped
waiting to be a cross and a woman
at home rinsing a cloth white as she could
and Joseph of Arimethea still thinking the rock

he had hollowed at phenomenal expense
was going to be his, forever,
not Some Body Else's, for a spell . . .
So when the bag snaps on *your* doorstep,
flies open like leather wings
and you see instead of feathers
the tucked-in jars, the notched tubes,
the salves the spices
the lovely stuff of the flesh,
ask him in, go on, in for a moment.
There's no telling what else he might show you —
what mountain he has in mind
you may cast yourself from,
what price that your hair shimmer
like a diving hawk.

Liberal

Consider this:
   A man who feels for the people.
   A friend to the ill-favoured.
   Never a word against the bar-
barians assuming Roman dress.

Reconcile this:
   A believer in man's potential.
   A voice raised against the games
   where human flesh is sport.
   A man whose eyes fill at music.

You might at least concede:
   No man went hungry from my door.
   No woman was molested.
   No child was imposed on.
Humanitas inevitable as breath.

I who might have, have
   never raped, pillaged, extorted;

abused office or position;
    concealed; interfered with art;
stood between any man and sunset.

And yet as you say,
    I have killed a god. I have made
    of impartiality a farce.
    I have dabbled in chaos, I,
Pilate. Who vote as you do.

Who Doesn't Know?

We began at the feet of the urbane Greeks.
We who learned how philosophy speaks
        Through the strong hand
        As much as the trained mind.

Augustan government is the divine plan
For preventing man as mere man
        Tearing *societas* apart.
        It muzzles nature's shout.

We set a border, *ergo*, we understand.
We define by our edges. The grand
        Structures of art, of writing,
        Are the pressures of rule delighting

The unclaimed spaces, the open skies
That swarm with their wild energies
        Until the pen, the chisel,
        Impose thought as final.

Government and art, one may say, align.
Each is the advancement of that line
        Where law barbarity subdues.
        Romans *über* Jews.

Yet to be misunderstood is part of the job.
A nation given to religious mob-
   Rule, a god whose chat
   From a cloud is what

Lex is based on! Our Rome
They cannot conceive is where man came
   To assume his perfected role.
   Humanity *is* control.

Rome is arches instead of huts.
It is stone highways replacing bush.
   It is the end of whimpering lyric.
   It is the communal epic.

And what I, Pilate, half guessed
Before their shabby myth was crossed,
   The terror I inferred —
   Suppose God was Word?

God glowing in the cell of each mind?
Hierarchy itself no more than sand?
   The fact of blood and flesh
   Outwitting death?

Thus Rome itself dismissed. Time
Rolled like a schoolboy's string. Fame
   a mere candle's flap.
   Imperium — so much crap!

The axle has been unbolted. The stars
Fling their manes. The certitude of Mars
   An old man's broken cake.
   The line for white, for black

Blurs in the furnace of a dead mouth.
The mind shimmers at such drought.
   Man goes tarted as god.
   Where is *civitas* to be had?

Keep Moving, Please

In some quiet museum look quietly sometime at the parchment
pages, at the intricate cages of language, the elaborate colourful
divagations where capitals flare out, the monkish sensual
carnivals of calligraphy and penwork, gold-leaf the centuries
glance off much as your own eye floats above rubric, whorl,
over prophet and disciple with their peg-like figures,
        the whole cast
of creation in that field-day of hagiograph, ecclesiastical romp.
Sooner or later you spot me, pantomime Roman judge.

The illiterate for whom Jupiter is the name of a racehorse, Mercury
a grey line to serve notice of his fevers — there is always Pilate
he knows of. Pilate in his purple rig-out, his diminutive towel
dabbing aesthetic wrists, his patrician cool untampered,
such exquisite disdain. Democracy's pulse quite flutters
with prescience of his fall! The First Station of the Cross, then,
J Condemned to Death. Can't you hear the brass at the ready?
The big drums? The horns? *Mr Pilate, you're on!*

Before that AD/BC line was much talked of, before *paganus*
the country yobbo became a name for us all, that's me running
        the tracks,
the studio stuntman where Sunday's train hoots out in glory,
the tomb suddenly tunnel as grace whooshes through, lovely
refurbished Jix there riding the smoke-stack, steamed up
for the Ages, Pilate's fancy toga caught in the sleepers!
The school fat boy's always Herod. The class runt plays me.
I get a few comic lines. I talk posh. My rings flash.

Specular self, diminished image, I shave history
each morning. There is no core to freedom. No blank script.
Horace'll tell you of changing skies, Cavafy about your
City which beats in you as a heart (you, its map and clock).
The surf's insistent paws scratch at every coast. The dogs
at your side change names, the mountains gather different
snows, the same sun conducts its business with any bones to hand.
An antipodean note from Pilate: home is where I'm not.

VINCENT O'SULLIVAN

Them

Clarrie Smythe let's call him there was one of him
in Kotare Avenue I used to see him on my *Star*-
round sitting on a white veranda one hand slower than
the other, a daughter who called him 'Father' as though
old Clarrie gave a gippo's stuff for a bit of side; there was one
behind the shops he was Grace Wallace's grand-dad
that was enough for glory surely without the medals
he was supposed to have;
      Arch Cook's uncle who sang on the trams
who took his teeth out so he could whistle a decent tune
was another of them;
      there was one in Browning Street
down from the Weet-Bix factory he'd played in the Forces'
team after the fighting; he liked more
than anything else to sit in the corner of a room
and hear someone do a turn on a tin-whistle or a mouth-
organ so long as the women bloody stayed in the kitchen
and no one asked him what he thought as he said
about bloody *anything*. Some good mates had died
for peace so let's have some shall we? (His fingers
mind you the ladies reckoned were ready
like a rake if you didn't watch where you sat.)

There were Clarrie Smythes but not many of them.
They were the old blokes who made sure the memorials
didn't hog the scene entirely. When they wore red poppies
they were letting on there's places bigger than Westmere,
places a danged-sight meaner.
     There's quiet streets though and white
verandahs you think of when the poppies are budding in mid-
air and all you want is to get back there in one piece.
They let us in on that one too.
     If you watched them properly you knew
why they liked the reef's spread ink and the mangroves
changing colour a dozen times in a morning and to hold
a fish beating your hands down at Cox's Creek
was as good as an All Clear;
     Clarrie saying *By Christ boy*
it's a corker day knew what he was saying.

Morning Talk

The forsythia with its pale threads instructs
a dull house in its lesson against dullness.
The cactus is a lesson of a different kind.
The grossness of magnolia flags in, flags
the eye across wet spaces, insisting
in its way no more than *leathery, green,*
the shaken rags of season.
                    You walk
by a band rotunda on an early morning
the glitter of the railtracks quiver off
their future, a boy's bicycle spokes the flicking
lawn. There is a pond where a brownish splinter
declares the fish.
            A bird invisible in its
quickness cracks glass against the ear.
The flow of the river is alive as skin.
                    At the centre
a spoon across a plate in an ordinary room.
You walk as far as the window,
                the rotunda's top rested
on a froth of new October changes
the picture, quite.
            Electing from here
or there says, 'A different life, entirely.'
The boy's bright bicycle already melted
the fish surfaced redly in our moments
of absence the brazen enough magnolia
quietened down, as taste goes.
                    Sideways
is straight ahead to new composures.
Reflections spill diversely.
                Reality's
rabid marrow fattens with a wobble.
See, something not quite picked up
sets the neighbour's bitch circling
its glorious tang of wheels.
The bee at the looped forsythia, the hot laburnum,
pitches through brilliant fact.

ALISTAIR PATERSON

(Born 1929)

from *Odysseus Rex*

The black ships
with their bright shields are gone
       the warriors & their sword bearers
have fallen into the sea —
into the sunless hollows of the earth.
          The wind has taken them
Circe has captured them
the waves have smothered them
      & Odysseus is left with their silence:
holding to the wreckage of the world
he recognizes it —
            exhausted, he struggles
towards Calypso's island
         towards a rock-bound coast . . .

★

The night opens its crevices
those dark fissures
         in which are concealed
your hands, eyes, voice
           the moment
when nothing suffices —
not the distraction of books
          nor conversation
neither ache, hurt, nor howl
       the casual glance of strangers

I take out the cards
& shuffle the pack, turn up
         the King of diamonds
the ace of spades
          the humourless Jack —
construct theatricals

construe fictions putting in
                  an ambitious courtier's
tortuous schemings
                   the Cardinal's plot . . .

Under the cliff
where the ocean lurches
                   there are shadows dressed
as if in mourning —
Agamemnon, Hector, Achilles
                  are — all of them — dead
& countless others lie
unburied & unwept
                  amongst the ruins of Troy:
Teiresias got it right
                     & you alone still live . . .

As for myself —
an impenetrable wall
                  surrounds me, & somewhere
far off where I can't find it
there's a sky that's indigo blue
                  that slowly recedes
grows dark, turns black
becomes a white-hot ball
                  a clenched fist
an insidious pall
                that moves in endless spirals
. . . . .

★

Odysseus drifts
                towards the shoreline
is lifted by the seawaves
slides into troughs
               half crazed & almost blind
from the salt
             he fights against the tide rip
is driven Eastward
under loud & echoing cliffs
               past rocks & islands

ALISTAIR PATERSON

past rain-swept headlands
                    & away from
          the beckoning coast . . .

    ★

But it's the advertisers
who are telling you
               the things you need to know —
that Mattel has produced
a technological first
               in the home video industry
& embodied in the intellivoice module
a compact unit
                   that connects
to the intellivoice master component
& provides a new generation —
                the final perfection
of intelligent home video games
that speak to the operator
          & help him to direct his play
through a variety of
              realistic character voices . . .

    ★

And when you're not playing —
when you need something else
              to fill in your time
you can recite a canticle
             for the Great Whales
& the Hunters of Whales
for all the Denizens of the Deep
               & 'those
who go down to the sea
            in ships . . .'

How lifeless & forsaken
          is Smeerenburg
that was for so long
frequented by workers:

                a plain (white) with snow
melting at the water's edge
& strewn with red tiles
                        (with rubbish)
the bones of whales
rotting ropes
                        & graves
            so many graves . . .

Who would have known
                'death had undone so many'
or guessed
the discovery of islands
                of white bear, silver fox
harbours crammed with walrus
bursting with seals —
                winged by an unimaginable
plenitude of birds
should come to it:
                        such slaughter —
                        & so much of it . . .

And where is Leviathan
                lifting from the deep
the harpooners
(Basque, Dutch, Scottish)
                        waiting for the Killer
the Baleen, the Sperm
where are the whaling ships
                        the chaser
shore stations, chandlers
longshore-men —
                        the first
                        & last of them . . .

On that improbable shore
                        that terrible beach
the sea renews its violence
(heaves through the mist)
                the sun rises, sweeps to its fall
the albatross

ALISTAIR PATERSON

rides in silence
                    that unfathomed air
of wave-girt
rocks, of reefs & islands
                              the upflung
              edge of the storm . . .
  .   .   .   .

★

And while this is happening
                    somewhere on the broad Aegean
Odysseus who has slept with women
who has laboured, fought
                              & swung an oar
amidst his fellows
can neither sleep nor stay awake
                              but drifts towards Ogygia
savouring the impeccable cold
the raw & unforgiving light
                              of the stars.
It's the story of his life —
of the future & the past:
                    a clash of arms, the conch
sounding in his ears
the ripe edge of living
                              of life
pressed hard against his throat
                              the sea's sounds
& the sounds of the earth —
that insatiable drinker of blood
                              & eater of children.

Homer has set it in verse —
where Odysseus has been
                    everything he's done
all that he's known
                    & what he has seen:
that spring is ephemeral
                    summer an illusion
with the cities of the North

holding out against
           those of the South —
their defenders weary
embittered, tired of life.
        The sea has captured him:
its cold fingers
          thrust at his eyeballs
& he collapses in on himself
falls under the force
      of his own gravity knowing
everything he values is lost
        & all he believes in.
Alone in the sea & the dark
he calls on Athena
        rages against Poseidon.
  .   .   .   .

*

Meanwhile, somewhere else & far off
    the tide falls from the mangroves
children wade through the shallows
their thin legs straddling the earth
        travellers like all of us
    they are fish beneath the water
      clouds above the water
trees whose movement is breathing, growth
    a stretching of leaves, branches, roots.

It is discovery, the dumb
    & particular voices of rocks, stones
the flurry of blood, the flow of the lymph.
They have their directions, they pause
    they run, walk between the dark roots
    the tall grasses & shallow salt pans —
      & with such quizzical eyes
    such curiosity it could be the first
      or the last of their days.

But it's neither of these —
    merely a continuance & a renewal

as natural, spectacular
as the wind's rising, the sun's fall
    the diurnal drift & sweep of clouds.
    They are extensions of ourselves
        travellers with the delicate
arms & hands of girls. They go separately
follow the dolphin's path, enlarge the world.

.   .   .   .

★

Under
the clean, white sails of childhood
          a boat
moves over still water
& with such certainty, such grace
    one can see the physics behind it:
triangles, hemispheres —
          complementary forces.

It moves
beneath that steep hill
        where, in company with
his fellow townsmen (the last of them)
my grandfather lies under stone —
          lies fugitive
his bones amongst
       long forgotten bones . . .

And soon
there will come a time
      when no one remembers him
who, living, passed his life
a stranger
      moving in front of strangers . . .
He lies with his fellow townsmen
        in the shadows

of hills
& mountains, lies where
      morning breaks from silence

a tolling of bells
the far crying of gulls —

               where boats
move over still water, their sails
             bent to the sun . . .

JOANNA PAUL

(Born 1945)

the Course

trying to feel the bottom of this poem
feel its circumference
ground on something hard.

the salt marsh
seemed to go on for ever.
2½ hours
tracking 1½ miles of
tidal mud & marsh
from the round roosting point
Otefelo Head, observing
distant heads arms feet, the
bus driver a tea wagon.

PLANTAGO CARORUPUS
SALICORN AUSTRALIS
TRIGLOCHLIN STRIATUM
SELLIERA REPENS
SAMULUS REPENS
SHOENUS NITENS

traversing the grey marsh, it was
fluent with colour —
red russet yellow pink indigo
the floating horizon iridescent
    water; those low lying naked
succulents changing colour
from zone to

zone; SALICORN AUSTRALIS neutral, but now its long smooth thallus is pink to pinkish grey, & among the little dark round leaves of SAMULUS REPENS, SELLIERA RADICANS thongs flash fleshy green; in ponds ancient snails are grey then pink now russet brown; the men have stopped talking & stoop very quickly intently picking up snails peculiar to ARAMOANA 3 mm long soft narrow brownish hidden among roots of LOCHNOGROSTIS LYALLI & LEPTOCARPUS SIMILIS

salinity fluctuates from zone to zone, in wet & dry.
LOCHNOGROSTIS tolerates fluctuation is averse to sea
water

while WHEAT (our standard) cannot survive the presence
of salt
MIMULUS REPENS, SELLIERA RADICANS, SALICORN AUST
RALIS *show in ascending order their saline*
tolerance.

WHEAT may germinate in sea water
while SELLIERA RADICANS depends on fresh
water at germination for low salt levels in
which to rear young plants

SALT MARSH PLANTS are confined to salt marshes
but planted elsewhere, say in a well composted
garden thrive & grow taller. They don't like
the salt marsh but they can stand it.

as I was walking tired thru cold rain to warmth
across the salt marsh beside but not exactly with
2 talking old professors — a young chap in a
round yellow hat was sitting on his rucksack
watching me

we stopped abreast
13 wooden stakes
hemming in
the sea
&
between the invisible coastline & the invisible horizon,
a symmetrical & pointed island
floating
between the 6th & 7th stake
Sunion. 'Hellas'
I said. We were standing just above the outlet
of Dunedin City Sewerage.

I only know Greece (the islands) from poems
he said.

the bus rounded
a great round water tower, concrete
at Rotary Park

JOANNA PAUL

high over the peninsula
& down, past norman ' ' lime kilns
over lava flow on limestone

to Allans Beach.

We all talked, walking also or wading
thru sand like salt
to a rocky outcrop, with pools

where the upper margin of the rocky shore
extended vertically, above our heads
marked out by periwinkles

In a rubbery pouch of brilliant transparency
someone found a glassy shrimp, only its eyes
defined

what is the purpose of transparency
no purpose unless camouflage
most of the plankton are clear
but those at the surface of the ocean
prussian blue

unknowing

I reached a blue rock pool
round & deep
clear & still
empty & alive.

Music at Marama

   i)   the pianist lifts her tall neck
       her towering neck, playing Schubert
       & summer throws red carpet red
       into the face of the blonde girl
       fingering the music.

ii)   these girls have not conferred about
      their dress the pianist in blonde
      flouncy blouse green satin skirt
      & new white pumps is evening
      dressed for Brahms,
      Janet in purples clashing sings
      new music
      only the girl beside the pianist
      is dressed naturally, & looks out
      of place.

iii) the soprano stands against the
      piano like a T-square face fierce,
      hands knotted, striped skirt
      become piano, necktie the india
      red of mezzanine or window
      russet, her pleated collar caught
      into the worry of her face;
      voice very loud — only her
      breasts are left not knowing
      what to do & rise & fall
      in their own rhythm, pinkly
      shadowed, gently lit.

iv)   this girl's face is brown shadowed
      impassive as a jug; it is under
      her hands over her shoulder
      that the song takes place

v)   when someone in the audience
      puts up a hand to screen the
      winter sun, that big plump
      white illuminated hand melts
      into the white flesh of forehead
      to be framed by shiny tangled
      brown hair, & plushy blue
      creased cloth on well filled frame

      that moment is pure English
      Renaissance while on the stage
      flutes bubble fin de siècle Paris.

vi)   the piano goes continuo
the violin up & down in the
Baroque manner; why is face
important bow slithering from
note to note she hangs her
hair like a brown curtain;
beauty she should know is
insignificant beside the
human requisite of eye
nose mouth.

vii)   there is tarpaulin over the balcony
the piano is draped
Chris at the switchboard
'this music should be rich, exciting,
also rich' proffers only hair
today I shut my eyes & ears
& hear
Lilburns childhood clocks.

Wind / Ash / Sun / Sand / Sea

Wind

(sitting down to write a poem

with a glass of

Ash

return to Coromandel

'Go'

Miss 3 throws

six

dont count that

Sun

In the evening

we like to sit

(he in the sitting room with the

T.V.

((She has a record in her bedroom

in the kitchen is the radio

Sand

and read:
(((The *Character* of the pains varied very
much: most frequently they were of a hammering,
throbbing or pushing nature . . . pressing & dull . . .
boring with sense of bursting . . . pricking . . . rend
stretching . . . piercing . . . & radiating . . .

                        PETERS, 1853

Sea

looking down on plates that flowed

colour

we said: we sd

he sd — he said:

do you / believe in everlasting?

life
—
TITLE;

MERIMERI PENFOLD

(Born 1920; Ngāti Kuri ki Te Aupōuri)

He Haka

Ko te ao e ngunguru nei!
Au! Au! Auē hā!
Ko te ao e ngunguru nei!
Au! Au! Auē hā!
I a ha ha!
Kia whakapākehā au i ahau?
E kore! E kore! E kore!
Kia whakapākehā au i ahau!
E kore! E kore! E kore!
I ā ha ha!

Upokokōhua!
Taurekareka!
Upokokōhua!
Taurekareka!
I ā ha ha!
He tangata! He taniwha!
He taniwha! He tangata!

Ko taku kiri?
E pango e!
Ko taku pango?
Pōkerekere!
I a ha ha!
Tū whakapakaka ki te rā!
Tū whakapakoko ki te ao!
He taniwha! He tangata!
Au! Au! Auē hā!

Posture of Defiance

The world groans in anguish
Indeed! Alas!

404

It is in anguish!
Alas! Indeed!
It is! Alas!
Me an honorary white?
Never! No never!
Never an honorary white!
That will never be.
So be it.

Your head be cooked!
Slave you are!
Head desecrated!
Slave that you are!
Man it is! Or is it monster!
Demon or man!

My skin?
It is black!
How black?
Pitch black!
That I am.
I stand to bake brittle in the sun.
I stand and grimace at the world.
Demon it is! Or is it man?
Aue! Aue! Aue!

Translation by Merimeri Penfold

Tāmaki-Makau-Rau

Poua ki te hauāuru, hora ana ko Manukau
Poua ki te rāwhiti, takoto ana Waitematā.
Maiangi ana i waenga, ko Tāmaki-makau-rau,
Tara pounamu o nehe rā, tau tuku iho ngā tūpuna —
Rangi e tū iho nei, Papanuku rā e tau nei!

Tāmaki e! Panuku e! Makau-rau e! Paneke e!
Tau whakairo a te wā, ngā tai e tangi nei —
'Tematā, te hīnga o te rā, Manukau, te tōnga o te rā!

Takoto rā te takoto roa — tōia mai nei e te wā
Mai i te heunga o te pō i te ao, ka ao, te ao hōu!

Tau wahangū o 'matā e, huri ake rā, ka tūohu.

Nei ngā whare kōrero: Maungawhau, Maungarei,
Maungakiekie, Rangitoto, he piringa nō te tini,
He tohenga nō te mano — tū atu ana he pakanga,
Hinga mai ana he parekura! Aa! Mau ana te wehiwehi!

Tauiwi, maranga, e tau e — me he kāhui kūaka, auē,
Ki runga te tauranga nei! Ko Tāmaki-makau-rau!
Ka ū ki Waitematā, ka piki ki Maungawhau —
Ki Manukau, kua tau! Ki Maungarei, kua eke!
Hinga ana te wao a Tāne, tū mai ana ngā marae a Hōu!

Tamaki-Makau-Rau

Placed in the west, Manukau spreads out!
Placed in the east, Waitemata stretches out.
Between there rises Tamaki-makau-rau,
greenstone pendant of the ages, the beloved passed down
Rangi standing above, Papanuku lying here!

Tamaki shifts, Makau-rau changes!
The beloved of time, and the sounding tides,
'Temata at the rising sun, Manukau at the setting sun,
lying here, lying long, hauled up by time
when night was parted from day, day, the new day!

Silent beloved by the ages, turn and see!
Here are the homes of speech: Maungawhau, Maungarei,
Maungakiekie, Rangitoto, grasped by the many,
contested by multitudes — battles fought,
and battles lost! O what terror!

Strangers, come, settle like godwits
on the landing-place! It is Tamaki-makau-rau!
They land at Waitemata, climb Maungawhau,
they rest at Manukau, mount Maungarei!
The forest of Tane falls, the marae of the new men lie here!

Translation by Margaret Orbell

Tērā Ko Rereahiahi

Tērā ko Rereahiahi, ko (te) Māhu Tonga,
Kōrikoriko mai rā te kiko o te rangi
Kori ana, ka pū ake te tau o te ate
Rere ana ki ngā hihi whetū i runga
kia tiaho iho hei kura, te tara pounamu e tū!
 Nā te kune, te pupuke
 Nā te pupuke, te hihiri
 Nā te hihiri, te mahara
 Nā te mahara, te hinengaro
 Nā te hinengaro, te manako e.
Tērā te waka nā Te Hau, nā Hohepa i whakatere
Papaki ana te ngaru ki te rae o te tumu e karanga nei
Uhi iho ki ngā pokohiwi o Koro matua
Ripo ana (i) nga rua taniwha wānanga e noho pipiri
Te tauranga hoki (mō) ngā uri heke mai te taha raro o te motu e
 Ka hua te wānanga
 Ka noho i a rikoriko
 Ka puta ki waho ko te pō
 Ko te pō nui te pō roa
 Ko te pō turituri te pō pēpeke
 Te pō uriuri, te pō tangotango
 Te pō wāwā te pō tē atea
 Te pō tē waia
 Te pō i oti atu ki te mate e!
Kīhai te karawhiu o te kupu i tau i mau
Kīhai hoki te kei o te waka i nohoia i tērā
Ka tārawa takiwā ka tau (i) te kupu a Ngāti Whātua
Kapohia atu ana e Kui, e Ani ka rere he wero kē
Tangi ake ana te kī a Whae, 'E tama, whakakikongia rā
 te karanga.'
Ka mau te waka teretere, ka hoea e Ngāi Tahu ki tōna tauranga e
 Nā te kore i ai
 Te kore te wiwia
 Te kore te rawea
 Ko hōtupu ko hauora
 Ka noho i te ata
 Ka puta ki waho te rangi e tū nei e
Whakarongo, tirohia mai hoki ēnei rawekenga a rātou
(I) taea nei te hōhonu o te hinengaro te whāwhā

MERIMERI PENFOLD

(I) taea nei te taumaha o te manako te wero e kui, e koro mā,
(I) roto i ngā wānanga pū kōrero, whakapapa, karakia
Ehara hoki te wānanga a te hinengaro nō nāianei ake e
Ko te rangi e teretere ana i runga (i) te whenua
Ka noho te rangi nui e tū nei, ka noho i a ata tuhi
Ka puta ki waho te marama
Ka noho te rangi e tū nei ka noho i a te werowero
Ka puta ki waho ko te Rā
Kōkiritia ana ki runga hei pūkanohi mō te rangi
Ka tau te Rangi, te Ata tuhi, te Ata rapa
Ka mahina, ka mahina te ata i Hikurangi
Ka noho i Hawaiki ka puta ki waho
Ko Tāporapora, ko Kuku-paru
Ko Tauwharenīkau, ko Wawauātea
Ko Wiwhi-te-Rangiora e.
Tērā ka noho te rau tau te whare wānanga
Rere ana te awhi a te hunga rangatira o te rohe
Nā Parore, takoto ana tā Ngāti Hine mai i te wao a Tāne
Ka peke, pakū ana te waha o te hunga rangatahi
I noho tahi nei i a 'Mihinga i tōna tūranga
Ko Whare tērā i te kei o te waka a Tuia
Nā rātou rā i tuitui ngā rawekētanga
Pērā hoki te piri mai a te whānau whānui
E papata e noho puku nei i runga o Horotiu
Rere ana te koha tapu, tū ana te whare hei tūpuna
Tērā te Tumu ka pā atu te puna Te Pane o te Ika
Whakatinanatia mai ana ko Hine-ahu-one e tū
Te tuku (mai) te puna o ngā whare wānanga o te motu
Tū nei te Ao Mārama (te) toka te mahi wānanga
Tau mai ko Pāki, ko Hine me te whānau rangatahi
Hei tuhi, hei raranga i te pueru whakahirahira i te tupuna
Ko Tāne-nui-a-rangi e tū nei i runga o Waipapa e
Nau mai e Koro e
Nau mai nau mai!

There is Venus

There are Venus and the Southern Cross
glittering on the body of the sky
a thought stirs, rises from the deep inside
and flies up to the rays of the stars
to shine there as an ornament — the greenstone mountain stands!
    From the conception the increase
    From the increase the thought
    From the thought the remembrance,
    From the remembrance the consciousness
    From the consciousness the desire.
That canoe was set afloat by Te Hau and Hohepa
its wave crashed on the forehead of the chief who calls you now
it sprayed on the elder's shoulders
and spilled into the cramped caves of the dragons of learning
on that landing-place where the children of the north arrive.
    Knowledge became fruitful
    It dwelt with the feeble glimmering;
    It brought forth night:
    The great night, the long night,
    The lowest night, the loftiest night,
    The thick night, to be felt,
    The night to be touched,
    The night not to be seen,
    The night that ends in death!
The challenge did not land, it was not taken up
The stern of the canoe was left empty
It floated at random, until Ngati Whatua spoke
and Kui and Ani came with a new idea
The chief's mother said, 'Son, answer their call!'
Now the drifting canoe was held and Ngai Tahu paddled it to land.
    From the nothing the begetting,
    From the nothing the increase,
    From the nothing the abundance,
    The power of increasing,
    The living breath;
    It dwelt with the empty space,
    and produced the atmosphere which is above us.
Listen, see how our ancestors probed the universe
they grasped the very depths of thought

they took up the challenge of weighty matters, those old women
    and men
in oratory, genealogy, and discussion with the gods
for intellectual knowledge is no new thing.
    The atmosphere which floats above the earth
    The great firmament above us, dwelt with the early dawn,
    and the moon sprung forth;
    The atmosphere which is above us, dwelt with the heat,
    And thence proceeded the sun;
    They were thrown up above, as the chief eyes of Heaven:
    And the heavens became light,
    The early dawn, the early day,
    The mid-day. The blaze of day from the sky.
    The sky above dwelt with Hawaiki, and produced land,
    Taporapora, Kuku-paru,
    Tauwharenikau, Wawau-atea,
    Wiwhi-te Rangiora.
Now the university's centenary came
The chiefs of the region offered their help
Through Parore, Ngati Hine's gift came from the forests of Tane
the young people leapt up and cracked their mouths
While 'Mihinga sat with them
and Whare stood at the stern of the canoe Tuia
that group which bound meddlesome strands together
bringing the wider family closer
that teeming, self-contained multitude on Horotiu
gave their sacred gift, and the shell of the ancestral house was built
the chief went to the source at the fish's head
Hine-ahu-one the dining hall came to life
the well-spring for the universities of the island made its gift
Te Ao Marama, the academic wing stood as a foundation for
    teaching and
Paku and Hine arrived with the family of young people
to carve and weave a significant garment for the ancestor
Tane-nui-te-rangi, the meeting house, standing here on Waipapa.
Welcome, old man!
Come, welcome!

Translation by Anne Salmond

KUMEROA NGOINGOI PĒWHAIRANGI

(1922–85; Te Whānau-ā-Ruataupare, Ngāti Porou)

Ka Noho Au

Ka noho au i kōnei, ka whakaaro noa
He pēhea rā te huri a te ao katoa —
Ngā rongo kino e tukituki nei i te takiwā,
Ngā whakawai e hau nei ngā tamariki!
Kua kore noa he ture hei arataki
Te mana, te ihi ka takahia mai!
Kia kaha tātou ki te whakahoki mai
Te mauri ora me te wairua! Auē, ngā iwi e!

Tapaea ngā hē katoa ki runga rawa,
Kei a ia te ora me te mārama!
Kapohia te aroha nui o te Ariki
Māna e kaupare rā ngā kino katoa!
Whītiki, maranga mai, horahia rā
Ngā kupu hei oranga-ā-tinana e,
Kia noho ai i raro i te maru e
Te Rangimarie, te Rongopai, auē me te aroha!
Te Rangimarie te Rongopai! Auē, ngā iwi e!

I Sit Here

I sit here and keep wondering
About what is happening to this world
The bad news that afflicts us
The distractions that tempt youth!
There are no laws to show the way
To the mana people trample down!
We must be strong, we must bring back
O my people, our living mauri and our soul!

Give all our troubles into the care
Of the One above, with whom is life and light!

Hold fast to the love of our Lord
Who will turn aside all evils!
We must gather our strength, rise up
And speak the words that will sustain us
That we may live in the shelter
Of God's love and peace!

Translation by Kumeroa Ngoingoi Pēwhairangi

Poi E

Wahine: Patua taku poi, patua kia rite
　　　　Tāpara patua, taku poi e!
　　　　E rere rā e taku poi porotiti
　　　　Tītahataha rā
　　　　Whakararuraru e
　　　　Porotakataka rā porohurihuri mai
　　　　Rite tonu ki te tīwaiwaka e.
　　　　Ka parepare rā pī-o-i-oi e
　　　　Whakahekeheke e kia korikori e
　　　　Piki whakarunga rā maminga mai rā
　　　　Taku poi porotiti taku poi e.
Tane:　 Poi e
　　　　Whakatata mai
　　　　Poi e
　　　　Kaua hei rere kē
　　　　Poi e
　　　　Kia piri mai ki au
　　　　Poi e
　　　　Awhi mai rā
　　　　Poi e
　　　　Tāpekatia mai
　　　　Poi e
　　　　ō tāua aroha
　　　　Poi e
　　　　Paiheretia rā
　　　　Poi! Taku poi e!

Rere atu taku poi
Tītahataha rā
whakarunga whakararo
Taku poi e!

Poi

Women: Strike my poi, strike together,
double strike my poi,
fly my poi, my round poi,
fly past
this obstacle
like a spinning top spinning towards me,
just like a fantail
flitting aside and chirping,
fluttering down, hopping about,
flying flirtatiously upwards,
my round poi, my poi.

Men: Poi
come closer
poi
don't fly away
poi
fly closer to me
poi
embrace me
poi
entwine me
poi
our love together
poi
binding me
poi, my poi!

Fly away my poi,
fly past,
up and down,
my poi!

Translation by Te Aomuhurangi Temamaka Jones

413

Whakarongo

Whakarongo
Ki te reo Māori e karanga nei
Whakarongo
Ki ngā akoranga rangatira
Nā te Atua i tuku iho
Ki a tātou e
Pupuritia, kōrerotia
Mō ake tonu.

Tirohia
Ngā tikanga tapu a ngā tīpuna
Kapohia
Hei oranga ngākau! Auē!
Tēnā
Kia purea te hau ora e
Ngā kupu tuku iho
Mō tēnei reanga.

Listen

Listen
to the Maori language calling.
Listen
to the chiefly teaching.
God gave it to us.
Remember it, speak it
forever.

Search
the sacred traditions of our ancestors.
Grasp them
to safeguard our welfare! Aue!
Here
affirm the vitality of language,
the sayings that proceed from it
for this generation.

Translation by Te Aomuhurangi Temamaka Jones

FIONA FARRELL POOLE

(Born 1947)

from *Love Songs*

Seven wishes

A straight account is difficult
so let me define seven wishes:

that you should fit inside me neat as the stuffing in an olive
that you should stand inside the safe circle of my eye
that you should sing, clear, on the high rock of my skull
that you should swing wide on the rope of my hair
that you should cross rivers of blood, mountains of bone
that I should touch your skin through the hole in your tee shirt
that we should exchange ordinary tales.

Serenade

I have wanted you for 12 months now.
Stood on the corner under
the lamp. Dancing.
You slammed your mouth shut.

I have wanted you for 12 months now.
Stood outside your window.
Sung to you.
You switched out your eyes.

I have wanted you for 12 months now.
Earned my bread.
Woven my blanket.

So I eat.
So I sleep.

FIONA FARRELL POOLE

Spring

That duck racing for the reeds
on wheeled feet and after her a
drake penis dragging a plastic
hose inches of it zoom into the
reeds and all that rough spring
stuff. Tulips in mincing rows
fart scarlet cats nest under
the Civic Centre and pop
kittens like black peas and you
strip your white winter body and
paint the bedroom lickety lick
madonna blue because nothing's
sacred and everything's blessed.

Pastorale

You follow the railway line
down past the cheese factory
over the bridge and there it is —
Arcadia.

To the right, sheep.
To the left, on the
diagonal, a creek.
Young totaras (23,
conical, a random
distribution). And
just coming into the
picture Daphnis
in dark glasses
Chloe in blue jeans.
Light fizzes on grass
legs sandals.
Light frames bliss in a paddock.

There is a delicacy in the exchange
each stroke applied with care.

It is important to maintain a balance
to find the colours proper to this scene.

───────

That was one for the box
one to put away.
Fold the sun neatly.
A cork in the grass the
sheep and the trees
wind in hair and
plane droning distant.
And you talked.
And I talked.
And you laughed.
Hold each sound tight
till the lid's down

and the light's
out.

Passengers

Name	By what ship arrived	Present address	Remarks
Emily Graham	'Chile'	Top of Stafford St.	Common
Amy Graham	'Chile'	ditto	do.
Anne Brown	'Chile'	Pellings Cottages	Clandestine
Miss Moran	'Chile'	ditto	do.
Miss Parsons	'Chile'	Back of Waverley	do.

Police records, Dunedin, 1876

Anne Brown's Song

I first spread my legs
on a London street
and the shillings came easy
put shoes on my feet.
(I've lain on clay
and I've lain on sheet . . .)
And men with rough fingers
have staked out their claims

and gone off up country
no addresses no names.
There's gold in my crannies
there's gold in my crack.
Come miners and diggers
I'm down on my back.
There's a crack in the ceiling
a draught at the door
my back aches my mouth's salt
but there's time for one more.

A nice little bar
with a lamp and a chair
and frosted glass windows
to keep out the air
(there's a crack in the ceiling
a draught at the door)
and no man to empty
his load in my box
no fingers no breathing
no crabs and no pox
and I'll pile up the shillings
to keep in the heat
till I lie in the clay
till I lie in the sheet . . .

Mary McGonigle, 18. Domestic servant. Donegal. 'Blue Jacket' 1867.
Caroline Taylor, 12. Domestic servant. Origin unknown. 'Mystery' 1859.
Jane Lawry, 15. Domestic servant. Cornwall. 'Queen of the Mersey' 1862.
Mary Lawry, 18. Domestic servant. Cornwall. 'Queen of the Mersey' 1862.
Sarah McConnell, 14. Domestic servant. County Down. Emigrated 1870s.

Nineteenth-century ships' records

Mary Lawry's Song

Open the door Mary.
And who shall I say called?
Only a rough wind
scraping his boots
on the Rock and Pillar.

Answer the bell Mary.
And who was it rang?
A cocky sun tipped
his hat dumped his swag
on the doorstep and
off up the valley.

Polish the spoons Mary.
And are we expecting company?
A crowd: thick cloud
a rose a young appletree.

Set the tea Mary.
And who shall I set it for?
A quiet man who
comes in each night and
goes out each morning.

Lucy Rainbow, 21. Domestic servant. Rochdale. 'Maori' 1858.
Died of 'nervous debility' on voyage.

Lucy Rainbow's Song

Lucy sits under an African sun
stitching her shirt and when
she has done, Lucy will wear it
and people will stare and say
'Lucy, your hair, there's
weed in your hair' and people
will smile and say 'Stay yet
a while'. But Lucy will step
on the cold white foam
over the water till
Lucy is home

light as rain
light as cloud
light as any sea bird . . .

FIONA FARRELL POOLE

Clara Roskruge, 16. Domestic servant. Cornwall. 'Indian Empire' 1864.
Charlotte O'Neil, 17. General servant. Origin unknown. 'Isabella Hercus'
    1871.
Ann James, 33. Laundress. Abergavenny. 'Light Brigade' 1868.
Harriet Attiwell, 20. Domestic servant. Leicestershire. 'Cameo' 1859.
Eliza Lambert, 14. Domestic servant. Surrey. 'Mystery' 1858.

Nineteenth-century ships' records

Charlotte O'Neil's Song

You rang your bell and I answered.
I polished your parquet floor.
I scraped out your grate
and I washed your plate
and I scrubbed till my hands were raw.

You lay on a silken pillow.
I lay on an attic cot.
That's the way it should be, you said.
That's the poor girl's lot.
You dined at eight
and slept till late.
I emptied your chamber pot.
The rich man earns his castle, you said.
The poor deserve the gate.

But I'll never say 'sir'
or 'thank you ma'am'
and I'll never curtsey more.
You can bake your bread
and make your bed
and answer your own front door.

I've cleaned your plate
and I've cleaned your house
and I've cleaned the clothes you wore.
But now you're on your own, my dear.
I won't be there any more.
And I'll eat when I please
and I'll sleep where I please

and you can open your own front door.

ROMA POTIKI

(Born 1958; Te Arawa)

Tarawera

all I wanted was a tree
and a burning,
a hot stripping of the senses.

lift the shroud from the mountain,

basalt and iron
ferrous slit of the earth,
thick lipped ancestor.

scoria and dust
a red blister biting.

a womin plants a whenua
skin to skin
in black and white
a return to the source.

a gull flips,
over the valley
spagnum absorbs
the shocks
slow steps
rocking on the slopes
a procession
a movement
out
over the rim
a slide, a fall,
pouring to the bottom.

masked in chalk
walking on powder
the make-up of the mountain.

ROMA POTIKI

clean channels / direct passage
up the face,
one of many,
racking the shadows.

stone facts,
panels drop.

in sun —
one man,
sleeps on her flanks
a solid embrace.

rods connect,
hammers and tapes
record a response
live needles press, in sleep —
skin that burns
on waking.

hold tight
grip, till knuckles bleach — translucent
giving everything
back / to bone.

theres new blood on the mountain.

for a father in hiding

take me away
i used to travel.

i hear the breath of the people
in each corner
'and scraping at the glass.

someone must have sent the dreams
of meeting houses
low and dark,

earth floors
and slits for windows,
each old face watching silently.

and i am searching, searching,
for the smallest entrance.

blind horses
scent the air
that blows through you.

palazzi

sitting out on the palazzi
with my back to the open lounge
my lowered lids let the shine in.

a white porcelain bowl, used each morning,
the only religious ceremony left today — break fast.
an old one from the testaments.
it came from a rubbish dump at Kohukohu.

saw an italian sun and thought about fast cars on the slopes.
red cars 'n long scarf women. a trip on the grey gravel of europe.

i'd wear me blue dancing shoes and take me
fishes eyes.
daydreams on a cracked concrete slab in Rotorua.

the present

it wasn't really a nautilus
some shiny sea egg
a sac
pear full and fragile.

ROMA POTIKI

flaying fish cast yr smokey rims
and breast milk pallor.

you came from a cold-blooded mating
into warm hands
that passed you to a womin
whose nose fits perfectly into yr orifice
changes her
to a hawk without wings.

beauty cascading through opalescence

sea and air.

PŪTAHI CULTURAL GROUP

(Leader Mark Kopua, born 1962; Ngāti Porou)

Mā Wai Rā E Kawea ngā Tohu o Ērā

Mā wai rā e kawea ngā tohu o ērā
Kua makere ki te Pō o Tū.

Ka kinikini mai te mamae e ahau
Kia whakutuutu rā te karanga o ngā tīpuna
Hurihuri noa au, i te ao, i te pō
Ko te makariri kei kōnei, ko te ahuru kei kōnā.
Kimikimi noa au, ki whea, ki whea
Ki te ara whakahokinga, te ara ki te aka matua
Kei te kumekume ngā kohimuhimu ki taku manawa
Kei te hāparapara, tīhaehae, ka utuhia i te roimata
Auē — taukuri e.

E i ana i roto, tukua, tukua
Kia hoki atu ki te one tipuranga
Kei reira taku pito.
Auē — taukuri e.

Kaurori, kaurori ngā uri o roto i te pō
Whanawhana, takahuri, tīhore ka wehe, ka pō, ka ao.
Ka whakamatatūtia, ka oho mahara, ka riro ki te ao
Kia kite rā te hinengaro i ngā tuku iho mā
O ngā tīpuna
Kua marino e te wai, kua rarau e te puehu
Ki te pā o te aroha, nā ngā ringaringa tīpuna
Whano — whano tū mai te toki
Haumi — hui e taiki e!

Who Will Carry the Emblem

Who will carry the emblem of those
who have gone to the underworld?

A pain gnaws within me
beckoning me to answer the call of my forebears.
I turn restlessly day and night
for it's cold here, the warm where I should be.
I search far and wide, but where, where?
Where is the way back, the way to my father's root, my beginnings.
Whispers nag at my heart,
cutting and tearing it, till my tears well up —
Alas, the pain.

Inwardly I am driven to turn back,
to return — return home, to my birth-connection.
Alas, the pain.

The inheritor within me staggers, staggers about in the darkness,
bent back and forth, twisted, laid bare, divided between the dark
     and the light.
Be wakeful, awaken memory, come into the light.
Then hearts will recognise those beliefs
that are from the ancestors.
The water will be calmed, the sediment settled
by love's touch, by ancestral hands.
Go — go, grasp the ceremonial adze,
Join together, assemble!

Translation by Pūtahi Cultural Group

Te Ahi Paura Auahi E

Te ahi paura auahi e auē, Te ahi paura auahi e auē,
me rapa atu i tō tīmatanga auē, i roto i ngā whakapapa auē
me whakanuia ki Mahuika he toa, he wahine toa, he ariki, he toa
Nā Maui Pōtiki te whaiātanga auē

I tōna tinihanga ka riri a Mahuika.
Kei a Tāne-nui-o-rangi te oranga o te ahi e
Kei te kaikōmako, kei te tōtara me te pukatea
Auē rā Mahuika e kore koe e ngaro atu
Ko ngā kaitiaki kei te wao nui a Tāne

Ko wai te wahine? Te matua?
Ko Te Pō, nā Te Pō
Ko Papatuanuku — ka puta mai te mokopuna
Ko Hine-ahu-one
Te ira tangata he wahine nā Tāne, ka hangai te tara
Ka puta ko Hine-tītama
Ka moe i a ia ki tōna matua, ka tahuri ia, i tahuri ia
Ka heke, heke iho ki Rarohenga — auē
Tapaia tonu ia i tōna tapahanga
Ko Hine-nui-te-pō

Ka takai rā Maui Pōtiki i te Tikitiki-a-Taranga
Murirangawhenua te tipuna,
Nāna te iwi kauae e hī ana te whenua, hī ana te whenua
Wahine toa, maranga. Maranga, maranga mai!

Little Smoking Ember

O little ember smoking away, O little ember smoking away,
let me search for your beginnings in our genealogies.
I pay tribute to Mahuika a warrior, a warrior woman, a queen,
    a warrior.
It was Maui Potiki who bewitched her.
His deceit earned the rage of Mahuika.
She gave the comfort of fire to Tane's hordes,
The kaikomako, the totara, the pukatea.
Aue, Mahuika, you will never be destroyed —
Tane's great forest has your guardians.

Who was the woman? The parent?
It was Darkness, and born of Darkness
was Papatuanuku — who bore the child
Hine-ahu-one, Earth-formed-maiden, who was

427

the first human, and wife of Tane. He moulded her vagina
and Hine-titama, Dawn-maiden, was born.
She married her own father and turned, turned,
and descended to Rarohenga — aue.
She then changed her name
to Hine-nui-te-po: the Great-maid-of-darkness.

It was Maui Potiki that Taranga wrapped in her topknot
Murirangawhenua was his grandmother.
It was her jawbone that fished up this land, that fished up
    this land.
Warrior women, arise. Arise, stand tall!

Translation by Pūtahi Cultural Group

KUINI MOEHAU REEDY

(Born 1941; Ngāti Porou, Te Awemāpara)

Te Mana Motuhake

Tangata tonu e tangi nei
He ara mana motuhake
Ki tēnei ao
He ara poutama ki te rangi e
He oranga mō tātou katoa
Atamai ki au

Kua tae ki te wā ngā iwi
Tutehu nei i te pō
Maranga mai kōkiritia
Te kaupapa
Mana te tū te ihi
He mana motuhake
He ohākī tuku iho
Nā rātou mā

Ara te mana
ara te toa
Tawhiao
Mahuta
Te Whiti
Ko Rikirangi
Tapaia ngā hara
whiua ki te ao
Ngā tai pounamu he tohutohu
Atamai ki au

The Special Mana

People still grieve
for a way of separate mana
in this world,

a stairway to heaven,
survival for all of us
including me.

People, the time has come
to push through darkness,
to raise up, to advance
the proposal.
Stand with the prestige,
a special mana —
a last wish
of those who have gone.

That is the mana,
that is the bravery,
Tawhiao,
Mahuta,
Te Whiti,
Rikirangi.
Cancel our debts
throw them to the world —
The tides of pounamu are a symbol
even to me.

Translation by Te Aomuhurangi Temamaka Jones

E Te Tau

E ako e te tau i te reo Māori
Te reo rangatira o ngā mātua tūpuna
He taonga rā nā te Atua
Puritia kia mau
Kei ngaro e te tau e

Rukuhia e tama ngā wai o Waiwhetu
Whakatau e hine te tauira o Te Aroha
Horahia whānuitia ki ngā kōhanga
Puritia kia mau kei ngaro e te tau e

My Loved One

Learn Maori my loved one,
it is the noble language of your ancestors
a great treasure from God.
Maintain it
Lest it be lost my loved one.

Let the life stream of Waiwhetu cleanse you my son,
Let the house Te Aroha be the example of your pride my daughter.
Share it with all other kohanga
Maintain it lest it be lost my loved one.

Translation by Kuini Moehau Reedy

NIGEL ROBERTS

(Born 1941)

Beauty / Truth / Genius & Taste etc.

I am wearing
a pair
of Brett Whitely's
socks.

How I came by them, is
another poem
but you may be aware
of the expression
'great artists steal & the poor
borrow'

Well I borrowed
the socks from Brett
as he borrowed
a cup of sugar
from Francis Bacon.

I would
like to think
that Brett wore them
when he painted Patrick
White; as this lends
a painterly quality
to the socks
& a literary seriousness
to the poem.

The socks, sadly
are unsigned —
this may worry a hole
on their investment, or
your comfort be
attributed

to the Master of Laminex
    Pro Hart.

        Beauty
            Truth
    Genius & Taste etc.
      go for a walk
    if I wear Brett's socks
        or find
    that painting & sculpture
is the furniture
    of the beautiful & the rich.

      The Beauty
           Truth
Genius
      & Taste etc.
    of the unique object
is confirmed
        by its price —
    this gives a gloss to
  inequality
      & makes hierarchies
        thrilling.

    The first printmakers
were right
      the unique market sucks
  where the best
    are pensioners
    of their craft
or support it
marking the cribs of Milton.

      This
unique object
      is for sale.
This poem
      is for sale.

> 'Brett's socks
> grey with elastic
> tops & Australian content.'

> It will harmonise
> & be at home
> with the leather
> & the chrome.

The Gulls' Flight

The gulls' flight
is low
flat
& hard

they go
to sea
to the edge / where
the day's fire
is lit

they go
as shiftworkers
to the dawn.

The New Age Class Listings

The Jewish Community Centre offers these:
Kindergym, Little Flippers, Creative Chinese Cooking
for Singles, & Men in Transition — a course for men
exploring their options.

The Open Education Exchange has listed
Baseball for Beginners, whose résumé is this:
Ever had a secret desire to play Baseball, but
were intimidated by grimaces, contemptuous mutterings

or eyeball rollings? then maybe
Baseball for Beginners can turn that around in
a personal & emotionally supportive atmosphere.

There is NO overt sex in a course for Women —
Orgasms are good for you. This
is led by Verna Betts, who knows how mellow & together
you can be.
Verna owns a sensuous supplies store & has taught
at the Institute of Human Abilities

The East Bay Socialist School is Shattuck Avenue
has the course for all of you, who started
Das Kapital, but never finished.
There will, on the 2nd, be a seminar
on the Jonestown Catastrophe — as the People's Temple
was considered a Left organisation, the seminar
will hope to show how The Left can provide
a sense of community, without being driven to extremes.

Is there a system of geographical power points, that
contributes to people's success, in various locations?
Astro Cartography answers these questions &
by computer calculating your horoscope, geographically
can put you in the right place & at the right time

We have to call or write: The Atlantis New Age Bookshop
for information on their weekly classes in ESP —
&, should we need to, we can recharge our batteries &
deepen our meditations
with pyramids from their wide selection.

The classes, at Birth Body & Breath, include
Treasure Mapping, Affirmations, & Physical Immortality.
There, on the first Saturday of every month is
Leonard Orr, the founder of Rebirthing, & a well-known
Prosperity Consultant, who is conducting seminars on
Loving Relationships, the way we want them.

In Psychic Judo, which is taught at the Monastery of One
we can learn how to avoid being manipulated, & how
to manipulate those, who are trying to manipulate you.

NIGEL ROBERTS

We can learn how to change our myth of self, without
anyone knowing it, & how, to Hex, Bless & Cast a Control Net
& how, to get another person to say yes.
In the seminar, Women as Space / Man as Time, we can
prepare the terrestrial mind for an encounter with
a cosmic intelligence.

The Great Oaks School of Health is expanding
its community —
& needs persons who believe that by hard work, exercise
fasting, positive thinking, kinesiology, acupressure
reflexology, massage, colour therapy, herbs, homeopathy
vitamins, clay, colonics, sensory deprivation tanks
& sauna,
we can return to a more natural & simple way of living.

Deon Dolphin of Open Channels is an ordained minister
mother, gourmet cook, past lives counsellor, rebirther
& liaison between the old & new age. Deon
who is an affiliate of The Safe Space Youniversity
claims that by clearing our past lives, we can be more
here now, by going back there, then.

The San Francisco Medical Research Foundation Inc
believes The Vision of Oneness, the principle
& foundation of The New Age, & that this unity can
be summed up in the motto: In God we trust, as found
on the back of the United States Dollar Bill.
The Foundation recommends their Elixir of Life:
a pure, alchemical, homeopathic remedy containing
distilled water & pure gold, which works by changing
the blood's vibrations, so that negative thoughts & emotions
are chelated & absorbed by the pure gold.
It is available from Ralph Ornstein, President
& Professor of Alchemical Sciences, University
of Light, Apt. 50, 207 Gough St; San Francisco.

The Tao of Abundance will give those, who have
a record of success, a jet assist towards greater
accomplishment, with much less effort & vastly
expanded satisfaction.

436

It is for those who want real results, in
the real world —
A trainee testifies: 'The best training I've taken
& I've·taken a lot of trainings.'

Attention. Pay Attention. Pay Attention to Attention.
Give your attention to A Gurdjieff Oriented Workshop
which is led by Chris Elms.
Chris deals with money, sex, & jobs, as the route
to the fastest realization.
This group will change your life; don't call unless
you can tolerate that. Meets weekly. Very few openings.

Ready to consummate your spiritual search?
Write: Shortcut to Enlightenment
Box 16101, San Francisco
and save yourself years, even lifetimes
of treading a seemingly endless path.

IAIN SHARP

(Born 1953)

from *Why Mammals Shiver*

25

If gaunt men wheel carts
outside your window,
demanding the dead,
give the dead to them.
It's a reasonable request.

These are flexible times.
The sky is empty of gods.
Go ahead then. Laugh.
Nothing stares down.

If your legs are firm,
dance on them.
Tables, tombs, washing-lines, wires —
the venues are plenteous.

If your legs are feeble,
broken, enormous, missing,
or if your back snaps,
be pleased with stillness.
Rest. Dream deeply.
Planets will swim over you.
The earth too will spin.

The Perfect Bones

I'm afraid to walk the long beach.
I'm afraid to leave the fire.
The dark ocean grinds its teeth.
Thirsty gods wait eyeing our blood.

Friends who left the fire were swallowed.
Their spat-out souls wail high in the wind.
Moon-hued trinkets sprinkle the sand,
broken bits of us peeled by the sea.

Share with me the warm cave.
Caress the flesh cold ghosts covet.
Beside the hearth your face is amber.
Hold me now with your perfect bones.

The Title Poem

Where has my love departed?
I chased her penumbra
along the walls and pavements.
Now I cannot see her.
I cannot see.
A darkness descends
and swallows me entire.
I stretch my arms.
I grope for objects.
There is nothing.
Where has my love departed?

Oh, she is waiting, she whispers.
She is very patient.
She is trying to kidnap
the blind person.
She will lead him by the hand
over the wide estuary,
the dark plateau,
to where the wind-harp whistles
and all manner of birds rejoice.

He will like it there.
He will smile.
His blind eyes will glisten.

IAIN SHARP

Remembering Childhood Winters

First snow was comforting —
a sparkling white coverlet
drawn over the lumpy world,
over the eyes of the dead.
After the haphazard sifting,
the ballet of falling lacework,
life was left so simple
for a day or two small children
in balaclavas and mittens
shaped the land to their fancy.
In fields of frozen footprints
huge, round, carrot-nosed amputees
sat lopsided and grinned.

The Pierrot Variations

In the weak winter sunlight
the churchyard entices Pierrot
as he leans on his chipped bones,
dreaming of lapsed chances
and pure eastern thought.
'The secret awaits perception
through eyes unclouded by longing.'
Ah, Pierrot reveres Lao Tzu
but he longs, he longs
and beyond his ache sees only

flowers that pine for the sun,
the yearning of the stars
across enormous distance
for one another's glamour,
the dance of dark oceans
entranced by the moon
which circles and circles our sphere —
everywhere a helpless longing,
a desperate desire.

Pierrot, for example, craves
the dimpled back of Elizabeth,
her slim perfection.
With his massive heart he craves
an orderly existence.
He craves undying fame,
the judges so charmed by his song
they weep in gratitude, and yell:
What a radiant contribution!
What an artefact!
Pierrot will endure forever.

And the sun, of course, descends.
Fires flare in a thousand homes.
The darkness every winter
surprises defenceless Pierrot,
yet, look, the Milky Way murmurs,
the lachrymose moon persists.
Its small messages ricochet
from countless urban windows,
against the seething ocean,
among the churchyard leaves.

Air

Air can do anything. It has that kind
of flexibility. You know this because
you live in it. You live in the air
and you peek out your window,
you hold out a feather,
you wait for special announcements
that come to you over the air,
you attend to the wires,
you breathe it in,
and check for evidence of tempests,
such as runaway trees, truant windows,
your neighbours' rooftops puffed abroad,
or your neighbours borne aloft.

IAIN SHARP

When the air is well-disposed,
when it zigzags,
when it entertains bright insects
I suggest you go and meet it.
Be bold. Take off your cardigan.
Tango in a backless gown
with the air against your
vertebrae. Send up a kite.
Send up your legs
like Nini Paws-in-the-Air.
Feel the sky. Filter the breeze.
Fill a polythene bag
with your exhalation
and post it by sea to a blue whale
as a gesture of fellowship,
an emergency aqualung.

Then proceed to an airy spot
and build with a nonchalant air
a white dome which doubles
as a bust of C. K. Stead.
Perch on its summit and part
your hair with a silver comb.
Lean back. Wave to the whales.
Drop a paper helicopter
down through the atmosphere. Smile.
Smile like a Hollywood Pharaoh.
The world is unruly but it's yours.
You're its heir.

PITA SHARPLES

(Ngāi te Kikiri-o-te-Rangi, Ngati Whatuiāpiti)

E Rere te Hukarere

E rere kairerere
E rere kairerere te hukarere
Ki runga i te kuia e
Makariri mokemoke
Mō ana mokopuna
Mō tōna kāinga e
Maringi
Ringi mai ngā roimata
Roimata
Ringi mai ngā roimata
Mō tōna kāinga e

Ka piki ara piki
Ka piki ara piki te hūpeke
Ki rōwhare kōhatu e

Te whare tiaki
Taonga tipuna
O ngā iwi
O te ao e

Ka kimi
Kimi ōna taonga
Taonga
Kimi ōna taonga
Nō tōna kāinga e

Ka tangi te kairangi
Ka tangi te kairangi ki te kite
I ngā taonga Māori e
Manaaki mahana
I roto i Amerika
Noho marie

443

PITA SHARPLES

Ngā kura e
Kua oti
Oti pai āna mahi
Ngā mahi
Oti pai āna mahi
Mō tōna kāinga e

E rere kairerere

The Snow Fluttered Down

The snow fluttered down
on the old lady.
She was cold and lonely
for her grandchildren,
for her family at home.

The tears
streamed down her face,
tears for her home.

The old lady climbed the steps
and went inside the great stone building,
the building which housed
the ancestral treasures
of the peoples
of the world.

She searches,
she searches for the treasures,
the ancestral treasures
from her home.

Then the old lady cried,
she cried when she discovered
her Maori ancestral pieces.
The treasures were blessed and warmed
although far away in America.
The treasures were allowed to remain
in peace.

The work of the kuia
was now completed.
She had finished
the task at hand
for the people at home.

The snow fluttered down.

Translation by Pita Sharples

Hine-ahu-one

I Kurawaka i tāraia te oneone e
Hei tapairu e he wahine tipua e
Hine auē Hine-ahu-one
Ko te pūnga o te ira tangata

Nā Tāne-nui i maminga i a Hine-tītama e
Mai i taua wā i tāmia mana wahine e
Hine auē Hine-ahu-one
E ara whakatikaia tātau nei e

Hinemoa, Mahinārangi e
Hinemātioro, Muriwai
He mano wahine e mau ai te mana e

Wairaka, Hine Āmaru e
Rongomaiwahine, Te Puea
He wahine kaihautu rangatira ariki e

Mā wai e awhi i ngā wā o te pōuri e
Māu tonu rā e hine ko koe rā i takahia e
Hine auē Hine-ahu-one
E ara hāpainga āu tamāhine e
Hine-ahu-one

445

PITA SHARPLES

Hine-ahu-one

It was at Kurawaka where the earth was fashioned and given life.
It was the form of a woman ancestress.
It was Hine, Hine-ahu-one.
She is the origin of the human race.

It was Tane-nui who first practised deceit on Hine-titama.
From that day until now the dignity of women has been oppressed.
So Hine, Hine-ahu-one,
return to correct your people.

There was Hinemoa, Mahinarangi,
Hinematioro and Muriwai,
countless are the women who have
upheld the mana of the people.

There was Wairaka, Hine Amaru,
Rongomaiwahine and Te Puea —
many were the women leaders and high chiefs.

Who then will embrace you in sad times?
It will be a woman even though
she be downtrodden by men.
So Hine, Hine-ahu-one,
Arise and uplift your daughters.
Yes Hine-ahu-one.

Translation by Pita Sharples

Takiri Mai te Ata

Takiri mai te ata
Ka totoko te aroha
Pūmahara o te hanga
Ka wehe i ahau
Nā ko tauiwi
Takahi te auaha

O te iwi
Nāna i whakatū
Kaupapa Ingarangi
Ki roto wharekura
Kia whakakotahi ai
Ngā whakaaro ki tērā
Ki tā te Pākehā e
Tāmoea te pūmanawa
O aku mokopuna
Auē taukiri e!

Pērā Waikohu whenua
Whārikitia ana te motu
Rite ki Tūkorehu
Hīpokina tihi maungapae
Ki mānia
Tāmia tikanga
Ko te reo o Koro mā
O ngā whakatipuranga e

Tawhirimātea
Ki te tono mai
Āu tamariki
Hei hoa mōku
Ki te whawhai
Ki te patu hoariri
Riaki kohu kino e

Auē mā Tūparara
Te pūkohu
Pūawhe ki tua
Pūawhe ki kō
Mā Haupauma
Te pana ki waho e
Ko te hikitanga
Huakanga
Ki te whakatū wānanga
He kura Māori
Ko te reo rangatira e

Nā ko Kōhengihengi
Ka tuku

447

PITA SHARPLES

Hei mau kaupapa
Taonga
Kawe kawe
Kawe ki maunga
Kawe ki awariu
Kawe ki te tino kōpū
O te whenua e
Auē kia whakahokia
Te mauri motuhake
Te mana
O tuairangi
Ki te iwi e.

Dawn Breaks

As dawn breaks there
sorrow wells up inside me
as I contemplate what
is lost to me.
For it was the strangers to this
land who trampled the creativity
of my people.
It was they who established
the English Curriculum
within our schools
so that all in this country
should think as one,
as the Western values of the white man,
so crushing the natural
talents of my children.
Alas, the pain.

It is like a great fog
blanketing the land,
like Tukorehu, Deep Mist himself,
covering even the highest mountains
and the lowest plains,
suppressing the very customs and
language of my ancestors,
generation after generation.

448

Tawhirimatea
send
your children
to assist me
in the battle
to destroy the enemy,
to lift this evil mist.

Send forth Tuparara, Violent Wind
so that the great fog
be driven away,
be driven outside.
Send Haupauma, Head Wind to evict
the great fog.
It is the removal,
the uncovering, so that we
can establish our schools of
learning, build Maori schools
embracing our own noble language.

Now send forth
Kohengihengi, Gentle Wind
to carry the message,
our treasures,
to transport these
to the mountains,
throughout all river valleys,
and indeed to the very bowels
of this land.
Only then can
our spiritual force,
our mana
of ages gone
be restored to our people.

Translation by Pita Sharples

ELIZABETH SMITHER

(Born 1941)

Temptations of St Antony by his housekeeper

Once or twice he eyed me oddly. Once
He said Thank God you're a normal woman
As though he meant a wardrobe and went off
Humming to tell his beads. He keeps
A notebook, full of squiggles I thought, some
Symbolism for something, I think I've seen
It on lavatory walls, objects like chickens' necks
Wrung but not dead, the squawking
Still in the design, the murderer running.
He's harmless, God knows. I could tell him
If he asked, he terrifies himself.
I think it makes him pray better, or at least
He spends longer and longer on his knees.

A verse letter to Tonia

Someone is chiming at the piano
Between the stroke of bells
Something stands up to face the sun.
I have missed the talk by Margaret Drabble
But your letter in its tent
With its piled deserted mattresses
Reminded me of the Princess and the Pea.
I wonder if she slept at all
Knowing the weight and sensitivity of
Royal blood, composing in her head
A shorthand proclamation
(Probably beginning We regret to inform)
Like a rejection slip? Several people I know
Are good at these sort of poems
It's more like my first marathon.

450

Here's something very private: a dead leaf
Has just fallen slowly at my feet
Which I've regarded as a private sign for years.
It caught on the branches of a fern as it fell
Like a body from the tenth floor bouncing
From balcony to balcony and landing on
A mini car which it squashes flat
So someone comes out and exclaims My car!
My precious possession! You mustn't
Speak of your body as blotched, it could
Be listening, after all it has the equipment.
Another leaf, smaller, has landed by my left foot
The only trouble with signs is their meaning
It probably means I should abandon the poem.
I had a strange visit from a friend recently
We had not met for 20 years (this is what
I was going to tell you if I wrote
A proper letter.) We sat in the garden
And I was talking too much as usual
And I think she was watching me with a view
To analysis (Room with a view?)
But I cut her short by saying
(I'd just read about it in a book of essays
On novelists) that where the old mores
Those that are imposed from without I guess
Like handling a knife and fork properly,
Leaving a calling card, not drinking the finger bowl,
The absence of these and their corollaries
Tend to make us look to others' opinions
As a judgement or mirror image as though
Suffering from amnesia we are trailing clues
From a consensus of friends and foes.
The next day we went to the graveyard
And the old school: nothing came back
Except there was a new lily pond
And along the bush track by the river
Where we tramped in black stockings
The same thrushes flew up with outstretched wings.
None of the graves were in order
I couldn't find the subject of my novel
But you would have liked several things I saw:

ELIZABETH SMITHER

Two children's graves with a tiny lamb
Perched on the headstone reminded me
Of signalling from windows when the parents
Are asleep. A family called Jones
Had a pink marble mattress curled
Like bedding airing or a back hunched
In a love posture, a very vigorous missionary.
My friend got tired and lay across
The grass graves of five soldiers
Which seemed promiscuous; I had
A wild desire to chain smoke. After a time
The air became heavy and we escaped.
Perhaps the best thing is a philosophy —
That means an accretion like certain tastes
Losing the resistance to garlic, living on vegetables
(Remember your father's garlic sandwiches?)
I think you should wear a rose always
Like an exterior heart while you harden
The interior heart until it breathes
The impressions you command for it:
The other rose can wane while the heart unfolds.
The insect living in your ear was such a creed
Details one builds with then prunes
Like brushing the shoulder of a black coat.
I loved your description of the sand
And the way you described the sea
Made me think of full-length mirrors
Lying sideways in the sheen before
The wall of water shatters like a wine glass.
It's just past noon. The lawn is littered
With leaves now, only the bamboo leaves
Move in a freckled way, the heat's found out
My cave. I'll type this and swear
I can't write better, at least that's eternal.

from *Casanova's ankle*

Casanova's ankle

Casanova was turned by an ankle
Over and over. His glance ascended
To towers of conquest, snares set
In the shade of trees. Too bad
He had to toil as well in the trap
To free the booty used
And stained by capture. Distasteful
Somehow what he possessed
When the time for possession came.
It was better in the stalking light
With the moon half-hid
Following the scented glove, the ankle.

Casanova sated

This little mal I sleep through, untriste
Untriste my weapon, my treatise
This little sleep like a liqueur
Sipped between dawn and leavetaking
The white starlight assembling garments.

Casanova's pied à terre

Time to take off the dust sheets and go through
The list of black addresses, code
The letters and file them, burn some
Wash the hands in ashes, hope the heart
Plucked from the fire will endure
In someone's pocket. Endure in a laboratory more like
Unless I sleep some nights single
On a camp bed, lamp lowered, diary gutted.

Casanova in prison

Lovers may be hemmed up in a wall
But the wall is fatal to love
Or love's wit, philosophy.

Only in a crowd is secrecy
Only in journeys conquest
The bare wind over the dust.

Miss Darwin and the rosemary bush

I know the second the rosemary's scent came back.
Two days before I'd moved it
In one of my spurts of
Righteousness rather than gardening.
'Wrench it' someone said.   I paid no heed
Breaking the soil up with a pickaxe
For it to go in, tugging it out
Of the place I thought was unpropitious
(No one asked the bush) pick-
Axing the hole deeper while the rosemary
Lay swooning beside it.   I cut
A worm or two in half I think
Repulsive violence of gardening, feeling
It in the self, hurrying on
To the torturer's teabreak.   Finally anyway
It was in, in my propitious place.
But scentless.   I smelt it as I poured
The water over it that evening.   It was
Scented when I carried it from place to place
Like a Sabine maiden, I remember that.
It's your scent I love.   I didn't speak
To it exactly, it's worse than that
I believe plants hear like God
Thoughts as they form, not even
The outward expression we're so proud of
A shoddy thought well-earthed
But the feathery roots, their impulse.
This morning I came back to it: scentless
As I'd feared, moved the weeds around it
Thinking God knows what all the time
That she who kills a plant murders
That weeds have their uses which ought
Not to be ravished.   And I thought of

Some companions for the rosemary
Other plants in unpropitious places
A half-choked iris, two vines
That had gone the wrong way
And were covering a retreat.
In the end, knowing it could read
My thoughts, I tried to clear
My head even my heart of any signals
For I knew it must despise me for
Amateurism, even my amateur love
I could imagine the iris and the rosemary talking
Like two bronchitics 'When does her shift end?'
Or 'Only two more injections to go for her'
Or just a look, maybe I'd left them weak as that.
So I put the spade away and around the base
Where the worm was covered, where it seemed
I could be safely gentle at the last
I plumped the cushions round, forgot
What it was to be human, communed no more
But dumbly did in the last few weeds
And the scent came back, strong as though
The rosemary had farted, a warm gust
And when I approached my face
The leaf ends, like forgiveness, were full of it.

Nights spent with women

One who drew out of her case
A tattered negligée with a trailing hem
Left over from a decade's old honeymoon
She herself with cropped hair
Trailing the negligée like an old bear.

One who slept pillowless
Her face flat against the sheet
So when I woke first she seemed to be
A White Russian pressed against the earth
In a labour camp kissing the snow for berries.

One who slept under a poster of sailors
Left over from a Film Festival: three
Larger than life heads of men
Who were reflected in her mirror
Wearied but not from looking at women.

One whose country house
And absent husband made fearful
So she slept with a shotgun under her side
And under my pillow my head touched
The edge of a small box of cartridges.

I remember the flower girl in the hospital
Tidying up the leaves and petals
Each morning when the floors were new polished
Then whisking away at night
Air guzzlers, tame sharing roses.

Winter's natural position

Among the negative, once you are in
It is important not to take a defensive position
Draw your roots up slightly, timorously hold out leaves.

The capacity of the negative expands
With the action exerted on it: the pressure
To survive, if visible, can be dearly bought.

After penetrating anything look indifferent
Is a counsel with many applications:
It is winter's natural position.

Professor Musgrove's canary

In the humid months a miner's canary
Inserted in the doorway of a lecture room
Would have died I swear it

The theatres were olfactory, a stench
Whose elements escape, it could be
Stone perhaps and intellectual grief

Except the smell of universities is never simple
The canary would never have stood it
That's for certain, a maw

In which the brightest bird
Would have done the decent
Curled up in its cage, like a dead carnation

It's less in spring, quite gone in winter
Still we must deposit
Something in these buildings

That summer re-heats and re-serves us
I think rightly we deserve it
Man must live with his own learning.

The Creative Writing Course faces the sonnet

Something formal, say a silver jug
By Cellini or espaliering apples
Can be approached by two methods:

Usefulness: Cellini was known for spouts
And espaliering apples is practical
In a narrow garden with one wall

Or envy: Who gave the popes these millions
Who left these fossils of great beauty
Which still fruit in irony?

KENDRICK SMITHYMAN

(Born 1922)

Reading the Maps   An Academic Exercise

All grid co-ordinates on this sheet are in terms of
false origin

Today when I was leaving you were gone
to the Library, hunting. So I couldn't say
what I wanted to say. No matter.
At nine I phoned about the mice and rats
which infest us, and departmental cats.
Are they procurable or not? No matter.

On the wall in front of my table are four
map sheets of Hokianga. One weakly faded,
the main part of a research scheme gone
mainly down the drain. Even when bought
it did not tell the truth (if truth I sought)
about that district. Some roads were gone

already, some were petered out to tracks,
some only projected. I quibble. It was truth
I pressed after to the blazing four
dusty points of the local compass, ground
by ground hunting for Mahimai and found
how legend bred him still, not one but four,

five or more versions of his Life and Times
in their ways different but yet held true for some
around those parts. They've not roads, mere tracks
in scrub or scruffy bush, beaten, halfway lost,
uncertain where they go, or stay. What cost
to follow them? What gains? Tracks are just tracks.

Or legends of them, getting nowhere much;
otherwise, fictions of any parish's mild dreams
mounted towards a future where times
would not work out of joint. Those sad dreams ailed

materially, the vision in them failed,
sailed off like so much junk caught up in Time's

hard-driving westerlies or blustering tides,
dumped among mangroves, slumped like driftwood on water
frontages. 'The tourist will find much
to interest him, from . . .' From here to there,
hunting or haunted. Finding, found out where
roads disappear or don't amount to much.

Like schemes which I'may think of, truth to tell.
No matter — no, that isn't true. Dusty, bitter
our ways work out, crudely move like tides,
nonetheless turn; comes turnabout in flow
and ebb, they matter. Down at the Head glow
finely the dunes. Promise still rides the tides.

★

TO GIVE A GRID REFERENCE ON THIS SHEET

PAY ATTENTION TO LARGER MARGINAL FIGURES AND TO THOSE PRINTED ON THE FACE OF THE MAP VIZ $_8$30			
Point 270' Rawhia			
East		North	
Take west edge of square in which point lies and read the figures printed opposite this line (on north or south margin) or on the line itself (on the face of the map)	10	Take south edge of square in which point lies and read the figures printed opposite this line (on east or west margin) or on the line itself (on the face of the map)	42
Estimate tenths eastward	5	Estimate tenths northward	6
East	105	North	426
Reference 105426			

Now I know where I stand, where I stood.
Within limits. All grid coordinates on this sheet are
true only in terms of false origin.

★

Leave the highway just past a store
almost opposite this shortcut through the gorge.
You want to bear west beyond the store,

back of the district high school. As you go
you raise an abandoned church (which is here)
with a small marae. Shortly, the river.
Follow its bank for a bit, until
a farmer's yard, between the cowbail and pigpens.
So drive slowly. You'll need to.
The map says the road ends there. Not true.
You are now right under a stone face.
See the quarry sign? Drive
into the quarry, keeping to the hill side
(because of a fall on the other hand to the river).
You skirt a shoulder. Look for an unformed road
lifting suddenly, steep. But get over the crest,
you're on top of packed sand.
Carry on to the Head. You cross
the old tramway which used to go up to
the Harbour, remains of the one time main road
to gumfields (south of the river and this next
river) out from the edge of the Forest. It went on
down the coast, then climbed inland on the line
of a Maori trail. Of course, the map doesn't
say anything about that. Maps can

tell you about what is supposedly present.
They know little about what's past and only
so much about outcomes. They work within
tacit limits. They're not good at predicting.
If everything is anywhere in flux
perhaps we may not read the same map twice.

★

A DEFENCE OF RYME

*Nor must we thinke, viewing the superficiall figure of a region in a Mappe that
wee know strait the fashion and place as it is. Or reading an Historie (which
is but a Mappe of men, and dooth no otherwise acquaint vs with the true Substance
of Circumstances, than a superficiall Card dooth the Seaman with a Coast neuer
seene, which always prooues other to the eye than the imagination forecast it)
that presently wee know all the world, and can distinctly iudge of times, men
and maners, iust as they were.*

Samuel Daniel

THE BOOK OF THE ROAD

Out on A 61 for Ripon
Left at Ripley on B 6165
  to Pateley Bridge
Paeley Bridge through Grassington
  on B 6265, to connect
B 6160, through Kettlewell, Starbotton
  and Buckden
Turn left at Buckden and follow
  Langstrothdale Chase to Hawes
  (not numbered)
Hawes-Bainbridge on A 684, cross to
  Askrigg and on (no number) to
  Castle Bolton

Have lunch there?

Castle Bolton, over Redmire Moor to Reeth
Reeth into Arkengarthdale
Turn right beyond Langthwaite over
  Scargill High Moor to meet A 66
Right again, to B 6277, there left to
  Barnard Castle

Allow time to see castle, medieval bridge and
  inn where Dickens wrote *Nicholas Nickleby*
  (so the Treasures book says) and esp.
  Bowes Museum (if open??)

From Barnard Castle backtrack on B 6277
Watch for turn off (unnumbered) to
  Egglestone Abbey
(Have tea there or in town?)
Then follow River Tees to get back to
  A 66 for Greta Bridge (isn't that Dotheboys
  Hall?)
Carry on A 66 to Scotch Corner, down A 1
to turn off on A 59 through Knaresborough

KENDRICK SMITHYMAN

NOTE: Roman road beyond Oughtershaw on way
    to Hawes and site of fort at Bainbridge
    From Greta Bridge A 66 follows a Roman
    road (no name)

*

We may not read the same map twice,
especially where sands are on the move.
I speak loosely because thinking
not of a map's ineptitude but of
some shiftless nature which is prior.
Maps merely feign to represent the case.
Shiftless? A shifty case, more like,
unsure in its election as well as
in its origin, in its ground
of being as well as in its becoming —
neither works any way too well
for this instance. Are we not assuming
that what one has here to purport
to use as an example will survive
scrutiny? Somehow, has survived?

You follow me: I talk of what we have
and have not, of a sandhill lake
which comes and goes. Or maybe, came and went
since when I was last probing there
forestry men and engineers intent
on reform were then debating
how best to right an aberrant nature.

Their maps could not properly cope
with it. It was offence to natural
justice, natural right, and law.

It came and went. Worse, it was essential
when not existent. Boundaries
tentatively it had, often flouted.
It had? Check my legal fiction.
Rather, they had. Sometimes three lakes flaunted
themselves, sometimes two, or only
one, or none. Not only sands were on the move,

the lake dissolved, moved, reappeared,
will dwindle, again quicken. In remove
a presence, in presence a fact
substantial, insubstantial form
no less? This play with arid words,
dry as lake beds where cloudy midges swarm
until extinguished, the dunes made
to conform to rational order and
rabid, but useful, their surgent pines
established turn to increase wayward sand.

Something we know lost, gained by that.
Then how, best right aberrant nature?
Terms of reference not precise,
you guess, we may not read the same map twice.

*

REFERENCE

On the sheet in front of me on the wall
two sections REFERENCE.

The section on the left has

Roads	Two way One way Unmetalled Track	Bitumen, Concrete or Metal
Railways	Double track Single	
Bridges		Concrete Wooden Suspension Footbridges

with some other things about Main Electric Transmission lines,
Distribution lines, Conventional spacing, Wooden poles and Actual
positions

Pylons   No

463

I am leaving out all the signs for them, you understand? Also, anything to do with telephones, tramways and the distinctions of Principal from Smaller stations.

The section on the right has

Keys to bush, trees, plantations, scrub, scattered scrub, hedge or short row of trees, fence (prominent), swamp, mangrove, drain, sand, shingle, cliffs & terraces, stop bank, rocks, building, church, cemetery, windmill, radio mast, additional clues for trigonometrical stations with permanent signals, spot heights in feet above mean sea level, sketch contours at 100′ intervals, and bits about post and telegraph services. Outside the limits of the code are two other notes, how to recognize a pa, and rock outcrops with large boulders.

Given all that you should be able to operate
within or without prescribed or designated limits.
You may yet have to go to the wall.
How was I ever able to find my way there?

★

HOW TO GET BACK BY MAGNETIC BEARINGS

    True North, now, that is one thing.
    This another, how to get back
    (wherever that was) magnetically drawn
    to harbour. Instruct me, all I ask,
    instruct me how — this *plus*, or lack
    as *minus*, evidently apply — to unmask
    a not altogether dissembling
    map? True, is true of false origin.

TO CONVERT A	TO CONVERT A
MAGNETIC BEARING	GRID BEARING TO A
TO A GRID BEARING	MAGNETIC BEARING
ADD G–M ANGLE	SUBTRACT G–M ANGLE

TO OBTAIN G–M ANGLE
add the Annual Magnetic Change
multiplied by the number of years
since 1965 to the G–M angle for 1965
$1° = 60'$
Annual Magnetic Change $+3'$
G–M Angle for 1965 $16°30'$ for
the Central Grid Line of this sheet

You may not read the same map
twice. On such least point we may agree
without implying more. Or may we? Add or subtract,
something's still to be read as before
contemptuous of cartography
as of art or art's surrogates, its sniffling poor
relations which I ape, thumb at lip
lacking bearing, puerile seen-through act

so you say. As you say.

*

SYMBOLS

I cannot see our land clearly.
It comes and goes because covered with symbols.
Isn't this symptom of a psychotic state?

Take England now. In England I was given
to hold in my hand a necessary guide to
SYMBOLS USED ON THE MAPS, to hold as I was driven.
'O take fast hold' — that's Sidney, in *CS 32.*

Eleven different sections of symbols on one sheet,
twenty of them in one section. Here's from
another:

> Castle or house with interesting interior
> Abbey, priory or other ecclesiastical
>   building (usually in ruins)
> Parish church
> Castle or house in ruins
> Archaeological monument

465

KENDRICK SMITHYMAN

> *Garden (usually attached to private house)*
> *Botanical gardens*
> *Zoological gardens*

but no *Interesting church*. Interesting churches are
in Symbols Used on Town Plans, another section.

Another section, of another life.
Here I am told how to find a *Frontier post*.
I shall go down to the river which may be

demented. I shall go on hoping to cross over.
Perhaps this is a frontier. We have crossed
frontiers before this.

Here is a sheet of paper. Write on it for me.
Go on, write on it. Why do you write *No.*?
What number do you mean?

★

LEGEND

I

this landscape landfall.

II

A map so new you wouldn't read about
it, a loop road which hadn't been built
in hill country behind Tokomaru Bay.
Way forward proved the way back.

Like a one track mind it pressed as far,
died under a mount, a none too significant
mound. So have we all, well truly spent.
Well, there was the mount. On its round

emphatic the bull, who rose to design.
His neck arched, the masculine pouch,
his weapon cooling, out to prove
that way forward is the way back

466

III

where maps may need a change in legend for

IV

this masculine landfall/landscape

and seascape. Together, your un-
certainty in seeing, grit and spray
confronting or bedevilled, those dun
sands drove at berm and cliffs while away
in their distance sea leagues with
the land's league collogued were one,
classically distant. Could you well say
how far in space or time you were astray
from plainjane rivermouth, that plebeian

rivermouth beyond the quarry,
beyond the mundane?
                    On the wall
fronting me I pinned, years ago, a wry
black *toro* from a Spanish bottle
to further esemplastic
legend's proclivity
for becoming and *there* would do as well
as anywhere, near Mahimai's burial
place. As chance worked, it's not very

far from the beach where (December
'69, was it?) the skyline
crests learned how to break with their severe
old puritan habit, its condign
bearing, stood — preliterate,
hieratic — risen clear
above confusion the young bulls in line,
preternaturally clear. They define
and redefine what you perhaps swear

is land that cannot wear myth's host
plausibly, an unlikely stock.
Surveyors missed them running out the coast

467

but legend needs. We are what dreams shock
briefly to become; this you heard
long since. Then where, at cost,
shall we amazed be forced to press the rock
channel deep, final, face him who will lock
and batten on us? Fictive, will most

prove fact? Way forward is way back
baffling to wayward plan or chart,
a maze the end and origin, track
not made good though trick you got by heart
sorely. I speak of the Minotaur
at the heart of us, the black
kruptos, that animates each crafty art?
All pay him tribute, kill him off, and start
to run his course again shiftless, bleak

V

as fallen masculine scape tumbled
headlong. Sprawls, fold on fold. Heaves,
scarred hide. Promise still rides.

South and east they have fire by night
in their skies. Here, to the north a mast,
a television repeater station catches
signals. What sign/signal/symbol for
the Muse? Perhaps

VI

on a hilltop a crossbred Jersey sire.
His progeny champ below, mouse-coloured
in their rat run. He bellows, hefts clods.
They caper excited, I am shit-scared

clinging then to one strand of No. 8
fencing wire the guard rail of a swing
bridge over a creek, just discovered
that several planks ahead are missing.

The bulls come gathering either end and
as well as my pack there's all the camera gear.
He bellows and bullocks. They collect, they dance.
We are offered, in season. In season
not at the dark heart, out in the open

VII

are taken, being promised. *As/Was*
Mahimai and probably Rutherford
(if that was his name) who disappeared
in a cloud of bullshit, who said he spent
ten years of himself back of Tokomaru.

That was the first season I went looking
for Mahimai and Rutherford, sidetracked
into hunting after graveyards' wooden
headboards, their iconography lost style.
About them maps are reticent.

I swung between: a family burial ground,
and the Wesleyans' plot. With those boards
which we cannot read and the grave of
their millenarian teacher, Heke's tohunga
Papahurihia. The vates? They deny

VIII

but we need more to the legend, and for

★

A QUESTION OF SCALE

To bring it all to scale, the given
    is 1:63360, 1 inch to 1 mile,
        and is outmoded.

That, given. Also false origin
    is given as base from which we work, almost capable
        until outmoded.

KENDRICK SMITHYMAN

To bring it to scale I was driven
  or drove headlong, taking whatever a telltale dial
    on an outmoded

dashboard said was nearly true of *Then*
  and *There*, the literal. Metaphor too, and parable
    long since outmoded.

C. K. STEAD

(Born 1932)

from *The Clodian Songbook*

2

Clodia's pigeon pair
              one on egg-guard
the other at large
or roosting above tomatoes
heavy with their siftings —

              she likes the hard peck
they give her fingers

                    she likes their talk
of rolled oats
under the awning.

Ignoring my parallel season
        she ripens in her deck chair
              eating the stained fruit.

I too like that tang on the tongue
                    softness of feather
pain of the sharp peck.

3

That prow drawn up on shingle
                    under willows where the early
                                lake fishermen
                        cast into stream-flow —

put your ear to its heartwood
you'll hear slap of salt
snap of sail

                                rush
of long nights straining under bellying moons
                    northward to Suva.

                              On her side
like the star Cross she lies under
given over to calm and reflection
                         Catullus' yacht
            hot youth of Catullus.

7

            Air New Zealand
                    old friend of Catullus
    you offer a quick hike
                    to Disneyland
                    the South Pole
    Hong Kong's hotspots
    to ease a jealous ache.

        Thanks brother
                    but I'd rather
    you flew downcountry a message to Clodia

Tell her she's known to her 300 loveless lovers
    as the scrum machine.
                    Tell her
        Catullus loves her
    as the lone lawn daisy
                    loves
            the Masport mower.

13

Fucking, I feel at one with the world
Clodia
it's like rowing into heaven.

                Through glass
        the moonlit ferns and pongas
sculpted in the grove of Priapus
                    approve.

            On this coast are white
    wine
                and oysters.

from *Paris*

5

Here's Catherine Deneuve she's walking under klieg lights
against a garish mural brilliant in the deepest bolgia
of the new Les Halles — hesitates, lights cigarette,
walks on. The cameras love her and so do you.
Take her to coffee in your head. Take her to bed.
On the escalators gipsy children have picked your pocket
and in the dingy gendarmerie you hammer out a statement.
Disguised as a spaniel she waits in a nearby café
drinking thé citron and rehearsing her fabulous lines.
Through cloud-cover out of sight the force de frappe is drilling
for the first blue sky when they will drape their jet-trails
at an anniversary over the Arc de Triomphe.
Forever new, Catherine looks up and smiles.
'Fat girls die young,' say the graffiti, 'and that leaves
little old women.' You feel yourself drifting away
over traffic, through the jostle of falling leaves,
above the cold shoulder of a statue staring down whitely
at a girl on a bench in the Luxembourg Gardens weeping
at the thought of Catherine Deneuve. Your name may be Truffaut
but there's no end in sight. This Paris is like a disease.

6

Losing yourself you keep your hold on grammar,
and now by way of crescendo a white dove flies out
of the face of Magritte, or is it by way of diversion?
You have come a long journey to enter the bathroom of Pierre
        Bonnard,
to take to task Picasso in the light of a cubist dawn,
to look through Matisse's windows at the palms of his hands
as they're blown against the blue of a Mediterranean night.
Loneliness has honoured you with a singleness of vision
that admits you to the frame. There is no charge.
The morning is a paradigm of vermouth, cool and dry
and heady as you walk across the Pont Neuf already
making for the end of a story. Paris, take this down:
the sweeper is losing his argument with the breeze,
the leaves are storming the Bastille, a priestly cassock

wants heaven now, this world is climbing and flying;
the thin pale clouds are enacting nineteen-forty
for a silent movie; everything is written on the river
in a foreign language, everything engraved on the sky
with a silver tip. Paris, you ancient sewer,
my spectacles and my shoe-leather embrace your ways.

8

This is where the President of the Republic spends his afternoons.
Here's the street where his motorcade passes. From this dais
he pins on ribbons and medals and kisses wrinkled cheeks.
He's the one who decides whether fish in our southern ocean
should wear water wings or grow two heads.
Sometimes he leans to the left sometimes to the right,
sometimes he's ten feet tall, sometimes he accepts diamonds
but the bombs go off on time. Here's his mistress.
She has two breasts, both of them strangely beautiful
when seen from the south. This is the Rue de la Paix.
Here's the boulevard where workers from the regions march
demanding a bright new numeral for the Republic.
This is the Quai d'Orsay, this the Aerogare des Invalides.
Climb aboard and we'll take you for a picnic in the Bois
where there are no bombs. Paris will never again
suffer the indisposition of the boots of a foreign invader.
Even the army will fight. Be careful of the hard-boiled eggs.
In Le Déjeuner sur l'Herbe of Manet only the lady is naked.
In the eyes of the President are tears for the love of France
while he pours the wine. Nor will the franc be devalued.

10

Now is the night we used to call Symbol of Death
but there's water through branches and lights and stars on
      the water.
Showing at the cinema on the far side of the square
is your movie with Catherine Deneuve — yes already it's made.
She kisses you in a mirror and the cats on the mansard
quote Rimbaud at the moon, which answers in French.
The glass doors open inward, the shutters push out,
and there beyond the balcony railing it runs
the silver ribbon of your thought rebuffed by the light.
Here you can see why Chagall's lovers float up

through branches to join the stars — it's the shortest route
to a high old time and not as difficult as walking.
In the Rue Mazarine your table is waiting in a window.
Will she be there with her neat and busy bush?
Go out among these hands that are pure conjecture.
As wine touches the tongue, as the eyes exchange,
as a voice caresses an uncomprehending ear,
do not neglect to dictate these informal strictures
with all their whims of glass, their glosses on lust,
to the Paris of Paris that's nobody's dream but your own.

Going to Heaven

                    married one
                    fathered three
travelled far
            wrote (say) a round
                            dozen
died and

★

mangroves
moongroves
            salt on a light wind
                            rattling
cabbage trees
blinds
        and on the bland night
broadcast
                    a dog
two moreporks
        a nameless night-shriek
                a million-piece
insect orchestra

★

C. K. STEAD

                          green dark
colourless
green
                and the moon still
                              in water
on water
              in a glass by the bed
shakes at a
ghost-step

★

                    all this sounding
                              silence

nothing changed
                          50 years
turning on itself
in sleep

★

                      such a long way
to come back
was always
                                that
summer
                      even in rain
                        on a sack
stock-still
                              astride
the grey pony
                                above
the brown dam

★

what lays the stone
                                stare
down
                          thunder
            and a bitch of a
                  non-existent

it was the wrath of
            it was the rock
of

Hephzibah! Hephzibah!
Beulah!
                (Moriarty!)

            backward dog

go bite your tail!

*

            and all the time
                    it goes
greening down slopes
            trees a decade taller
                a decade broader

            and yourself
one fuck nearer your last
                rising to look at

            a white cloud's lovely
satisfied/self-satisfied
                        trailing
over its earthly mirrors

*

            along the ridge-top
                    threading
among sky and cloud

(who rode to heaven
on a horse?)
            young 'head-in-air'
astride the grey
pony
                    above
the brown dam

*

477

C. K. STEAD

here are shellpaths
                    bareboards
underfoot
                    and a
breeze from the sea

*

breaks as always
all over
                    another sunday
here is heaven

                    take off your
clothes and
                    lie down

                    prepare for
(again?)

takeoff

After the Wedding

1

After the wedding comparing notes with
Cousin Elspeth and Cousin Caroline
about our childhood bareback riding
on the Kaiwaka farm —

                    How, fallen with your
10-year legs did you get back up
even supposing he stood for you?

Cousin E remembered vaulting from the back
of her pet pig.
                    I used the ruts worn deep
by the cream sledge — stood him in the hollow
and leapt from its edge.

                    Elspeth
and her sister, blonde babies
under the trees I climbed —

                    wooden verandah
hot dry garden sheltered by macrocarpa
dogs panting in shade
                    my face black
from the summer burn-off.

2

In sleep I still trace those tracks
below gum trees
                    skirting the swamp
through bush to that pool of pools
where the small brown fish suspend themselves
in shafts of light.
                    My feet sink
midstream in heaped silt
clouding the flow.

                    Water had cut its way
through black rock greened with moss
down to that glassy stillness overhung
with trees.

            In the rock cleft
a deep hole water-worn and cold and dark —

I caught the eel that lived there
                its sinuous spirit.

3

In recollection summer is forever
renewing itself even in the thickest
leafmould shade.
                    It draws a life
from heat in the ploughed field
where I gathered fossil gum
                    or in the hayfield

or in sunlight above the flame
above the dam.

       Cousin Elspeth, Cousin Caroline
cantered bareback
             fell
(years after me) from the same horse.

4

Weddings are full of God and the word of God
and the word God. I wonder what they mean.
To be one with your body, your body one with the world —
more than a marriage, it's a consummation

bracken and oil-flame like red cellophane
flapping on the hill-slope
            Eden
won't ask you back, you must make your way
in dreams, by moonlight, or by the broad light of day.

5

There was another stream, a creek
on the far side of the road
where the old house had been.
       It ran through reeds
silent.

The moons repeat themselves
the moreporks retort
the eel and its sibilants
are fluent

    an old chimney stands.

6

It's not what the landscape says
but the way it's said which is a
richness of saying, even of the thing
said —

        that finely articulated slope
a few words at the water

the breathy manuka and the precise
pernickety ti tree

        a long last sentence of cloud
struck out by the dark.

After the wedding
I lie in darkness
I see something that might be myself
        step out for a moment.

It makes the moon
look at itself in water
        it makes the stars
gaze.
      It hears a nightbird and something
            that rustles
in reeds.

It sees itself called
        to light up a silent
vast
        beautiful
                    indifferent
waste —

mirror to the mystery
mirrored.

7

Break it
        (the mirror)

the Supreme Intelligence
is always silent
                  and death will come
in the guise of just this stillness

or another

        but that was always the case.

8

'Marriages are made in Heaven'
                  — not so.

We marry to be nearer the earth
cousins of the fur and stalk
           talking together

that brown water reflecting
those green hills.

JOHN POUTU TE RANGI STIRLING

(Born 1922; Te Whānau-ā-Apanui, Ngāi Tahu)

Kua Whiua

Kua whiua atu ki te rangi
Kī mai hoki he tangata ora
Ki te ao mārama e

Ka tutuki ngā kapua o te rangi
Te taha o tēnei Apakura
Hei whakamārama i te ao

Hikitia rā e te iwi
Tōu mana
Ki runga rawa, kia kore ai
E tūkinotia

Pupuritia mai rā te aroha
Te kupenga o te oranga
Kei kōnei rā te wairua

Urutomotia te whare nei
O ngā taonga kua hoki mai
Karakiatia, kōrerotia, e te iwi
Mihitia, tangihia, taukiri e.

I Have Sent

I have sent up to the heavens
because the living say
there's a bright light.

The clouds meet above
near Apakura, the lament
to enlighten the world.

People, raise
your mana
up high so that
it may not be destroyed.

Cleave to love,
the net of well-being
where lies the spirit.

Enter this house
of the treasures that have returned.
Bless and talk about them, people,
greet them, mourn for them, taukiri e.

Translation by Te Aomuhurangi Temamaka Jones

Ka Pā tō Hoe

Ka pā tō hoe
Tērā te haeata takiri
Ana mai ki runga o Aoraki

Uia mai ko wai
Te waka ko Takitimu
Uia mai ko wai te iwi
Ko Kāi Tahu e

Takenga o Aoraki
Ko Tahu Pōtiki
Te tipuna nāna nei
I toha ki Te Waipounamu

Haere mai
Te manuhiri tūārangi
Uia mai ko wai te iwi
Ko Kāi Tahu e

E karanga, e karanga atu nei
Haere mai.

The Oar Strikes

The oar strikes
Alas! There's a gleam of light
on Aoraki.

Ask me who is the canoe?
It is Takitimu.
Ask me who are the people?
It is Kai Tahu.

Tahu Potiki,
chief of Aoraki,
is the ancestor who spread the seed
all over Te Waipounamu.

Welcome
distinguished guest.
Ask me who are the home people?
It is Kai Tahu,

Calling, welcome, welcome to you,
Welcome.

Translation by Te Aomuhurangi Temamaka Jones

HORI TAIT

(Born 1923–81; Tūhoe, Te Arawa)

He Koha Kī

E tā e taku mokopuna
Te mana whakaheke o ō tūpuna
Homai ō taringa kia ngaua ehau
Mai kore e tau te whakaaro nui ki a koe
I hangaia mai koe i te wāhi ngaro
E te mea ngaro
Nō reira ō titiro ō whakarongo
Ō whai kī
Me pupū ake i te wāhi ngaro
Arā i tō ngākau

E tā whakatipuhia tō mana
I runga i tō mana whakaheke
Me aro koe ki te hā o te tangata
Hangaia te tangata i tāna i kī ai
I tāna i pai ai
Whāngaihia kia ora te tinana
Kia ora te wairua
Kia noho tahi ai i runga i te rangimarie
Whakauhia ki te kākahu mahana
Ki te whakaaro nui

E taku mōkai he wā poto noa koe
I waenganui i te wā kua hipa
Ki te wā kei te tū mai
Nō reira kia tere te whakarata
I tō ngākau ki ngā āhuatanga
O tōu nei wā
Haere, whāia te mātauranga
O te Pākehā kaingarawahia
Hai kīnaki i tō kai tūturu
Ko tō kai tūturu ko te mātauranga o ō tūpuna

E hika mahia ngā mahi kia rite
Tōna whānui·ki tō te whenua
Kia tika ai hoki ko tō taumata
Ehara he koha kī nā taku kuia
Tēnei te tangi ake ki a koutou e

A Gift of Words from my Grandmother

My beloved grandchild,
inheritor from my ancestors,
left me speak in your ear
in the hope you may be inspired
you were created by the unseen,
yes, by the unseen,
therefore what you see and hear,
what you say —
let them well from the unseen,
your inner being.

My child, base your mana
on the mana handed down to you.
Pay heed to the dignity of people,
people made in His image,
His excellent image.
Care for them in body,
care for them in spirit,
so that body and spirit will be in harmony.
Wrap them in the warm cloak of wisdom.

My child, you are only a moment
between two eternities — past and future,
so hasten, and come to terms
with the circumstances
of your time.
Seek the knowledge of the Pakeha,
consume it
as an appetiser for your true course
which is the wisdom of your ancestors.

HORI TAIT

Let your deeds be
as wide as the earth
to justify a place in the sky.
A gift of words indeed, grandmother —
I weep for you and for you all.

Translation by Hori Tait

BRIAN TURNER

(Born 1944)

Jack Trout

I drive the rod tip forward
and the tapered line uncoils
and stretches on the clear
lumpy water
where it rushes between weed
and yellow leaf-lagged rocks
out from a line of weeping willows.

The fly, a slim caddis imitation,
pricks the water, (the nylon trace
like a murmur of film
across a bleary eye),
as my staring eyes
strain to follow its jiggling course
downstream towards me.

There it is, mite-small,
and there, bending after it,
the pale shape of curious trout.
I draw breath, tense, wait
for the flash of white
from the corner of the mouth,
the jump or flick of nylon
and . . . *now*, I strike.

The fish sheers in panic, turns,
but the hook is set. We are
strung together in a fatal bond.
The surface scutter says
I do not have him yet,
that he is far from spent,
his red yellow brown black and white splendour
still belonging in the river.

The rod tip is pulled hard down,
his tail thwacks the water
as he flexes and coils,
strives to rub out the hook
on a flake of rock, or roll
the trace around him
and snap it with a manic shrug
of his shoulders.

He begins to flounder near the surface.
Through the shocking murk
of pain the slow heave of his breathing
deflates me. For a moment
I hope the line will part
so he can return
to flick and suck and idle
in the ripple I dragged him from.

But no, I draw him slowly
through shallows thick
with a puky-green slime
and toe him carefully ashore.
There is gravel in my boots,
in my chest, as I hit him twice
behind the eyes, once to
decide his fate, and once
for mercy's sake.

Coming Home

Coming home late through the smoky
fuzz of late autumn, winter rackety
on the elbows of birch trees,
a storm of finches pecking an apple.

I feel some things are never
lost in the conspiracy of evening,
the garnered and gathered
puddling silences of chill air.

490

I find you, wet hair glistering,
lying in a bath of foam, so I soap
your back, my hands revived
by your smooth skin, its perfect slither,

and then I go in my dubious mind
to stand in the damp and addling
dark beside the beetle-browed barn
and wait for tribulation to pass, music to begin.

Nichita Stanescu

You say you 'live inside a full-stop'
even though you hate them
and much prefer to 'whistle up the moon'.
'A single great life' seethes
in your tired, wrought
Romanian's face.
                    The hurt we inflict
upon animals and trees haunts you,
is raw as wind accompanying rain.
Nothing is pure enough
to cleanse centuries of infection.

A moon rises white
and floats like a full-stop.
The light is as clear
as the tears that flood your eyes,
wet your stubbled cheeks.

Each life is a 'great life',
but some are greater than others.

BRIAN TURNER

Listening to the Mountain

for Peter and Phil

The clouds lift off Flagstaff
relaxing in the sun
while the city gets on with dispensable business.

The cumulus jostle but not in earnest
and nor is the wind, teasing the sky's scalp
and ruffling the skin of the harbour.

Each day the sun's hauled further west
so there's no question
it's spring.

Late, the sun begins to shine
as cloud abdicates, and late
the spirit lifts, at last.

At a different magical time every day
the mountain comes into view
and frowns or shimmers.

The line of the ridge
dips then lifts and runs off
into the blue distance.

Sometimes I imagine the mountain
is sleeping in the sunshine,
sometimes I think I am dreaming

the mountain is dreaming
of places it will never get to see,
and sometimes I feel the mountain

knows what I am thinking
as it lies there smiling
and looking down on the city

and the thriving sea, and all
that I shall ever stand for
grows benignly like a mountain in me.

The blue burns and the mountains
turn blue and the streams
from the blue mountains flash wickedly.

Blue light clashes with white light
above where the rolling hills
are tanned and blistered beneath the sun.

A million tolerant stars or more
and one buxom full moon
look down upon the still dark waters of the pond.

Whatever I was thinking when the cirrus
touched the tops of the mountains
left me wondering where to go from there.

If we listen long enough
the mountain wind sifting through the tussock
will bring the music of water leaping from stone to stone.

The lark, so high it's but a speck
in the blue, sings a song to remember
when you feel despair.

Celmisia have no voice
except to sing of the flowers
that are not here.

The mountains know that many people
have lain among them and listened
to the yearnings that reverberate

from age to age, between the races
and shiver like fire and water, and shake
like stone among the creatures of the world.

BRIAN TURNER

The river issues from the mountain and gathers confidence.
It has the assurance of one who knows
that it will return to where it belongs.

___

The birds are so curious
they could be our friends.
Only the mountains know

where they have come from
and where they are going
and what will happen when we are gone.

High Noon

To approach the river
first we must cross a field
of hot stones.

They sit and swelter
like peasants
in grey overcoats,

their rounded backs
bearing the indiscriminate
weight of air.

I step between them
not wishing to be a burden,
not wanting to trip on others' care.

At the river's edge
I kneel, then wade in.
The water pushes into my mouth,

a thickening tongue.

Blind Child and the Moon

My family, I hear them speak
    of the weird sight of a daylight moon
        using words like ghostly,
ethereal, unearthly,

            and I have heard them
shout and say that
        the moon is huge and bright
            and fills the sky
with orange and yellow light,

            and their voices
convey delight and wonder
        at what they have seen: my father
            says it is magisterial
and very beautiful.

        To me their words
are like waves of music
        breaking in my heart
            yet what can I really
know of the source of these things?

            I have stood
on a hillside at night
        and held my parents' hands
            and tried to imagine
what it is that excites them so.

            In my ignorance
I say it is whatever I choose
        to imagine it to be, and,
            what I see depends upon how I feel
about the dark moon risen in my head.

HONE TUWHARE

(Born 1922; Ngā Puhi, Ngāti Korokoro, Ngāti Tautahi,
Te Popote, Uri-o-Hau))

Snowfall

It didn't make a grand entrance and I nearly
missed it — tip-toeing up on me as it did
when I was half asleep and suddenly, they're there
before my eyes — white pointillist flakes
on a Hotere canvas — swirling about on untethered

gusts of air and spreading thin uneven
thicknesses of white snow-cover on drooping
ti-kouka leaves, rata, a lonely kauri, pear
and beech tree. Came without hesitation
right inside my opened window licking my neck,

my arms, my nose as I leaned far out to embrace
a phantom sky above the house-tops
and over the sea: 'Hey, where's the horizon?
I shall require a boat you know — two strong arms?'
. . . and snow, kissing and lipping my face

gently, mushily, like a pet whale,
of (if you prefer) a shark with red bite — sleet
sting hot as ice. Well,
it's stopped now. Stunning sight. Unnerved,
the birds have stopped singing,

tucking their beaks under warm armpits: temporarily.
And for miles upon whitened miles around,
there is no immediate or discernible movement,
except from me, transfixed, and moved by an interior
agitation — an armless man applauding.

'Bravo,' I whisper. 'Bravissimo.' Standing ovation.
Why not . . . Oh, come in, Spring.

A Talk with My Cousin, Alone

And afterwards, after the shedding of mucus, the droll
  speeches and the hongi for my cousin in the box,
  we were called to meal at the long tables.
  But I hadn't come for that.

I could hear the Tasman combers shredding themselves
  nearby, wishing then for a cawing beak of sound
  to help me reassemble myself. Taking my shoes off,
  I trudged a steep dune; sand, a cool silken lisp
  spilling through my toes.

Bottomed on a hill of sand, I wondered wry dry leaves
  whether the pakeha marine authorities would sell
  us back ephemeral Maori land (now exposed to bird,
  bleached crab and shrimp) lying somewhere between
  low water mark and high.

A pounding gavel is the sun today — a brassy auctioneer:
  the sea, his first assistant. Of this, no instant
  favour offered me in stint. I cushion my elbows
  deeper in sand. I'm the only bidder.
  For this beautiful piece of land/sea-scape, I will
  start the bidding at twenty Falling Axes per square
  centimetre, said the sun looking hard at me for an
  ear-lobe twitch, or, other sign.
  Get stuffed, I reply, holding my middle finger
  straight up — and turning it. Slowly.

Idly I think, that after the eleven o'clock prayers
  tomorrow (and before lunch) my cousin will have
  gone to ground.
  'They may ban *tangihangas* in the future,' I say
  to him. 'Right now you're doing your job. This
  moment is forever as the splayed fingers of the hand
  drawn together, like a fist.' I look up at the sun
  and blink. The sun is beside itself, dancing. There
  are two of them.

HONE TUWHARE

A Song in Praise of a Favourite Humming-Top

I polish your skin. It is that of a woman
mellowed by the oil of the tarata,
humming-top. What stable secret do you

keep locked up in movement, humming-top?
skipping away daintily as you do, sidewise
lurching, nonchalantly coming erect?

Your drowsy sighs lull and beguile the people
the many who've come to hear your talk,
your whizz your buzz your angry bee-stung

murmurs — which are simply about nothing
at all. Ah, see: they're closing in —
stopping just short of whip range.

Eyeballs plopping like bird's eggs sucked
deep into your whirlpool, they're surging
forward again treading on each others' feet.

Lips stretched tightly over teeth, they grin:
find throat at last to shout; exclaim.
O, they will leave finally, when they've

finished fondling you, cooing over you like
a kukupa. I don't like it: each one of them
a thief's heart gladdened — but covetous.

This poem developed from a 'Spell for a wooden humming-top cut out and fashioned
from a totara; matai. Woods which alone hum and whine beautifully.' Author unknown.
Text in Edward Shortland's Maori Manuscript Notebook 2(b) (MS2) page 73. Hocken Library,
University of Otago, Dunedin.

Study in Black and White

A friend rang me last week as soon as he got
back from the Antarctic. Wonderful wonderful:
he seemed genuinely pleased to find me in
but in a careful voice asked if I could look
after something for him. I know,
you've brought back a lump of coal, I said.

I have a King Penguin in my fridge.
I look in on it every day as it stands there
with a huge egg between its feet, waiting . . .
Stolid, taciturn, it shares the fish with the
cat, the raw minced meat with me.
It stands there with its head absolutely still.
Only its eyes follow me when they are not
already glazed in sleep: I've grown fond of it.

And I'm not the only one.
In this house people come together mainly to
say true and surprising things about each other.
The light-hearted irreverent ones unhappily
have turned particularly grave; frequently
begging me to open the fridge door.
Wonderful, they chant, stroking it: truly wonderful.
I hate it when they go on like that.
Any moment now I'm afraid, they will deify it.

I should ring my friend
to ask if there is a ship or plane leaving soon
for the Antarctic: because I really think
King Penguin would be happier standing shoulder to
shoulder with his Royal brothers, each with an egg
at its feet, their backs to the wind and driven
snow, waiting:
for the F.A. Cup winners with the colourful jerseys
red noses, flapping arms, to trot on to the
snow-field in single file.

King Penguins should all kick off then and watch the visitors
really break up in a beautiful shower of soaring
eggshells and baby penguins wonderful wonderful.

HONE TUWHARE

A Fall of Rain at Mitimiti: Hokianga

Drifting on the wind, and through
the broken window of the long house
where you lie, incantatory chant
of surf breaking, and the Mass
and the mountain talking.

At your feet two candles puff the
stained faces of the whanau, the vigil
of the bright madonna. See, sand-whipped
the toy church does not flinch.

E moe, e te whaea: wahine rangimarie

Mountain, why do you loom over us like
that, hands on massive hips? Simply
by hooking your finger to the sea,
rain-squalls swoop like a hawk, suddenly.
Illumined speeches darken, fade to metallic
drum-taps on the roof.

Anei nga roimata o Rangipapa.

Flat, incomprehensible faces: lips moving
only to oratorical rhythms of the rain:

quiet please, I can't hear the words.
And the rain steadying: black sky leaning
against the long house. Sand, wind-sifted
eddying lazily across the beach.

And to a dark song lulling: *e te whaea, sleep.*

Tangi-hanga

Rest, Matiu. Lie easy
My voice grown tall has found legs

I sense your apprehension: know
that your canoe teeters
on inconclusive reefs of argument

I will beach your canoe
For I am your mother's kin
and she is my sister who before her
death wished only that her body
be returned to her people and lands
to the south: rest easy

I too have listened to the interminable
noise: an abomination of mock-lily
concern: my buttocks numbed beyond care
or art by arrogant speeches of welcome

Though my words to you are gentle
my brow is lined and crossed with anger

Northern blood of Matiu
hear me without preliminary
Your loud-mouthed declamations resolve
nothing

Observe: his ears are red and stuffed
sore with your bickerings
Together you've blinked the owls to sleep
the sea to embarrassed mutterings
A turd upon you all. On your collective
ignorance may the cunt of Hine-nui-te-po
squint a baleful eyeball before pissing

Agh! My thoughts gather in my mouth
like soured spittle: I claim Matiu

HONE TUWHARE

For tomorrow before the sun at noon can cast
fresh shadows on the road we shall have
shaken the dust from this place: this place
where more value is placed on the material
substance he leaves behind than the memory
of his pulse and heart for men.

It is finished: I turn away

Lament

In that strident summer of battle
    when cannon grape and ball
    tore down the pointed walls
    and women snarled as men
    and blood boiled in the eyes:
    in the proud winter of defeat
    he stood unweary
    and a god among men.

He it was whom death looked hotly on
    whilst I in adoration
    brought timid fuel to his fire:
    of all things manly he partook

Yet did it plummet down like a bird
    engulfing him as he headlong
    rushed towards the night,
    the long night
    where no dawn wakes to pale
    the quaking stars: farewell

Farewell companion of laughter and light
    who warmed the nights with the
    croaking chants of olden times: hear
    me now sing poorly sing harshly . . .

At dawn's light I looked for you
    at the land's end where two oceans froth
    but you had gone without leaving a sign
    or a whispered message to the gnarled
    tree's feet or the grass or the inscrutable
    rock face. Even the innocent day-dreaming
    moon could not explain the wind's wry mirth.

To you it seems I am nothing —
    a nobody and of little worth
    whom the disdainful years
    neither praise nor decry
    but shall abandon to fat
    and the vast delight of worms: farewell

Farewell farewell
    Let the heavens mumble and stutter
    Let them acknowledge your leaving us
    Mine is the lone gull's cry in the night
    Let my grief hide the moon's face
    Let alien gods salute thee and
    with flashing knives cut open
    the dark belly of the sky.

I feel rain spit in my face.

I bear no malice, let none stain my valedictions
For I am at one with the wind
the clouds' heave and the slapping rain
the tattered sky the wild solitude
of the sea and the streaming earth
which I kneel to kiss. . . .

This poem was suggested by a tangi in Sir George Grey's *Nga Moteatea.*

HONE TUWHARE

On a Theme by Hone Taiapa

Tell me poet, what happens to my chips
after I have adzed our ancestors
out of wood?

What happens to your waste-words, poet?
Do they limp to heaven, or go down easy
to Raro-henga?

And what about my chips, when they're
down — and out? If I put them to fire
do I die with them?

Is that my soul's spark spiralling; lost
to the cold night air? Agh, let me die
another hundred times: eyeball

to eyeball I share bad breath
with the flared nostrils of the night.
For it's not me I leave behind: not me.

Only the vanities of people:
their pleasure, their wonder and awe
alone remain.

Bite on this hard, poet: and walk careful.
Fragmented, my soul lies here, there: in
the waste-wood, around.

Dear Cousin

Some day soon old friend, before either
of us can throw our hand in, I'll say
to you: come.

Then, I'd roll out my threadbare whaariki
— to help you remember to take your boots
off — spread an old newspaper on the floor

and on it place a steaming pot of puha,
kamokamo, riwai, brisket-on-the-bone and
dumplings what we call: doughboys.

For sweeteners, I'd produce another pot
of boiled fish-heads with onions, cracking
open the heads afterwards for the succulent

eyes and the brains: that will be a special
treat, because we're both brainy buggers.
Then — because I know that you are also

a devout man — deeper than any prayer can
grab you — I would say simply: go for it.
And we'd crack a bottle or three together

you and me, swap lies and sing: happy days
are here again.
We would never hurt ourselves because we

wouldn't have far to bump our heads sitting
on the floor where only a small effort
is needed to roll over, rise on one knee

stand up — go out and wring your best friend's
neck. What do you reckon, Cous?

TE KURU-O-TE-MARAMA WAAKA

(Born 1914; Te Arawa)

He Pātere mō te Hū o Tarawera

Ka whāia e ahau te rere a taku manu
He rere whakatakariri ki te mahi a te tangata
Hurihuri kau ana i te mea e pā mai nei
E kore hoki a taea te pēwhea!

Tīmata mai ana i te tihi o Te Wāhanga, tāwera te paoa
Whakawhiti ki Ruawāhia, ki Tarawera
Whāia ake ana e te ahi e te toka
Ka kanapa te uira ka tangi te whatitiri
Ohorere ana ia ko Te Whakatopehanga, ki Rotomahana
I ngā māhanga whakahirahira nei
Te Tarata Otūkapuarangi
Kānapanapa ana roto o te atarau
Kore rawa ake nei e kitea e te tangata e

Whāia tonu ana ka hū te moana
Ka rere taku manu tītahataha ana i te tihi o Te Kumete
Kia mātai tonu ki Te Hape o Te Toroa
Koia nei te tirohanga iho nei
Ki te wai kenekene, ki te wai uriuri
Ki Okaro nei te mutunga o te riri
Tau tonu atu ana ki te tihi o Kakaramea
Kua oti nei te mea i rerea mai ai, e taku manu e!

Ka titiro whakamuri taku manu ki te whiu o te whenua o
     te tangata
Mārakerake ana mamaoa pungarehu te ngaronga o te iwi
Ko Ngāti Taoi ka moe tahi mai me Rangitihi
Wareware noa ake te riri o Paerau ki a Rangiheuea
Kātahi taku manu ka titiro roimata koroingo noa ana
Kua ngaro Te Ariki, kua ngaro Moura
Te tūnga whakahī o Moko te patunga a Te Tai Tokerau
Hāpai ake ana te titiro a te manu
Kei raro ngā ngaru whakapukepuke ana

506

Ākina ki te one i Punaromia
Te ūnga waka nei o Tūhourangi
Ko ahau te morehu
Kua ara mai nei
E koko ia e ara e . . .

A Patere for the Eruption of Tarawera

I follow the flight of my bird
a flight path of anger because of the deeds of man.
Circling in bewilderment at what is about to happen,
yet knowing the inevitability of fate.

It commences from the peak of Te Wahanga in a hanging pall
    of smoke.
From there it flits to Ruawahia, to Tarawera
closely followed by fire and brimstone.
Lightning flashes and thunder roars
startling my bird as it swoops down to Rotomahana,
to the beautiful Twins
of the White and Pink Terraces, Te Tarata Otukapuarangi,
glistening in the moonlight.
These sights that will never again be seen.

My bird flies along the boiling lake
zigzagging as it banks over the peak of Te Kumete.
To gaze upon the Hape o Te Toroa
where it sights
black waters dark and ominous.
Then finally to Okaro where the holocaust ceases
and my bird comes to rest on the summit of Kakaramea.
Because the reason for its flight is ended.

My bird looks back at the vengeance against earth and people.
Desolate under steam and ashes where now lie my people,
Ngati Taoi and Ngati Rangitihi side by side.
All enmity between Paerau and Te Rangiheuea forgotten.
My bird looks with tearful eyes as it whimpers in the dawn.
Te Ariki is lost and Moura also,
the foothold of Mokonuiarangi the victim of Te Tai Tokerau.

TE KURU-O-TE-MARAMA WAAKA

My bird lifts its gaze
while tossing waves crash against Punaromia,
landing place of Tuhourangi,
of which I am the survivor
standing proud before you
woe is me.

Translation by Te Kuru-o-te-marama Waaka

TANIWHA WARU

(Died 1988; Ngāti Rāhiri, Waiotama)

Ngā Roimata

Ranginui nōu ngā roimata
Te Ihorangi nāu te ua
Uanui, uaroa, uanganga, uawhatu
Maringi te wai kī pai te moana
Maringi te wai kī pai ngā roto
Kī pai ngā awa kī pai ngā manga
Te wai-ā-tea me te waimatua
Waiora, waitapu, waiinu, wairere
Tukua kia rere tukua kia maringi
Rite ki te wai i morimori i au
I roto i te kōpū o taku whaea e.

Tears

Sky Father, it was your tears.
Te Ihorangi, it was your rain,
great rain, extensive rain, hailstorm, fierce rain
that released water to fill the ocean,
that poured down water to fill the lakes
that filled the rivers that filled the streams.
The engulfing waters of the seas, the unpolluted water,
life giving water, sacred water, drinking water, rushing water
let it flow. Let it fall where it may —
like the waters that envelop me
within my mother's womb.

(Composed for Expo 1988.)

Translation by Taniwha Waru

IAN WEDDE

(Born 1946)

Driving into the Storm: The Art of Poetry

The music leads you out
        into a uniform evening landscape
    with a wide shining blue-
              grey body of water
                    dark smoky mountains
in the distance:
              a pale mantle, breath of its
thousands, reveals the city
                 at the far side of the water:
        close up
the white cotton-head dry flowers
            of Old-Man's Beard clematis —
the music takes you out into
            all this — the music plays
      from some radio
             in some house
behind you up the hillside —
                some 'semi-classical'
trash. Next
        it's the
flatness of the landscape fools you, so that
when you first see the mountains
           they seem
        impossible obstacles, until you begin to ascend
when you realize they're lifting you up
into the rainy architecture of the storm.

                All language is a place, all
        landscapes
      mean something. In the back seat
one passenger is taping up his knuckles.
A less violent carload of travellers would be hard
        to find, but we too
            have places we arrive at

and sometimes we can't
drive through.
      We have to
    stop, we must let the hidden meanings
out. The confrontations that may hurt us
into original thought.

            If you've been everywhere
this was worth waiting for. If you've been nowhere, this
feels like everywhere, your free brochure
'How To Get Lost & Found In New Zealand'
           where you stop for lunch at a
'tavern' that plunks you into Europe
      till you get the bill. $8. *For two!* Where you
             travel through farmland, 'cattle
  ranches' and
'meadows' full of sheep.
            If you believe this
      you're really
nowhere, the language sees to that
whereas somewhere
          you're still driving
into storms the mountains are about
to hurl down upon the nowhere brochure
imported trees and washbrick haciendas.
          Places the earth's crust is so thin
you may even meet the natives
       and be unable to resist buying their wares.

         The back-seat passengers are checking their
             helmets and groin guards
and some kind of ignorant fear
    has begun to enter the trip
the way a conclusion can bleed back toward you
through a narrative.
      The confrontations where
      you stop driving, you get out and stand
under hard rain and feel
storm waters burst through
      the rotten barricades

of your heart. You're up there
                              you can see
where you come from.
                        André Kostelanetz
playing footlight favourites
will not save you now
though not much art can manage such
                    immaculate conjunctions, the uniform blue-
grey vista
                awaiting your recognition
        back then, that
trashy muzak

14/8/81

The Relocation of Railway Hut 49

1

Yet why shouldn't I aim with 'tender'
the best stories begin
'you're not going to believe this but'
I'm still just a taut sailor
on shore leave in life
(time to get back in the tender)

like my tempest tossed great grandfather before me
'Tend to th' master's whistle'
two white doves flirt by the water
Heinrich Augustus and Maria Van Reepen
Barnacle Bill and the Scandinavian Princess
I couldn't either live away from
how light stirs in the surface
(time to attend to the water)

sounds bound once in the braids and weeds of seas
or how the waves wash my spring head in sun
fishscales glittering on my dead father's arms
through how many lives' gentle propulsion

his sea man ship escorted me here
(pit ease sake against sea men)

and you can see
how the pitted concrete face of the city
begins to show the short history
of an early disenchantment
(certain material securities have not stood up)

drown the books
let purpose buckle against something of no substance
the rainbows that fall into our open mouths
our legal tender of breath
(here's just a pet food kingdom)

and the kids in Fun City
aren't going to walk in one day and say
'Enough Space Invaders, it's the revolution'
(it's just a dog food factory)

it's the first few ships
Cooked Breakfast, *Bad Karma* and *Gaga in Toto*
stirring light into the water
whatever acids history serves us to fling
that I can't live away from
(imaginary mountains won't budge either)

just heave to live ear
listen see man pen meander
the moon drips light through my roof
wind croons in my ear
wherever I am there's no where to go
(chance is just another iron butterfly)

2

And you easy mark for the sick
vertigo of underemployed responsibility
better look out!
Know where to go!

IAN WEDDE

Is the light fading
will the Cruise Ship ram the atoll
how do you read your musical watch in the dark
and what happens next?

Way out west among black iron dunes
contenders are shooting up katipo venom —
now *there's* nationalism for you!

Heinrich Augustus sailed through
the Dangerous Archipelago
beneath unfamiliar stars —
hanged if he was born to drown
on an acre of barren ground.
No vertigo.

Mid ocean reek of reef
mermaid's braids uncharted smell of weed
stellar sound of grief's wreck
passion's gentle helm

'Must our mouths be cold?'

3

Nose to tail in the pool
the swimmers turning and turning

I enter the tainted bowl of my affections
my chemical chalice
eyes grape pulped by chlorine

Through how many lives' genital propulsion
his sea man's tender helm engendered
to end here to prosper

This line I heave to Heinrich Augustus
This mouth I warm for him

4

As ship rig pilot to this harbour
that the craft not founder
as reef and bar tender I sköl him
founder of my line

Disenchantment and an end of meandering
here he found her
by sea man's nurture to tend her
his delicate dove by the wind's waves

shoving moonlight up the bay
outside the door of 49
the fast clouds roar
their shadow steers the sea

I tendered for the relocation of hut 49
single men's quarters
Thorndon Quay Railway Yards
you're not going to believe this but
$50 and got it.

5

Outside the door of 49
will be a slender almond tree
pohutukawas will scratch the panes

Past all realism the pet food kingdoms
green ache of barren drowned
broken knowledge of disenchanter's art
grave few whirled

The nearby smokehouse leaking mists:
eels, trout, chicken
49 dim in smoke and autumn dusk
the delicate almond whirling its leaves

Ships tended for weather tides turn
keeping tides to leeward of their pick
and 49's the bower I line on
while everything under the moon swings

IAN WEDDE

Heart's vanity to prosper
brave new pastoral acre
in tended 49 my praise
pilots the smoky light through pain.

6 *der Fischer*
Hanging today the glass door in 49
Heinrich Augustus born in 1840
balance and an easy swing out
spliced his own tackle with a sewing needle
light casting its lures in
fouled the line and plunged in after it
sound of rain squall on the pane
double pneumonia in Blenheim in 1916
jammed any door I ever tried to hang
appropriate death for an old sea man
balance and illumination I can't do it
only thing missing was salt in the water
tomorrow, windows

7

Disenchanted city of few lights and less music
stand by pilot for ship rig
these clear stars of an Indian summer
one border your breath won't passport
harbour night watch man later
here in the dark no man's land
you draw breath like credit
how long can that last?

Steered clear of the army
ran to sea at fourteen and never been home
tending the tension right on pension night
schnapps intoning enlightenment
how much equity left in your barren domes
or hope in your heart pumping its orders?

My glittering dead father now
watch man pilot in his own death ship
remembered Heinrich's lone order and schnapps

'above all I respect his memory'
and all unnoticed by those armies
camped among their dazzling constellations.

Unnoticed Heinrich intoning Goethe
light entertainment
between their watch towers
the wasteful panting of your lover's breath
Hello goodbye I'm here I'm gone hello.

8

By the brave sail to prosper
on the strange sixth hour down under
drinking the new autumn air before me
amazing kitchenettes all sun set kissed
discover the world lovers at play
past all real ache men trod.

Spitting seeds from hut 49
orange's sweet cold cramps
sun kissed and tempest tossed
my little residence my making sense
the only conclusions ever reached
just heave to live here.

Barbary Coast

When the people emerge from the water
who can tell if it's brine or tears
that streams from them, purple sea
or the bruises of their long immersion.

They seem to weep for the dreams they had
which now the light slices into buildings
of blinding concrete along the Corniche.
Is it music or news the dark windows utter?

IAN WEDDE

Day-long dazzle of the shallows
and at night the moon trails her tipsy sleeves
past the windows of raffish diners.
The hectic brake-lights of lovers

jam the streets. My place or your place.
They lose the way again and again.
At dawn the birds leave the trees in clouds,
they petition the city for its crumbs.

The diners are cheap and the food is bad
but you'd sail a long way to find anything
as convenient. Pretty soon, sailor boy,
you'll lose your bearings on language.

Language with no tongue
to lash it to the teller.
Stern-slither of dogfish guttings.
Sinbad's sail swaying in the desert.

Only those given words can say what they want.
Out there the velvet lady runs her tongue
over them. And she is queen of the night —
her shadow flutters in the alleys.

And young sailors, speechless, lean
on the taffrail. They gaze at the queen's amber
but see simple lamps their girls hang in sash windows.
Thud of drums. Beach-fires. Salt wind in the ratlines.

Takes more than one nice green kawakawa
leaf, chewed, to freshen the mouth
that's kissed the wooden lips of the figurehead
above history's cut-water

in the barbarous isles'
virgin harbours. That hulk shunned by rats
bursts into flames.
And now the smoky lattice of spars

casts upon the beach
the shadow-grid of your enlightened city.
And now I reach through them — I reach
through the eyes of dreaming sailors,

faces inches from the sweating bulkheads,
blankets drenched in brine and sperm.
Trailing blood across the moon's wake
the ship bore out of Boka Bay.

Trailing sharks, she sailed
for Port Destruction. In Saint Van le Mar,
Jamaica, Bligh's breadfruit trees grew tall.
In Callao on the coast of Peru

geraniums bloomed like sores
against whitewashed walls.
The dock tarts' parrots jabbering
cut-rates in six tongues.

The eroding heartland, inland cordillera
flashing with snow — these the voyager forgets.
His briny eyes
flood with chimerical horizons.

'I would tell you, if I could — if I could
remember, I would tell you.
All around us the horizons
are turning air into water

and I can't remember
where the silence ended and speech began,
where vision ended and tears began.
All our promises vanish into thin air.

What I remember are the beaches of that city
whose golden children dance
on broken glass. I remember cold beer
trickling between her breasts as she drank.

IAN WEDDE

But my paper money burned
when she touched it. The ship
clanked up to its bower, the glass towers
of the city burned back there in the sunset glow.'

Cool star foundering in the west.
Coast the dusty colour of lions.
The story navigates by vectors
whose only connection is the story.

The story is told in words
whose only language is the story.
All night the fo'c'sle lamp smokes above the words.
All day the sun counts the hours of the story.

Heave of dark water where something
else turns — the castaway's tongue
clappers like a mission bell.
Unheard his end, and the story's.

Raconteurs in smoky dives
recall his phosphorescent arm
waving in the ship's wake.
Almost gaily. The ship sailed on.

NGAPO WEHI

(Born 1934; Whakatōhea, Tuhoe, Te Whānau-ā-Apanui, Ngā Puhi)

I Te Tīmatanga

I te tīmatanga
Ko te Pō nui
Ko Te Pō roa
Ko Te Pō tangotango

Auē!

I te tīmatanga
Ko Te Pō nui
Ko Te Pō roa
Ko Te Pō tangotango

I tīmata mai Te Ao
I roto i Te Pōuri
Ko Te Kore ko Te Pū
Te Weu, Te More, me Te Aka

Te Ahunga Te Aponga
Te Kune iti Kune rahi
Ka whānau mai ngā tama
A Ranginui me Papa
Ka wehea, rāua
E Tāne-nui-a-rangi-e
Ka puta mai
Ko Te Rā, Te Marama, Ngā Whetū
Ngā otaota ngā rakau Auē!

Puta mai i te pō
Ko te ao mārama

NGAPO WEHI

In the Beginning

In the beginning was
the great night
the long night
the dense night.

Aue!

In the beginning was
the great night
the long night
the dense night.

The world began
in the darkness:
the void, the source
the rootlet, the tap root, the fibrous root.

The generation, the collection,
the small swelling, the large swelling —
the sons of Ranginui and Papa were born.
The parents were separated
by Tane-nui-a-rangi.
Then there appeared
the sun, the moon, the stars,
the plants and the trees. Aue!

From the night came
the world of light.

Translation by Miriama Evans

HELEN WATSON WHITE

(Born 1945)

Whitebaiters

They are sliding to catch the
last sun on water, the day
as summed in a small wave's
turn of watery phrase

Moon-like their movements
slow stalking the evening
along a road that snails
have already imperceptibly

altered, scrawl-trawling the
flat-bottomed river with
its waxy impressionable
floor. Their moon-boots

black and weightless make
waves of no more substance than
the patterned sea-signature
imprinted on a sole.

Neither fish nor fool are
they in their slowness
knowing how to look (sly
and sideways) and where

and what (they make no
secret) they search for. The moon
is their messenger, ushering in
answers to a million trivial

questions in quick-penned lines —
the fish news — paper-thin and print-
fresh on the incoming
tide.

Plants speak

Plants speak out
in their pertness though
the audience is a-
sleep in the alcoves

Windows keep a late
watch and in the wide
night lights thicken
and glaze

The season is not
mellow somehow; the dark
is embarrassingly
alive
            I emerge from
an underground society
wearing my

house like a crown

Hope

In the season of fortune the
light kept shining when

least expected. Hope was
the only consequence
the will was the way

She knew what she wanted
without dread of too much

care; no more special prize
being offered, she wore her
lust like a flower

ACKNOWLEDGEMENTS

For permission to publish the poems in this anthology, acknowledgement is made to the following poets, publishers and copyright holders:

Fleur Adcock: Oxford University Press, London (*Selected Poems*, 1983; *The Incident Book*, 1986)

Rob Allan: *Untold*; *Landfall*; *Antipodes*

Arapeta Marukitepua Awatere: Estate of the author

Eric Beach: Saturday Centre Poets, Cammeray, N.S.W. (*In Occupied Territory*, 1977)

Tony Beyer: Melaleuca Press, Canberra (*Dancing Bear*, 1981); Hard Echo Press (*Brute Music*, 1984); Caxton (*The Singing Ground*, 1986)

Peter Bland: McIndoe (*Selected Poems*, 1987)

Jenny Bornholdt: *Landfall*; Victoria University Press (*This Big Face*, 1988)

Rangiahuta Alan Herewini Ruka Broughton: Estate of the author

Alan Brunton: Red Mole Enterprises (*And She Said*, 1984; *New Order*, 1986)

Alastair Campbell: Te Kotare Press (*Soul Traps*, 1985)

Meg Campbell: Te Kotare Press (*The Way Back*, 1981; *A Durable Fire*, 1982)

Janet Charman: Allen & Unwin (*The New Poets*, 1987); New Women's Press (*2 Deaths in 1 Night*, 1987)

Te Taite Cooper: The author

Curnow, Allen: Auckland University Press / Oxford University Press (*You Will Know When You Get There*, 1982); Auckland University Press (*The Loop in Lone Kauri Road*, 1986)

Wystan Curnow: *Morepork*

Leigh Davis: Jack Books (*Willy's Gazette*, 1983)

Monita Eru Delamere: The author

John Dickson: Untold (*What Happened on the Way to Oamaru*, 1986); Allen & Unwin (*The New Poets*, 1987)

Lauris Edmond: Mallinson Rendel (*Wellington Letter*, 1980); Oxford University Press (*Salt From the North*, 1980; *Catching It*, 1983; *Selected Poems*, 1984; *Seasons and Creatures*, 1986; *Summer near the Arctic Circle*, 1988)

Murray Edmond: Oxford University Press (*End Wall*, 1981); Caxton Press (*Letters and Paragraphs*, 1987)

Kim Eggleston: Strong John Press (*From the Face to the Bin*, 1984; *25 Poems*, 1985); *Untold*

Acknowledgements

David Eggleton: Penguin Books (*South Pacific Sunrise*, 1986)

Riemke Ensing: The Lowry Press (*Letters-Selected Poems*, 1982); The Griffin Press (*Spells from Chagall*, 1987)

Anne French: Oxford University Press (*All Cretans Are Liars*, 1987)

Bernadette Hall: *Untold*; *Landfall*

Michael Harlow: Hawk Press (*Nothing but Switzerland and Lemonade*, 1980); Auckland University Press (*Today Is the Piano's Birthday*, 1981); Auckland University Press / Oxford University Press (*Vlaminck's Tie*, 1985)

Dinah Hawken: Victoria University Press (*It Has No Sound and Is Blue*, 1987)

Arapere Hineira: Waiata Koa (*Kokako Huataratara*, 1986)

Te Okanga Huata: Estate of the author

Keri Hulme: *Untold*

Sam Hunt: Penguin Books (*Collected Poems*, 1980; *Approaches to Paremata*, 1985); Whitcoulls (*Running Scared*, 1982)

Kevin Ireland: Oxford University Press (*Practice Night in the Drill Hall*, 1984; *Selected Poems*, 1987); Islands (*The Year of the Comet*, 1986)

Michael Jackson: McIndoe (*Wall*, 1980; *Going On*, 1985)

Louis Johnson: Mallinson Rendel (*Coming and Going*, 1982; *Winter Apples*, 1984); Antipodes Press (*True Confessions of the Last Cannibal*, 1986)

Mike Johnson: Voice Press (*The Palanquin Ropes*, 1983)

Shane Jones: The author

Te Aomuhurangi Temamaka Jones: The author

Timoti Karetu: The author

Hera Katene-Horvarth: Estate of the author

Piki Kereama: The author

Hugh Lauder: Caxton Press (*Over the White Wall*, 1985); *Untold*

Michele Leggott: Caxton Press (*Like This?*, 1988)

Graham Lindsay: Ridge-Pole (*Public*, 1980); Auckland University Press (*Big Boy*, 1986); *Untold*

Rachel McAlpine: Mallinson Rendel (*Recording Angel*, 1983)

Heather McPherson: Spiral (*A Figurehead, a Face*, 1982); Tauranga Moana Press (*The Third Myth*, 1986); Allen & Unwin (*The New Poets*, 1987)

Cilla McQueen: McIndoe (*Homing In*, 1982; *Anti-gravity*, 1984; *Wild Sweets*, 1986)

Harvey McQueen: Caxton Press (*Against the Maelstrom*, 1981); Black Robin (*Oasis Motel*, 1985); *NZ Listener*

Acknowledgements

Aunty Jane Manahi: The author

Bill Manhire: Allen & Unwin / Port Nicholson Press (*Zoetropes*, 1984)

Pā Max Takuira Mariu: The author

Hirini Melbourne: The author

Trixie Te Arama Menzies: Waiata Koa (*Uenuku*, 1986)

Michael Morrissey: Sword Press (*Closer to the Bone*, 1981; *She's Not the Child of Sylvia Plath*, 1981); Auckland University Press (*Taking in the View*, 1986)

Elizabeth Nannestad: Auckland University Press (*Jump*, 1986)

John Newton: Untold (*Tales from the Angler's El Dorado*, 1985)

Ranui Ngarimu: The author

Gregory O'Brien: Auckland University Press (*The Location of the Least Person*, 1987)

Bob Orr: Voice Press (*Cargo*, 1983); *Rambling Jack*

Vincent O'Sullivan: Oxford University Press (*Brother Jonathan, Brother Kafka*, 1980; *The Butcher Papers*, 1982; *The Pilate Tapes*, 1987); McIndoe (*The Rose Ballroom*, 1982)

Alistair Paterson: Auckland University Press (*Odysseus Rex*, 1986)

Joanna Paul: *Parallax*; *Morepork*

Merimeri Penfold: The author

Kumeroa Ngoingoi Pēwhairangi: Estate of the author

Fiona Farrell Poole: Auckland University Press (*Cutting Out*, 1987)

Roma Potiki: Allen & Unwin (*The New Poets*, 1987) and the author

Pūtahi Cultural Group: The group

Kuini Moehau Reedy: The author

Nigel Roberts: Wild & Woolly, Sydney (*Steps for Astaire*, 1977)

Iain Sharp: One Eyed Press (*Why Mammals Shiver*, 1980); Hard Echo Press (*She is Trying to Kidnap the Blind Person*, 1985; *The Pierrot Variations*, 1985)

Pita Sharples: The author

Elizabeth Smither: Auckland University Press / Oxford University Press (*The Legend of Marcello Mastroianni's Wife*, 1981; *Shakespeare's Virgins*, 1983); Oxford University Press (*Casanova's Ankle*, 1981); Auckland University Press (*Professor Musgrove's canary*, 1986)

Kendrick Smithyman: Auckland University Press / Oxford University Press (*Stories About Wooden Keyboards*, 1985)

C. K. Stead: Auckland University Press / Oxford University Press (*Geographies*, 1982; *Paris: a Poem*, 1984); *Islands*; *Poetry Australia*

John Poutu Te Rangi Stirling: The author

Hori Tait: Estate of the author

Acknowledgements

Brian Turner: McIndoe (*Ancestors*, 1981; *Listening to the River*, 1983; *Bones*, 1985)

Hone Tuwhare: McIndoe (*Year of the Dog*, 1982); Penguin Books (*Mihi*, 1987)

Te Kuru-o-te-marama Waaka: The author

Taniwha Waru: Estate of the author

Ian Wedde: Oxford University Press (*Driving into the Storm*, 1987); Auckland University Press (*Tendering*, 1988)

Ngapo Wehi: The author

Helen Watson White: The author

BIBLIOGRAPHY

FLEUR ADCOCK
The Eye of the Hurricane. A. H. & A. W. Reed, 1964
Tigers. London: Oxford University Press, 1967
High Tide in the Garden. London: Oxford University Press, 1971
The Scenic Route. London: Oxford University Press, 1974
The Inner Harbour. Oxford: Oxford University Press, 1979
Below Loughrigg. Jesmond: Bloodaxe Books, 1979
Selected Poems. Oxford: Oxford University Press, 1983
The Virgin and the Nightingale: Mediaeval Latin Poems. Newcastle-upon-
    Tyne: Bloodaxe Books, 1983
The Incident Book. Oxford: Oxford University Press, 1986

ERIC BEACH
Lyrics & Blues. Wellington: Lisa Art Productions, 1971
Saint Kilda Meets Hugo Ball. St Lucia, Vic.: Makar Press, 1974
In Occupied Territory. Cammeray, NSW: Saturday Centre Poets, 1977
A Photo of Some People in a Football Stadium. Melbourne: Overland, 1978

TONY BEYER
Jesus Hobo. Caveman Press, 1971
The Meat. Caveman Press, 1974
Dancing Bear. Canberra: Melaleuca Press, 1981
Brute Music. Hard Echo Press, 1984
The Singing Ground: Poems. Caxton Press, 1986

PETER BLAND
My Side of the Story. Mate Books, 1964
The Man with the Carpet Bag: Poems. Caxton Press, 1972
Mr Maui. London: London Magazine Editions, 1976
Stone Tents. London: London Magazine Editions, 1981
The Crusoe Factor. London: London Magazine Editions, 1985
Selected Poems. McIndoe, 1987

JENNY BORNHOLDT
This Big Face. Victoria University Press, 1988

ALAN BRUNTON
Messengers in Blackface. London: Amphedesma Press, 1973
Black and White Anthology. Hawk Press, 1976
O Ravachol. Red Mole Publications, 1979
And She Said. New York: Alexandra Fisher for Red Mole Enterprises,
    1984
New Order. New York: Alexandra Fisher for Red Mole Enterprises, 1986

Bibliography

ALISTAIR CAMPBELL
Mine Eyes Dazzle: Poems 1947–49. Pegasus Press, 1950; revised editions
  1951 & 1956
Wild Honey. London: Oxford University Press, 1964
Kapiti: Selected Poems 1947–1971. Pegasus Press, 1972
Dreams, Yellow Lions. Alister Taylor, 1975
The Dark Lord of Savaiki. Te Kotare Press, 1981
Collected Poems. Alister Taylor, 1982
Soul Traps: A Lyric Sequence. Te Kotare Press, 1985

MEG CAMPBELL
The Way Back. Te Kotare Press, 1981
A Durable Fire. Te Kotare Press, 1982

JANET CHARMAN
2 Deaths in 1 Night. New Womens Press, 1987

ALLEN CURNOW
Valley of Decision. Phoenix Miscellany 1, Auckland University College
  Students Association Press, 1933
Enemies: Poems 1933–1936. Caxton Press, 1937
Not in Narrow Seas. Caxton Press, 1939
Island and Time. Caxton Press, 1941
Sailing or Drowning. Progressive Publishing Society, 1943
Jack Without Magic. Caxton Press, 1946
At Dead Low Water, and Sonnets. Caxton Press, 1949
Poems 1949–1957. Mermaid Press, 1957.
A Small Room with Large Windows. London: Oxford University Press,
  1962
Trees, Effigies, Moving Objects: a Sequence of Poems. Catspaw Press, 1972
An Abominable Temper. Catspaw Press, 1973
Collected Poems 1933–1973. A. H. & A. W. Reed, 1974
An Incorrigible Music: A Sequence of Poems. Auckland University Press,
  1979
You Will Know When You Get There: Poems 1979–1981. Auckland
  University Press / Oxford University Press, 1982
Selected Poems. Penguin Books, 1982
The Loop in Lone Kauri Road: Poems 1983–1985. Auckland University
  Press / Oxford University Press, 1986
Continuum: New and Later Poems, 1972–1988. Auckland University Press,
  1988

LEIGH DAVIS
Willy's Gazette. Jack Books, 1983

JOHN DICKSON
What Happened on the Way to Oamaru. Untold, 1986

LAURIS EDMOND
In Middle Air. Pegasus Press, 1975
The Pear Tree: Poems. Pegasus Press, 1977
Wellington Letter: A Sequence of Poems. Mallinson Rendel, 1980
Seven: Poems. Wayzgoose Press, 1980
Salt from the North. Oxford University Press, 1980
Catching It: Poems. Oxford University Press, 1983
Selected Poems. Oxford University Press, 1984
Seasons and Creatures. Oxford University Press, 1986
Summer Near the Arctic Circle. Oxford University Press, 1988

MURRAY EDMOND
Entering the Eye. Caveman Press, 1973
Patchwork. Hawk Press, 1978
End Wall. Oxford University Press, 1981
Letters and Paragraphs. Caxton Press, 1987

KIM EGGLESTON
From the Face to the Bin: Poems 1978–1984. Strong John Press, 1984
25 poems: The Mist Will Rise and the World Will Drip With Gold. Strong
    John Press, 1985

DAVID EGGLETON
South Pacific Sunrise. Penguin Books, 1986
People of the Land. Penguin Books, 1988

RIEMKE ENSING
Making Inroads. Coal-Black Press, 1980
Letters-Selected Poems. The Lowry Press, 1982
Topographies. Prometheus Press, 1984
Spells from Chagall. The Griffin Press, 1987

ANNE FRENCH
All Cretans are Liars. Oxford University Press, 1987
The Male as Evader. Oxford University Press, 1988

BERNADETTE HALL
Heartwood. Caxton Press, 1989

MICHAEL HARLOW
Edges. Athens: Lycabettus Press, 1974
Nothing But Switzerland and Lemonade. Hawk Press, 1980
Today is the Piano's Birthday: Poems. Auckland University Press, 1981
Vlaminck's Tie. Auckland University Press / Oxford University Press,
    1985

DINAH HAWKEN
It Has No Sound and is Blue. Victoria University Press, 1987

ARAPERA HINEIRA
Kokako Huataratara. Waiata Koa, 1986

Bibliography

KERI HULME
The Silences Between: (Moeraki Conversations). Auckland University
    Press / Oxford University Press, 1982

SAM HUNT
Bracken Country. Glenbervie Press, 1971
From Bottle Creek. Alister Taylor, 1972
South into Winter. Alister Taylor, 1973
Time to Ride. Alister Taylor, 1975
Drunkard's Garden. Hampson Hunt, 1977
Collected Poems 1963–1980. Penguin Books, 1980
Running Scared. Whitcoulls, 1982
Approaches to Paremata. Penguin Books, 1985
Selected Poems. Penguin Books, 1987

KEVIN IRELAND
Face to Face. Pegasus Press, 1963
Educating the Body: Poems. Caxton Press, 1967
A Letter from Amsterdam. London: Amphedesma Press, 1972
Orchids, Humming-birds, and Other Poems. Auckland University
    Press / Oxford University Press, 1974
A Grammar of Dreams. Wai-te-ata Press, 1975
Literary Cartoons. Islands / Hurricane, 1977
The Dangers of Art: Poems 1975–1980. Cicada Press, 1980
Practice Night in the Drill Hall: Poems. Oxford University Press, 1984
The Year of the Comet: Twenty-six 1986 Sonnets. Islands, 1986
Selected Poems. Oxford University Press, 1987

MICHAEL JACKSON
Latitudes of Exile. McIndoe, 1976
Wall. McIndoe, 1980
Going On. McIndoe, 1985

LOUIS JOHNSON
Stanza and Scene. Handcraft Press, 1945
The Sun Among the Ruins. Pegasus Press, 1951
Roughshod Among the Lilies. Pegasus Press, 1951
New Worlds for Old. Capricorn Press, 1957
Bread and a Pension. Pegasus Press, 1964
Land Like a Lizard. Brisbane: Jacaranda Press, 1970
Selected Poems. Bathurst, NSW: Mitchell College of Advanced Education,
    1972
Fires and Patterns. Brisbane: Jacaranda Press, 1975
Coming and Going. Mallinson Rendel, 1982
Winter Apples. Mallinson Rendel, 1984
True Confessions of the Last Cannibal: New Poems. Antipodes Press, 1986

MIKE JOHNSON
The Palanquin Ropes. Voice Press, 1983
Standing Wave. Hard Echo Press, 1985

HUGH LAUDER
Over the White Wall: Poems. Caxton, 1985

MICHELE LEGGOTT
Like This? Caxton Press, 1988

GRAHAM LINDSAY
Thousand-eyed Eel: A Sequence of Poems from the Maori Land March.
 Hawk Press, 1976
Public. Ridge Pole, 1980
Big Boy. Auckland University Press, 1986

RACHEL McALPINE
Lament for Ariadne. Caveman Press, 1975
Stay at the Dinner Party. Caveman Press, 1977
Fancy Dress. Cicada Press, 1979
House Poems. Nutshell Books, 1980
Recording Angel. Mallinson Rendel, 1983
Thirteen Waves. Homeprint, 1986
Selected Poems. Mallinson Rendel, 1988

HEATHER McPHERSON
A Figurehead, a Face. Spiral, 1982
The Third Myth. Tauranga Moana Press, 1986

CILLA McQUEEN
Homing In. McIndoe, 1982
Anti-gravity. McIndoe, 1984
Wild Sweets. McIndoe, 1986
Benzina. McIndoe, 1988

HARVEY McQUEEN
Against the Maelstrom. Caxton Press, 1981
Stoat Spring. Mallinson Rendel, 1983
Oasis Motel. Black Robin, 1985
Room. Black Robin, 1988

BILL MANHIRE
The Elaboration. Square and Circle, 1972
How to Take Off Your Clothes at the Picnic. Wai-te-ata Press, 1977
Good Looks. Auckland University Press / Oxford University Press, 1982
Zoetropes: Poems 1972–1982. Allen & Unwin / Port Nicholson Press,
 1984

TRIXIE TE ARAMA MENZIES
Uenuku. Waiata Koa, 1986
Papakainga. Waiata Koa, 1988 .

Bibliography

MICHAEL MORRISSEY
Make Love in All the Rooms. Caveman Press, 1978
Closer to the Bone. Sword Press, 1981
She's Not the Child of Sylvia Plath: Poems. Sword Press, 1981
Dreams. Sword Press, 1981
Taking in the View. Auckland University Press, 1986
Dr Strangelove's Prescription. Van Guard Xpress, 1988
New Zealand — What Went Wrong? Van Guard Xpress, 1988

ELIZABETH NANNESTAD
Jump. Auckland University Press, 1986

JOHN NEWTON
Tales from the Angler's El Dorado. Untold, 1985

GREGORY O'BRIEN
The Location of the Least Person. Auckland University Press, 1987
Dunes and Barns. Modern House, 1988

BOB ORR
Blue Footpaths. London: Amphedesma Press, 1971
Poems for Moira. Hawk Press, 1979
Cargo. Voice Press, 1983
Red Trees. Auckland University Press / Oxford University Press /
  Silverfish, 1986

VINCENT O'SULLIVAN
Our Burning Time. Prometheus Books, 1965
Revenants. Prometheus Books, 1969
Bearings. Oxford University Press, 1973
From the Indian Funeral. McIndoe, 1976
Butcher & Co. Oxford University Press, 1977
Brother Jonathan, Brother Kafka. Oxford University Press, 1980
The Rose Ballroom and Other Poems. McIndoe, 1982
The Butcher Papers. Oxford University Press, 1982
The Pilate Tapes. Oxford University Press, 1987

ALISTAIR PATERSON
Caves in the Hills. Pegasus Press, 1965
Birds Flying. Pegasus Press, 1973
Cities and Strangers. Caveman Press, 1976
The Toledo Room: A Poem for Voices: Pilgrims South Press, 1978
Qu'appelle. Pilgrims South Press, 1982
Odysseus Rex. Auckland University Press, 1986
Incantations for Warriors. Earl of Seacliff Art Workshop, 1987

JOANNA PAUL
Imogen. Hawk Press, 1978

FIONA FARRELL POOLE
Cutting Out. Auckland University Press, 1987

NIGEL ROBERTS
In Casablanca / For the Waters. Sydney: Wild & Woolly, 1977
Steps for Astaire. Sydney: Hale & Iremonger, 1983

IAIN SHARP
Why Mammals Shiver. One Eyed Press, 1980
She is Trying to Kidnap the Blind Person. Hard Echo Press, 1985
The Pierrot Variations. Hard Echo Press, 1985

ELIZABETH SMITHER
Here Come the Clouds. Alister Taylor, 1975
You're Very Seductive William Carlos Williams. McIndoe, 1978
The Sarah Train. Hawk Press, 1980
The Legend of Marcello Mastroianni's Wife. Auckland University
    Press / Oxford University Press, 1981
Casanova's Ankle. Oxford University Press, 1981
Shakespeare's Virgins. Auckland University Press / Oxford University
    Press, 1983
Professor Musgrove's Canary. Auckland University Press, 1986

KENDRICK SMITHYMAN
Seven Sonnets. Pelorus Press, 1946
The Blind Mountain. Caxton Press, 1950
The Gay Trapeze. Handcraft Press, 1955
Inheritance. Paul's Book Arcade, 1962
Flying to Palmerston. Oxford University Press for Auckland University
    Press, 1968
Earthquake Weather. Auckland University Press, 1972
The Seal in the Dolphin Pool. Auckland University Press / Oxford
    University Press, 1974
Dwarf With a Billiard Cue. Auckland University Press / Oxford
    University Press, 1979
Stories About Wooden Keyboards. Auckland University Press / Oxford
    University Press, 1985
Are You Going to the Pictures. Auckland University Press, 1987
Selected Poems. Auckland University Press, 1989

C. K. STEAD
Whether the Will is Free: Poems 1954–1962. Paul's Book Arcade, 1964
Crossing the Bar. Auckland University Press / Oxford University Press,
    1972
Quesada. The Shed, 1975
Walking Westward. The Shed, 1979
Geographies. Auckland University Press / Oxford University Press, 1982
Poems of a Decade. Pilgrims South Press, 1983

Bibliography

Paris: A Poem. Auckland University Press / Oxford University Press, 1984

Between. Auckland University Press, 1988

BRIAN TURNER
Ladders of Rain. McIndoe, 1978
Ancestors. McIndoe, 1981
Listening to the River. McIndoe, 1983
Bones. McIndoe, 1985

HONE TUWHARE
No Ordinary Sun. Blackwood and Janet Paul, 1964; reprinted McIndoe, 1977
Come Rain Hail. The Bibliography Room, University of Otago, 1970
Sapwood and Milk. Caveman Press, 1972
Something Nothing: Poems. Caveman Press, 1974
Making a Fist of It. Jackstraw Press, 1978
Selected Poems. McIndoe, 1980
Year of the Dog: Poems New and Selected. McIndoe, 1982
Mihi: Collected Poems. Penguin Books, 1987

IAN WEDDE
Made Over. Stephen Chan, 1974
Earthly, Sonnets for Carlos. Amphedesma Press, 1975
Spells for Coming Out. Auckland University Press / Oxford University Press, 1977
Castaly: Poems 1973–1977. Auckland University Press / Oxford University Press, 1980
Tales of Gotham City. Auckland University Press / Oxford University Press, 1984
Georgicon. Victoria University Press, 1984
Driving Into the Storm: Selected Poems. Oxford University Press, 1987
Tendering. Auckland University Press, 1988